Christoph Demmke / Timo Moilanen

Civil Services in the EU of 27

Reform Outcomes and the Future of the Civil Service

PETER LANG
Frankfurt am Main · Berlin · Bern · Bruxelles · New York · Oxford · Wien

Bibliographic Information published by the Deutsche Nationalbibliothek
The Deutsche Nationalbibliothek lists this publication in the Deutsche Nationalbibliografie; detailed bibliographic data is available in the internet at http://dnb.d-nb.de.

Cover Design:
Olaf Glöckler, Atelier Platen, Friedberg

Cover map: Júlio Reis
EU27-2007 European Union map.svg.
Wikimedia Commons, licensed by
CreativeCommons-Lizenz 2.5-de
URL: http://creativecommons.org/licenses/by/2.5/deed.de

ISBN 978-3-631-60466-3

www.peterlang.de

CONTENTS

List of Figures

List of Tables

Country Abbreviations

AT	Austria	Republic of Austria
BE	Belgium	Kingdom of Belgium
BG	Bulgaria	Republic of Bulgaria
CY	Cyprus	Republic of Cyprus
CZ	Czech Republic	Czech Republic
DE	Germany	Federal Republic of Germany
DK	Denmark	Kingdom of Denmark
EE	Estonia	Republic of Estonia
EL	Greece	Hellenic Republic
ES	Spain	Kingdom of Spain
FI	Finland	Republic of Finland
FR	France	French Republic
HU	Hungary	Republic of Hungary
IE	Ireland	Ireland
IT	Italy	Italian Republic
LT	Lithuania	Republic of Lithuania
LU	Luxembourg	Grand Duchy of Luxembourg
LV	Latvia	Republic of Latvia
MT	Malta	Republic of Malta
NL	Netherlands	Kingdom of the Netherlands
PL	Poland	Republic of Poland
PT	Portugal	Portuguese Republic
RO	Romania	Romania
SE	Sweden	Kingdom of Sweden
SI	Slovenia	Republic of Slovenia
SK	Slovakia	Slovak Republic
UK	United Kingdom	United Kingdom of Great Britain and Northern Ireland

European Union Abbreviations

EC	European Commission
EP	European Parliament
ECJ	European Court of Justice

I. INTRODUCTION

Civil service systems are a constituent part of our system of government. Modern government still depends to a great extent on the work of the national civil services and their employees – the millions of civil servants. In fact, the quality of life in Europe depends in many ways on those who work for government and on how government works as such. Furthermore, civil services have a democratic and ethical function; they should serve the society and the law, protect the population as well as function in a sustainable manner. For all of these tasks and duties the Member States have established specific civil services. No government functions as a private company or under labour law.

Despite the great importance of the civil services for the well-being of our societies, only very little comparative and empirical information exist about the nature of reforms and the reform paths of the national civil services. Even amongst academics, only little attention has been devoted to the field of comparative civil service reforms. What could be the reason for this? One basic explanation could be the enormous difficulties involved in carrying out comparative research in an area which, until recently, was considered to be a national competence and represents a branch of the politico-administrative system that has been influenced the most by national traditions and history.

Other problems relate to the challenges involved in comparing different national concepts and definitions of civil services. Moreover, there can be too little or too much attention on theoretical issues, too little or too much focus on historical explanations, a too general analysis without taking into consideration the many existing specific features of the national systems, avoidance of different linguistic meanings and definitions etc. In particular when comparing civil service systems, another problem stems from the question as to whether different reform concepts mean the same thing and whether the comparison is really comparing the same issues. The discussion around civil services is also related to many other issues which are seen as political, sensitive, confidential or even secret. Therefore, countries may be reluctant to become a subject of comparative research and release sensitive data.

Other challenges relate to the lack of attractiveness of doing research in a field which is often considered to be very complex, technical and dominated by legalistic approaches. Rhetoric also contrasts civil service reforms with new (good) managerial reforms and the old (bad) bureaucracies, civil services and bureaucrats. "The name given to the old – that against which the modern, reformed public sector organization stands out as superior – is usually something like traditional bureaucracy"[1]. However, it remains unclear as to what the new model actually is and how it contrasts with the old model - if this new model ever existed at all.

As we will see in this study, the reform of classical bureaucracies is actually a fascinating subject. It challenges many popular assumptions, increasingly puts into question traditional characteristics of civil service systems, but leaves us puzzled as to the outcomes of all reforms. In fact, although almost all European civil services are in a process of ongoing reforms, there is still very little knowledge and comparative information with regard to the nature and outcomes of these reforms. In the past, major studies have mostly concentrated on public management reforms, but focused less on the reform of the national civil services and HR-policies.

Since the publication *Public Management Reform: A Comparative Analysis*, from Bouckaert and Pollitt (2000)[2] until *Government at a Glance (OECD)* (2009)[3], awareness has been growing of the importance of government activities and public sector reform. In fact, the public sector is a major contributor to economic growth[4]. Moreover, it is commonly accepted that – besides the need to be efficient – an effective and appropriately sized public service is essential for social cohesion and a sustainable society. Education, health, security and other public services produce both desirable and essential outputs for society and economy[5].

This book presents an overview of the state of the art of the national civil services, the main reform trends that are taking place and the main outcomes of selected national reform policies in the field of HRM. The overall aim of this volume is to provide empirical evidence, facts and comparative statistical evidence in order to help experts and scholars to better understand the different national civil service systems, the nature of reforms and the changes that are taking place. This alone is risky business since civil service systems are very complex and technical. In many Member States civil service laws can easily fill hundreds of pages. Thus, any comparative study faces the risk of being far too superficial.

---

1 Christopher Pollitt/Geert Bouckaert, Public Management Reform: A Comparative Analysis, First Edition, 2000, p. 61.

2 Ibid.

3 OECD, Measuring Government Activity, Paris 2009.

4 Anthony Foley, The Size, Cost and Efficiency of the Public Service. In Administration, Vol. 57, No.1, p. 71.

5 Ibid.

This study thus represents basic research from which it may be worth continuing with more research into the different HR policies concerning such as leadership issues, developments in the field of working time, diversity management, anti-discrimination and pension reforms. This study may also serve as an instrument for a more rational discourse about the similarities and differences amongst the different national civil services.

Another question addressed throughout this book is: how do the national civil services deviate from the classical bureaucratic model, how do they differ amongst each other and where are the main reform trends leading?[6] We will also illustrate the important influence of traditions, national ideas and political developments on the design and structure of national civil service systems and civil service reforms. Thus, we agree that there is a connection between the culture of a nation or region, the way management in civil services is structured, how reform pressures are perceived and how reform priorities are adopted[7]. Therefore it contrasts with "the belief in the early 1990s that the worldwide trend of public management reforms in Western administrations would tend to converge to one single, common, universal "new public management" pattern"[8]. However, unlike Kickert's observation that civil services are very different and always linked to traditions and national identities, it also illustrates many common and partly converging reform developments in Europe. For example, a clear trend towards alignment of employment conditions in the private and public sectors and organisational reforms.

We will confirm an OECD analysis[9] which maintains that there is

- a transition from centralised to decentralised determination of employment condition,
- a shift from statutory to contractual or managerial governance,
- a development from career systems to post-bureaucratic (position systems),
- a delegation of responsibilities to managers,
- an alignment of pay levels with private sector practices and
- a change of special retirement schemes.

---

6 Walter J.M. Kickert/Richard J. Stillman, The Modern State and its Study, Edward Elgar Publishing, Cheltenham, 1999.

7 Kuno Schedler/Isabella Proeller (eds.), Cultural Aspects of Public Management Reform, Vol. 16, JAI Press, 2007.

8 Walter Kickert (ed.), The Study of Public Management in Europe and the US, Routledge, London and New York, 2008, p. 2.

9 OECD, The State of the Public Service, Paris, 2008, p. 23.

However, we also observe different and distinct reform paths amongst different country clusters, administrative models and civil service systems. For example, the current reform paths in Portugal and Spain, Austria and Germany or Latvia and Lithuania seem to differ widely. This reform process does not only challenge many traditional perceptions and traditional aspects of the bureaucratic civil services. In reality, it challenges the whole concept of a specific civil service and the traditional legitimacy of specific working conditions as such. Moreover, the often prevailing perception that civil services are reform resistant is clearly wrong. Instead, the tremendous pace of change is challenging the experts who have difficulties in understanding how and why the public services are changing[10]. Clearly, the reform of the national public services is moving through a fascinating but also disorienting period throughout Europe. Moreover, the current reform process is taking place in very different national contexts and before the background of widely varying traditions. In addition, the changing of some features has turned out to be more sensitive than others.

As a consequence, traditional features of the national civil services are increasingly disappearing. As one author points out, "Long-standing taken for granted assumptions and orthodoxies no longer hold. Traditional public services are under pressure to change and seem to be evolving – but into what?"[11] What has been achieved and what has been a failure? And where are we going? In this study we will try to answer the question of how the civil services have developed in recent years. However, it is also an attempt to contribute to a better understanding of the nature of the European civil services and to arrive at better definitions of the terms *civil service* and *civil servants*. From a practical point of view, the most important objective of this study is to compare civil service systems, organisational structures, as well as HR policies and HR reforms in the national civil services of the EU Member States. Here, the focus is on the employment of civil servants and status developments, recruitment-, mobility-, career development-, pay-, job security, decentralisation of HRM responsibilities and status reform issues.

In fact, this reform process is not without risks. Do reformers really know what they are leaving behind? Do they really know where to go from here? Is the reform trajectory really clearly defined? And will the reform path lead to better results? As we will see later in the following chapters, there are many uncertainties with regard to the outcomes of many reforms. What is known is that they

10 Arthur Benz, Status und Perspektiven der Politikwissenschaftlichen Verwaltungsforschung, in: Die Verwaltung, Nr. 3/2003, p. 369.

11 Ewan Ferlie/Laurence Lynn/Christopher Pollitt, Introductory Remarks, in: The Oxford Handbook of Public Management, Oxford, 2005, p. 1.

produce successes and failures. In fact, reform outcomes are ambivalent in nature. For example, most recent reforms have focused on performance management, diversity policies and pay reforms. However, relatively little has been done to avoid a fragmentation of HR management and to ensure fair HRM practices.

All ongoing reforms are challenging the classical bureaucratic model. However, what remains less clear is what will follow. What could be an alternative model for the old bureaucratic model? Where are the national civil services heading? Do we still need civil servants at all? In the last chapter we will attempt to find a solution to this challenge.

We would like to dedicate this publication to the European Network of Public Administration (EUPAN) and all the national and European experts who have helped and supported us in carrying out this study. We would also like to specially thank Thomas Henökl for his substantial support in the first phase of this study. Finally, many thanks to Tiara Patel for her friendliness and professional and speedy language check.

Christoph Demmke and Timo Moilanen
Maastricht / Berlin / Helsinki
February 2010

II. METHODOLOGY

1. Challenges in identifying comparative public administration models

Comparisons of the national public- and civil services have so far produced a contrasting picture[12]. Most of these comparisons are based on qualitative and literature research. Overall, there is very little factual and empirical evidence about structures, processes and policies in the national public services. The same is true as regards the nature of civil service reforms and evaluations in terms of their effects and outcomes.

Due to the difficulties involved in obtaining reliable data and carrying out applied empirical research, many theories reflect personal opinions, images and perceptions. According to Bouckaert and Pollitt, "There is a growing fashion for the authors of academic texts to 'confess' their own perspectives and likely biases"[13]. Often, some countries are praised as being reform-oriented countries, whereas others are seen as reform laggards although it remains unclear as to the basis on which these judgements and value statements are based.

Overall, many comparative publications about civil service reforms easily take the direction of ideological discourses. This is not surprising given the fact that it is very difficult to get reliable, yet comparable data from all 27 EU Member

---

12 See for example: Charles Debbasch, La fonction publique en Europe, Paris, 1981; Siegfried Magiera/ Heinrich Siedentopf (eds.), Das Recht des öffentlichen Dienstes in den Mitgliedstaaten der Europäischen Gemeinschaft, Berlin 1994; Yves Mény, Politique comparée, les démocraties: Allemagne, Etats-Unis, France, Grande-Bretagne, Italie, 5th edition, Paris 1993; Jacques Ziller, Administrations comparées, Paris 1993; Tony Verheijen /Alexander Kotchegura (eds.), Civil Service Systems in Central and Eastern Europe, Edward Elgar, 2000; Hans A.G.m Bekke/Frits M. van der Meer, Civil Service Systems in Europe, Edward Elgar Publishing 2000; Danielle Bossaert et al., Civil Services in the Europe of 15, Trends and New Developments, EIPA, 2001; Christoph Demmke/Danielle Bossaert, Civil Services in the Accession States, EIPA 2004; Christopher Politt/Geert Bouckaert, Public Management Reform: A Comparative Analysis, Second Edition, Oxford University Press, 2004; Ferdinand Müller-Rommel/Jean Blondel/Darina Malova, Governing New European Democracies, London, 2007; Walter J. M. Kickert (ed.), The Study of Public Management in Europe and the US. London 2008; Hans-Ulrich Derlien/B. Guy Peters, The State at Work, Comparative Public Service Systems, 2008; OECD, The State of the Public Service, Paris, 2008; French Ministere du Budget, Des Comptes Publics et de la Fonction Publique, French EU Presidency, Paris 2008; Jan-Hinrik Meyer-Sahling, Sustainability of Civil Service Reforms in Central and Eastern Europe. Five Years after EU Accession, Sigma paper no. 44, Paris, 2009; OECD, Government at a Glance, Paris, 2009.

13 Pollitt/Bouckaert, Public Management Reform, op. cit., p. 22.

States[14]. Moreover, different historical traditions and cultures[15] as well as different HR systems have a considerable impact on public management modernisation paths and on the outcomes of HR reforms. The relevance of context and diversity in European public administrations also has critical implications for the concept of mutual learning and the possibility to "import" so-called best practices from one country to another.

The same is true with regard to the differences in administrative culture[16]. Hofstede illustrated in Culture's Consequences (2001)[17] how values and organisational norms vary across countries. He distinguished countries by measuring five cultural elements: power distance, uncertainty avoidance, individualism versus collectivism, masculinity versus femininity and long-term versus short-term orientation. The great differences amongst the countries suggest that it would also be difficult to export good-practices from one administrative culture to another.

In addition to this there is the added difficulty of comparing and analysing the different (legal, political, organisational and HR-) instruments in different legal and administrative traditions and in many languages. This comparative study took 18 months and was carried out in English. Naturally, all discussion partners and respondents to questionnaires were asked to respond to a terminology which may not be understood universally across Europe.

Another challenge when comparing reform outcomes concerns the question of how to obtain honest and reliable answers to sensitive questions. It is true that growing administrative cooperation in the field of national civil services and the popularity of benchmarking have also engendered a growing interest in comparisons. Concepts such as *good/best practices*, *benchmarking* and *measuring government* have never been as popular as they are today. But are these concepts really easily applicable in a policy field which is so strongly dominated by national traditions and different cultures?[18] Most experts cautiously agree that

---

14 See OECD, La mesure de l'emploi public dans les pays de l'OCDE. Sources, Methodes et Résultats, Paris, 1997.

15 Schedler/Proeller, Cultural Aspects, op. cit.

16 Ibid.

17 Geert H. Hofstede, Culture's Consequences: Comparing Values, Behaviors, Institutions and Organizations Across Nations, Sage Publications, 2001.

18 Danielle Bossaert/Christoph Demmke/Marie-Laure Onnée-Abbruciati, L'evolution des fonctions publiques en Europe – une approche comparée des dévelopments récents. In Marie-Laure Onnée-Abbruciati, Le fonctionnaire est-til un salarié comme les autres?

comparisons and the identification of good practices are possible if more and better data on performance information can be generated and the work on comparable indicators is continued.

Another challenge represents the identification of administrative models. As such the use of models is ambiguous: "Not only is it difficult to know what the exact reference is about, but the word "model" is often used with an everyday language connotation (...). One of the most typical uses of this kind of concepts of models is illustrated by the recurring temptation to look at so-called best practices in public management. Comparing experiences can be very fruitful if it is done according to a carefully designed programme, but it usually ends up at best in misunderstandings, at worst in used-car salesmen attitudes..."[19]

One example is the so-called Napoleonic and Weberian (Prussian) model of public administration. Although both models are often seen as comparable, there are nonetheless a number of important differences. For example, Weber focuses a lot of attention on the importance of rules, but had little interest in the role of courts, corps and local administration.

In literature a number of experts have argued for the existence of two particularly strong models: "Most public administrative systems seem to be guided either by the Rechtsstaat model or by the Anglo-Saxon notion of the ''public interest''; very few systems fall between these two models, which appear to be inherently inconsistent and irreconcilable"[20]. In fact, at the beginning of the 21st century his distinction is no longer very helpful seeing as it is obviously very broad and too general.

Another possibility is to classify civil service systems as Weberian or neo-Weberian systems[21], Career or Position systems, New Public Service Systems[22] or Postmodern public Administration[23]. According to Bouckaert and Halligan[24],

---

Pensions de retraite dans les fonctions publiques en Europe, Bruylant, Bruxelles 2003, p. 5.

19 Jacques Ziller, European Models of Government –Towards a Patchwork with Missing Pieces, in: Parliamentary Affairs, No. 54, 2001, p. 102.

20 Guy Peters/Jon Pierre (eds.), Handbook of Public Administration, 1st edition, Sage 1995, p. 8.

21 Geert Bouckaert/John Halligan, Managing Performance, Routledge, New York, 2008.

22 Janet V. Denhardt/Robert B. Denhardt, The New Public Service, Sharpe, 2007.

23 Peter Bogason, Postmodern Public Administration, in: Ewan Ferlie/Laurence E. Lynn/Christopher Politt, The Oxford Handbook of Public Management, op. cit., pp. 234-257.

24 Bouckaert/Halligan, Managing Performance, op. cit.

the neo-Weberian system can be defined as a system where the rule of law constitutes the main frame for society. However, the civil servants are no longer merely bureaucrats; they also belong to the managerial profession, having a stronger focus on performance and customers. Moreover, private law is becoming more and more of a complementary instrument for public matters, whilst public legitimacy is increasingly based on the economy, efficiency and effectiveness[25]. According to Bouckaert and Halligan, there is a northern and a continental version of this model.

The OECD[26] as well as Bossaert et al.[27] classified the national public services into career system countries, position system countries or hybrid countries[28]. This classification resulted from the fact that – as a result of a broad range of other reforms in most public administrations over the last decade – there is no longer a civil service model that could be described as a 'classical bureaucratic career model'. Instead they adapt civil services to practices and processes applied in the private sector.

An empirical study by Demmke and Henökl (which was based on the examination of 17 indicators such as specific civil service employment rules, existence of lifetime tenure, specific pension scheme or degree of centralisation of HRM competencies etc.[29]) came to the conclusion that pure models no longer exist. Instead of clear-cut categories, there seems to be a trend towards hybrid systems that combine elements of more traditional Weberian and mixed public-private systems. The study also came to the conclusion that there are still considerable differences between the HR systems in the various countries.

In this study we adopted a similar, although more sophisticated methodology. The idea is to construct a model that reflects the main dimensions of traditional bureaucracy. First, we identified the central basic elements of traditional bureaucracy as described by Max Weber[30]. This approach allows us to use a set of indicators to measure the national civil service systems. Systems which follow the Weberian model are called traditional bureaucracies, and systems which deviate from it are called post- bureaucracies. In practice most of the countries lay somewhere in between these two extremes.

---

25 Bouckaert/ Halligan, Managing Performance, op. cit., pp. 41-42.
26 OECD, The State of the Public Service, op. cit.
27 Bossaert et al., Civil Services in the Europe of 15, op. cit.
28 Ibid.
29 Calculations based on a HRWG-survey in the Member States of the EU, EIPA, 2007/2008.
30 Max Weber, Wirtschaft und Gesellschaft, Volmedia, Paderborn, 1922, pp. 219-227.

The model consists of five main components: legal status, career structure, recruitment, salary system and tenure system. Each component has an equal weight within the model. Each component may consist of one or several sub items. The basic elements of this model are described below in Table 1. The table also shows the weighting of each item within its category.

Table 1: Traditional bureaucracy – post-bureaucracy continuum model

Main components	Component items (item's relative weighting within component)
1) Legal status	public law status (100%)
2) Career structure	existence of career structure (50%) career development centrally regulated (20%) entrance from the bottom (15%) promotions to other positions at mid-career or top-level not possible (15%)
3) Recruitment	special recruitment requirements (50%) recruitment centrally regulated (30%) private sector experience not relevant (20%)
4) Salary system	basic salary regulated by law (50%) wage system based on seniority (25%) wage system not based on performance (25%)
5) Tenure system	lifetime tenure (high job security) (40%) termination rather difficult (40%) job security differs from private sector (20%)

This approach allows us to address the question of whether the Member States are indeed moving towards new public service or post-bureaucratic civil service models. You can find more information about it on pages 187-189, 232-233 and 245-247.

We decided to refrain from using a classification for all those countries that deviated from the traditional bureaucratic model. The reason for this is twofold. First, it is difficult to identify an alternative universal model to the term 'bureaucracy'. Secondly, the differences amongst those countries with post-bureaucratic features are too great to be grouped into one category. Therefore, we decided to describe those countries simply as post-bureaucratic countries.

In our questionnaire Member States were also asked to identify those HR areas where working conditions for civil servants still differ from other public employees (e.g., with regard the right to strike). Here, one additional objective was to identify and to categorise those countries that have more aligned and private-sector like public services vs. those countries with specific public services. Other questions related to the organisational design of the national civil services (e.g., existence of career system, specific recruitment requirements, modalities relating to the access to the civil service, trend towards the decentralisation of responsibilities, reform of the seniority principle etc.). Our interest here was to gain evidence on whether (or not) the Member States are abandoning traditional hierarchical structures and flattening organisational structures, thus enhancing and delegating individual responsibilities, introducing more flexibility and opening up the national civil services.

In this study we agree that the contingency factors as well as institutional issues and the importance of politics, tradition and geography must always be seen in the context of reforms. At the same time (sometimes irrational) changes are a common feature of today's civil services. They are not resistant to change. In reality, they have been subject to multiple reforms, and stability has become an old-fashioned word. The good old times of leading role models (such as at the time of the Napoleonic or Prussian model and later on the bureaucratic model) are definitely over.

In fact, several studies have provided evidence that different historical traditions[31] and cultures[32], as well as HR systems, have had a considerable impact on public management modernisation paths. The relevance of context and diversity in European public administrations has important implications for the concept of mutual learning and good practice. In order to adequately tackle the questions of context and diversity and to go beyond descriptions of individual countries or cases, in this study the EU Member States were furthermore clustered according to their public administrative tradition. The relevance of these different traditions, such as the classic contrast between the continental public law systems and the Anglo-Saxon common law systems, is often found in comparative administrative research. In this study EU countries were assigned to the different public administration traditions as shown in Table 2.

31 Kickert (ed), The Study of Public Management in Europe and the US, op. cit.
32 Schedler/Proeller (eds.), Cultural Aspects of Public Management Reform, op. cit.

Table 2: Public administration tradition by EU Member State

Public administration tradition	Member State
Anglo-Saxon tradition	Ireland, Malta, United Kingdom
Continental European tradition	Austria, Belgium, France, Germany, Luxemburg, Netherlands, Slovenia
Mediterranean/South European tradition	Cyprus, Greece, Italy, Portugal, Spain
Scandinavian tradition	Denmark, Estonia, Finland, Sweden
Eastern European tradition	Czech Republic, Hungary, Latvia, Lithuania, Poland, Slovakia
New Member States (South-Eastern tradition)	Bulgaria, Romania

In this study we were able to go one step further and analyse whether these tradition clusters are actually supported by empirical data. For example, in which fields do Anglo-Saxon countries really have similar features? Or, what are the similarities and differences within the Scandinavian cluster? Our hypothesis was that tradition and geographical clusters would be logical. However, they may also lead to overly general perceptions about systems and reform processes. Therefore, it is also important to identify different reform paths. For example, assigning the Netherlands and Slovenia to the Continental European tradition, and Ireland and Malta to the Anglo-Saxon tradition seems open to discussion. Moreover, there are also considerable differences amongst the Eastern European countries. Comparing Spain with Italy also has its risks, as the Italian civil service is relatively young in comparison to the Spanish equivalent. The Italian system is also the result of a cross-fertilisation of different administrative cultures, including the Rechtsstaat tradition, the bureaucratic Napoleon tradition and local traditions from Lombardia and Veneto, Piemonte and Sicilia, Sicilie and the Vatican State. In particular the Lombardo-Veneto model and the French-inspired Piedmont model were very influential[33]. Spain developed its state administration following the centralised Napoleonic model and Prussian model. However, in the past 20 years the Spanish administrative system has changed considerably and it is much more plural in approach and more open to international influence

33 Marco Meneguzzo, The Study of Public Management in Italy, in: Kickert, 2008, op. cit., pp. 168-169.

than before[34]. After the reign of Franco it has also become much more decentralised than ever before[35].

Thus, another aim in this study is to gather more evidence about the differences and similarities amongst the different geographical and administrative traditions. Compared with the period thirty years ago, there now seems to exist a greater variety of administrative systems. For example, despite geographical proximity, the Baltic States have very dissimilar civil service structures. Also a comparison between the Czech Republic, Slovakia and Hungary may reveal only few commonalities. Moreover, even the Scandinavian position systems are not easily comparable. At the same time even the most traditional public services have introduced many forms of decentralised HRM systems, delegated HR responsibilities, weakened the tenure of employees and introduced different performance management systems. Consequently, the traditional bureaucracy has ceased to exist. But which model has replaced it? Is it possible that countries can "break" with their own past, values, norms and structures so easily?

2. Comparative approach

As already discussed, comparing civil service systems is a big methodological challenge. One important reason is the lack of a common definition of public service and civil service. Therefore, throughout the work on this study, a considerable amount of time was used in comparing and analyzing the different national definitions and concepts (see chapter IV for more details).

During the period from August 2008 to July 2009 two questionnaires were drafted, containing a number of open-ended and closed questions (see appendix 2 for more details). The first questionnaire was published on the EUPAN[36] website, and the Presidency of the European Union was contacted in order to ensure that competent national experts from all Member States would respond to the questionnaire. Consequently, the national representatives of the EUPAN's Human Resource Working Group (HRWG) were contacted and invited to respond. National experts were given a validation code in order to guarantee that only the official national respondents could submit their response on the EUPAN webpage.

---

34 Xavier Ballart, The Study of Public Management in Spain, in: Kickert, 2008, op. cit., p. 202.

35 Ibid.

36 European Public Administration Network. For more details about EUPAN please see its homepage, http://www.eupan.eu

The second survey was conducted by means of personal email. The response rate for both surveys was 100%, demonstrating a great interest in this study. After completion of the second questionnaire, the research team analysed and filtered all answers and identified those which were either still missing or unclear. In those cases the respective Member States were contacted on a bilateral basis in a "third round". Throughout the study, the Member States were eager to support the research team.

In order to cross-check, validate and to discuss the national answers, a roundtable discussion with representatives from all Member States was organised during the Czech and Spanish EU Presidency. Furthermore, preliminary results of the study were presented at the 52nd Meeting of the Directors-General of Public Service of the EU Member States under the Czech EU Presidency.

During this work we became increasingly aware of the difficulties and challenges involved. Due to the focus on structures, processes and HR reforms, this study never intended to assess which countries or administrations are more successful or better than others. Instead, this study intends to initiate a critical, open and constructive dialogue on positive and negative developments in the reform of the national civil services. Such a dialogue necessitates the ability to address difficult issues such as fairness, trust, competence and professionalism, and the courage to express openly dissenting opinions. We believe that the interest in contributing to this study and its findings – several are very promising and others are surprising in that they contradict some common sense doctrines of public management reform – can be interpreted as an indicator of the increasing level of awareness, as well as the growing care and diligence devoted to the implementation and handling of civil service reforms, and of the willingness to engage in such a dialogue.

III. THEORIES OF REFORM AND CHANGE PROCESSES

1. Where is the reform process in the national civil services leading?

Unfortunately, until today no public management theory offers a comprehensible theory and explanation of changing processes. When looking from the past to the present, however, it seems more likely that change will not result in a linear progress for the better, but rather to failures, successes, paradoxes, dilemmas and simple alternation. Choices must therefore be made very carefully.

Recent public management theories suggest that some reforms in the public sector are following the same path, whereas others are not. Some claim that partial convergence exists, whereas others are of the opinion that even among the most similar countries, convergence has been exaggerated. "These differing views may be founded partly on the sheer difficulty of doing large-scale comparative research on administrative change" due to the huge amount of material and linguistic barriers etc.[37] In his paper on clarifying convergence, Pollitt proposes a distinction between:

- Discursive convergence – more and more people are talking about the same concepts;
- Decisional convergence – the authorities decide to adopt a particular form, policy or technique;
- Practical convergence – public sector organisations begin to work in similar ways;
- Results convergence – reforms produce similar or identical results and effects[38].

Research about these different stages is obviously more difficult in relation to *practical convergence* and *results convergence*. In addition, convergence at one stage does not necessarily mean convergence at the next stage – far from it[39]. According to Pollitt, the "hypothesis proposed is that the extent of convergence declines rapidly as one moves through the four stages"[40]. Within the OECD countries there is considerable evidence of discursive convergence and also

---

37 Christopher Pollitt, Clarifying convergence, Striking Similarities and durable differences in public management reform in: Public Management Review, No. 4, Issue 1, 2002, pp. 470.

38 Ibid., p. 477.

39 Ibid., p. 478.

40 Ibid., p. 483.

some form of decisional convergence. There is, however, limited information on practice or results convergence.

Another powerful explanation for reform trends may be the existence of specific international values, fashions and political agendas that change over time. Pollitt claims that public management convergence has occurred much more as a result of replication of rhetoric, fashion and symbolism than the "grim dictates of the world economy or the functional necessity for increased efficiency"[41].

When looking back in time it indeed seems that every "era (…) has a few words that epitomise its world-view and that are fixed points by which all else can be measured. In the Middle Ages they were such words as faith, grace, God, nation; in the eighteenth century they were such words as reason, nature, and rights..." [42]. Today, these words seem to be globalisation, risks, efficiency, reform, change, flexibility, performance, decentralisation, transparency, citizen- and consumer orientation and sustainability. These "proverbs" (Simon) are in constant conflict with the classical civil service values such as neutrality, stability, hierarchy, impartiality, fairness, integration and standardisation. One could say that, where civil service values are "static" and "conservative", public and societal values are "fluent" and "modern". Today, also the so-called traditional and legalistic world of the national civil services is deeply influenced by the concept of change, the restless search for better models, ideas and solutions and the influx of new fashions and (politically) attractive values.

It is this tension between the different concepts and between tradition and modernisation that has provoked the crisis of the traditional civil service. Mostly, management science promotes the linear development belief that there is always a better way to do things. Management theory therefore often matches our own cultural belief that anything new is better and promising. For example, the introduction of new information technologies is generally seen as a very positive development which will enhance the transparency, efficiency and effectiveness of public services. Modernisation and change is a western concept that promises change, progress and a way to improve things. The best known claim for modernisation is the book from Osborne and Gaebler (1992)[43] in which the authors state that western societies are moving to a new "entrepreneurial" paradigm of public management, replacing outdated turn-of-the-century rule-bound design. It

---

41 Christopher Politt, Convergence, The Useful Myth ?, in Public Administration, Vol. 79, No. 4, Winter 2001, p. 934.

42 Dwight Waldo, The Administrative State, Ronald Press, New York, 1948, p. 19.

43 Dwight Osborne, T. Gaebler, Reinventing Government, Cambridge M.A., 1992.

is precisely because of this promise, it seems, that new public management theories were so popular.

In reality, however, "modernisation" is also an inherently ambiguous idea"[44] since "much depends on which meaning of "modernisation" is at issue"[45]. Today, some observers even claim that public administration in the 21st century has arrived in a new era of post-modernity[46]. Politicians mainly tend to give the new reform "proverbs" a positive meaning although these words are meaningless without a clear definition. Consequently, "Techniques for organisational engineering come and go with remarkable rapidity. New techniques come into fashion and old ones go out, much like the outfits modelled in Paris, Milan, and New York"[47].

In *The Art of the State* (1998) Hood distinguishes between four possible meanings of modernisation:

- Modernisation as deep change. As regards this concept, it would be at least questionable as to "whether fundamental social relationships will always change because technology changes (...) or whether common technology will lead to common organisation"[48]. In addition, another question is whether or not "old" public management issues could really be solved.
- Modernisation as irreversible change. Here, the claim of irreversible change is more rhetorical and cannot hold up in the face of sound logic (what about going back or turning in cycles?). Are we not turning back to some classical scientific management ideas when it comes to performance measurement, target setting etc.?
- Modernisation as convergent change. Although claims can be made for certain common internationalisation and convergence processes, there is no indication that the different public sectors are moving towards a common administrative model.
- Modernisation as beneficent change. "The fact that something is new or inevitable does not necessarily mean it is desirable"[49].

---

44 Christopher Hood, The Art of the State, Clarendon Press, Oxford, 1988, p. 195.

45 Ibid., p. 219.

46 See Ellen Mastenbroek, De postmoderne overheid: wens of werkelijkheid?, in: Bestuursweten-schapen, No. 2, 2003.

47 Joel D. Aberbach/Bert A. Rockman, In the Web of Politics – Three Decades of the U.S. Federal Executive, Brookings Institution, Washington D. C., 2000, p. 9.

48 Hood, The Art of the State, op. cit., p. 199.

49 Ibid., p. 206.

The current reform of public services perhaps best reflects a mixture of the second and third assumptions about change. While Government is not disappearing, it is nevertheless subject to great reforms. Traditional Government is transforming into "Governance" although this does not necessarily mean that we are taking a step forward in solving problems and offering better solutions. Moreover, the "evolving models of government are not intrinsically liberal or conservative, effective or not effective – they are simply different and new and thus require some careful thought on the part of those who care about good governance and well-functioning public administration"[50].

Overall, there is "more reform" than evidence about reform outcomes and whether the changing processes will produce better results. Today, there appear to be a number of basic concepts about the results and developments of civil service and public sector reforms.

- The first is that of a **linear development** from a known past to an uncertain future. This notion of change need not be teleological, but it does appear to imply that once we move through our one mode of organisation, or one way of doing things, we do not go back. According to this model, change is occurring because of **rational thinking** and individual and organisational self-interest. We subsequently learn new and better ways of performing our tasks and we progress. This thinking is typical of western thinking, since it is an idea based on trust of self-interest, egoism, rationality, progress and positive change.
- An alternative way of thinking about institutional change is to think of it as a more **circular, irrational or paradoxical process**. Rather than there being any linear progress, change may be achieved simply by moving governments back and forth. In this view there is less real progress, and more simple alternation…"[51]
- A similar approach describes reforms as the result of spontaneous crisis reactions, **value change** and **fashions** which are strongly dictated by the political class, the media and the citizens. For example, proponents of the risk soci-

---

50 Elaine Ciulla Kamarck, Public Servants for Twenty-First-Century Government, in: John D. Donahue/Joseph S. Nye (eds.), For the People, Can We Fix Public Service, Brookings Institution Press, Washington D. C., 2003, p. 134.

51 B. Guy Peters, The Future of Reform, in: B. Guy Peters/ Donald J. Savoie, Governance in the Twenty-first Century: Revitalizing the Public Service, McGill-Queen's University Press, Montreal, Buffalo, London, 2000, p. 426.

ety[52] suggest that the management and the prevention of all sorts of new, old and imagined risks dominate the discourse on public policies.

- Another way of thinking about change is the "**institutional robustness** hypothesis" or **path dependency theory**. Here a basic assumption is that national reforms must always be seen in the context of the national political system, decision-making process, national institutions, traditions and values.
- Finally, contingency-based theories claim that the choice of trajectories depends on certain **contingent variables** such as the costs and the size of the public service, political interests, complexity of the environment, level of government etc.

Today, it is widely accepted that evidence about the impact and results of many reforms is still insubstantial. Many methodological problems still exist in measuring the outcomes of reforms. Also, many national and comparative studies on performance management and performance measurement studies are more "preoccupied with describing the new measures, comparing measures from various countries and assessing the impact on accountability"[53]. However, little effort has been devoted to rigorous empirical verification of claimed results or to the identification of the causal relationships underlying them. Thus, today little is being done about reform outcomes. Nevertheless, we know a lot about reforms that produce different results. According to the German sociologist Schulze, the best of all worlds cannot be achieved, but it is worth searching for. The fact that this search will never come to an end is no reason to be pessimistic[54].

2. From bureaucratic role models to post-bureaucratic differentiation

Bureaucracies and civil service systems are said to exist since thousands of years in China and Mesopotamia[55] and then later on in ancient Athens and Rome. The term civil service was never a static and homogenous concept; its meaning developed and changed over time. In the beginning, civil servants were servants of the kings, queens, Lords and Royals; they had no rights and could be dismissed at any time. Although most of them belonged to an elitist, they were paid at the

---

52 For example, Ulrich Beck, Risikogesellschaft - Auf dem Weg in eine andere Moderne, 1986.

53 Melissa Forbes and Laurence E. Lynn Jr., How Does Public Management Affect Government Performance? Findings from International Research, Bush School Working Paper, No. 420, October 2004, p. 2.

54 Gerhard Schulze, Die Beste aller Welten, Carl Hanser Verlag, Wien, 2003.

55 Manfred Zach, Gauner, Pinsel, Chicaneure, Eine kleine Geschichte der Bürokratie, Tübingen, 2003, p. 12.

good will of the monarch. Civil servant positions were bought, acquired or sold. Nepotism and corruption was normal. In all existing systems, civil servants were supposed to be loyal (in the beginning to the Monarchs), to pledge allegiance and to obey the royal orders. Their main task was to collect taxes, to exercise police tasks, to prepare and manage wars and to protect the Monarchy. This historical role of (civil) servants as dependent instruments of the monarchy explains why later civil service concepts focused so much on rules, procedures and rationality. In fact, the objective was to make civil servants independent from particular and personal interests.

However, civil services and bureaucracy have more and diverse sources in the European landscape. The word "hierarchia" stems from Greek; the words *l'état*, *bureaucratie* as well as *l'office* are said to be of French origin. The term "Sheriffs" describes the first royal civil servants in the different counties under the reign of Henry II (1133-1189). In the medieval age, kings and queens increasingly "recruited" servants in order to collect taxes and to defend the territory of the monarchy. For the first time, this practice became a routine under the reign Philippe le Bel (1285-1314) who systematically concentrated on the recruitment of lawyers (who specialised in Roman law)[56].

The first sophisticated bureaucracy is said to have been established in Sicily under Emperor Frederic II (1194-1250)[57]. Sweden also developed a skilled central bureaucracy quite early in its history. This development began during the reign of Gustavus Adolphus, whose entry into the Thirty Years War (1618-1648) required the development of a powerful bureaucracy[58]. Attempts to create independent civil servants were also made by the Hungarian King Matthias Corvinus (1458-1490) who tried to strengthen the role of the central government against the assembly of the nobles and the regional power of the nobility[59].

Utopian ideas of the perfect administrative community had already been described in Thomas More's "Utopia" (1516), Tommaso Campanella's "The City of the Sun" (1602) and Francis Bacon's "New Atlantis" (1627). The first clear distinction between servants of the royals and servants of the state can be found in Thomas Hobbes' "Leviathan" which was published in 1651. The implementa-

---

56 http://www.vie-publique.fr/decouverte-institutions/institutions/approfondissements/histoire-fonction-publique.html

57 Hagen Schulze, Staat und Nation in der europäischen Geschichte, Munich, 2nd Edition, 2004, p. 29.

58 B. Guy Peters, The Politics of Bureaucracy, 5th edition, Routledge, 2001, p. 146.

59 Marco Meneguzzo, The Study of Public Management in Italy, in: Kickert, 2008, op. cit., p. 209.

tion of this concept can be found for the first time in France with the creation of the (relative independent) Conseil d'État du Roi, with its functions as legal adviser and administrative court. The Conseil d'État du Roi is generally considered to be the precursor to the Conseil d'État.

In Europe the emergence of independent and impartial civil services is closely linked to the emergence of the Republican State (firstly in France) and the Nation State (especially after the Congress of Vienna in 1815)[60]. In France, the public law status was "invented" during the French Revolution in order to link the civil servants to the State and not to the Monarchy[61].

However, the realisation of an independent civil service was more difficult than expected. At the end of the 18th century and until the 19th century, the absolute right of the "employer to discharge a worker coincided with the sovereignty doctrine in the public sector. Because employment was a privilege, not a right, it was subject to terms specified by government. Government is sovereign; it is inappropriate to dilute its management rights (...). Indeed for much of the nineteenth century (...) the spoils system dominated personnel policy. (...) Public office was perverted into a private fiefdom as arrogance, greed, and opportunism prevailed over honor, openness and prudence. Favoritism, cronyism, intimidation, corruption, waste, scandals and rampant dismissals were widespread in that squalid era. Rather than governance; its highest priority was to reward its friends, to grant favors for favors given."[62]

This practice changed slowly. Bekke and van der Meer[63] define modern civil service systems as depersonalised systems which differ from traditional modes of government. The biggest changes included the introduction of merit principles (including entrance examinations, job tenure, career service, political neutrality) which were adopted – as a moral guardian to democracy – and which should shield employees from politically inspired employment actions. "In all cases, and particularly in Britain, France, Prussia and Spain, the emergence of a central state in combination with the centralisation of authority is considered an

---

60 Hagen Schulze, Staat und Nation in der europäischen Geschichte, op. cit., p. 39.

61 "Le premier souci des républicains, dès la fin des années 1870, est de s'assurer des sentiments favorables des fonctionnaires à l'égard de la République : la fonction publique", http://diffusion.vie-publique.fr/decouverte-institutions/institutions/ approfondissements/histoire-fonction-publique.html

62 James S. Bowman/Jonathan P. West, Removing Employee Protection: A "See No Evil" Approach to Civil Service Reform, in: Leo W. J. C. Huberts/Jeroen Maesschalck/Carole L. Jurkiewicz, Edward Elgar, Massachusetts, 2008, p. 183.

63 Bekke/van der Meer, Civil Service Systems, op. cit.

important explanatory factor in the growing reliance of rulers of both military and civilian officials. The multiplication of government tasks and the increasing level of administrative specialisation eventually made the separation of the personal and the administrative household of the ruler inevitable (...). It was initially an organisational division, but it also symbolised a profound change in authority relationships. These changing roles represent an important institutionalised shift, as the authority relations of civil servants towards the ruler (gradually) became less personalised (...). Civil servants gradually evolved from personal servants in the service of the ruler to servants of the state"[64].

"Changes on the continent were actually realised as a consequence of the "Napoleonic" wars and conquests. Politico-administrative renewal was either imported or renewed..."[65] (...) "Instrumental in effectuating these changes was the establishment of the Rechtsstaat or in Anglo-Saxon terms the rule of law (...) This powerful idea had implications for the relation between government and the civil service system. (...) Step by step the legal position of civil servants in all countries was formalised and standardised (...) Merit instead of privilege was becoming the guiding principle"[66]. The status of the civil servants evolved into a protected status with many specific employment features that differed to ordinary employment patterns.

As such the creation of a modern civil service is a response to the emergence of the liberal state which was based on the rule of law. Despite this common frame, many civil service systems differed and had too specific reform trajectories. At the same time, criticism emerged in relation to the (often perceived inflexible) protected nature of the civil service. Consequently, civil service criticism is strongly linked with the emergence of a specific civil service. Both are at least two hundred years old.

Ironically, one of the first *modern* European civil services was not set up in Europe, but rather in India by the East India Company, distinguishing its *civil* servants from its *military* servants[67]. As early as 1793, the British government developed a civil service code for the territory of India "under which officials received reasonable if not lavish pay and conditions of service. The important question of promotion was regularised in accordance with the rule of seniority as laid down in the Charter Act of 1793. It was regarded as a safeguard against fa-

64 Bekke/van der Meer, Civil Service Systems, op. cit., p. 276.
65 Ibid., p. 277.
66 Ibid., p. 278.
67 Edgar Norman Gladden, Civil Services of the United Kingdom 1856-1970, Frank Cass, London, 1967.

vouritism and unfairness..."[68] In order to prevent corruption and favouritism, promotions within the company were based on examinations. The system then spread to the United Kingdom in 1854 (based on in the Northcote-Trevelyan report which was published more than 150 years ago)[69].

Lifetime tenure was first introduced in Bavaria in Germany in 1805[70]. Later on the so-called *Alimentationsprinzip* was established which obliged civil servants to devote their whole personality (and full working time) to the public employer. On the other hand the public employer was obliged to take care of the civil servant (and his family) for their whole life (from here stems the request to have specific pension systems for civil servants). In Prussia, the "Allgemeines Landrecht für die Preußischen Staaten" from 1794 contained 19000 paragraphs[71].

Elsewhere, different cities in Italy (and later on the State of Italy), different regions in Spain and parts of the Netherlands invented their own civil service models and further adapted them to regional and national tradition, culture and political needs. More and more, in all European societies it was believed that civil servants were linked to the authority of the state and could not be compared to other public employees or employees in the private sector.

Consequently, almost all Member States designed their public organisations in specific ways as they expected that certain behaviour on the part of civil servants would result from specific organisational features. Traditionally, a hierarchical and formalised organisational structure, clear and rigid career paths, lifetime tenure, full-time employment, seniority, advantageous pension systems and rigid remuneration systems were introduced in order to reduce as far as possible the risk of too much political influence, corruption, misconduct, the exercise of private interests and instability of government. Consequently, the traditional argument for a specific organisational structure was to produce a certain ethical status for civil servants who should be committed to the public good, neutrality, impartiality and to observing confidentiality and displaying expertise. In many countries, civil servants were therefore working in hierarchical organisations,

---

68 Edgar Norman Gladden, A History of Public Administration, Vol. II, Frank Cass, London, 1972, p. 251.

69 Stafford Northcote/C. E. Trevelyan, The Organisation of the Permanent Civil Service, Parliamentary Papers, Volume XXVII, 1854.

70 Matthias Pechstein/Rudolf Summer, Beiträge zum Beamtenrecht, Tuebingen, 2007, p. 58.

71 Hagen Schulze, Staat und Nation in der europäischen Geschichte, op. cit., p. 96.

had very specific recruitment procedures, specific ethical obligations, little mobility, varying working conditions and specific social security systems.

Since the notion of social services did not exist for a long time[72], most existing 'civil services' were tax services, military and judicial services and police services. Consequently, the most important task of the state sector was to *control* society rather than to *serve* society. The "Leviathan" (T. Hobbes) stood above society and governments were – until the 1970s – more concerned with the implementation of programmes than with the evaluation of their outcomes. Moreover, citizens were not allowed to question government authorities at all.

Within this bureaucratic structure, where the public service was closed off and separated from society and citizens, it was not possible for civil servants to the have the right to strike or the right to engage in collective agreements relating to working conditions. In other words, civil servants were seen as a different category of staff. Because of the specific treatment of civil servants, public perceptions arose of civil servants having different personalities, being motivated by different incentives, working less hard than employees in the private sector, being more security-minded, more rule-oriented and not very innovative.

In fact, the emerging modern concept of bureaucracy and civil service was by nature a "republican" concept that was designed as a counter concept to the traditional and charismatic power structure of the monarchist and medieval times. As such the bureaucracy as described by Weber was believed to be an instrument of power which was based on the principle of rationality. Its task was to enhance the stability of the state while limiting the influence of the (political) class. Yet, bureaucracy was not only supposed to be a new form of rational power, it was also believed to be more efficient and more ethical than any other organisational form until the 19th century.

Because of this promise, most new EU Member States in 2005 opted for structures with classical career paths. Today, most Balkan countries are moving in a similar direction. One major reason for establishing a career system is to "fight" the problem of political influence and patronage which had resulted from the Communist period.

However, in many central, Eastern and South Eastern countries, reforms come and go and it is still very difficult to predict where reforms will lead. Verheijen

---

72 For instance, until the 1950s only a few countries had anti-poverty programmes, or initiatives in the field of food safety, social security or environmental protection.

makes this very clear: "civil service developments has in most states been limited to the development and adoption of civil service legislation (…) The adoption of civil service laws in a large number of states in the region, however, has not resolved the problems of instability and politicisation and has rarely led to the development of a well-working system of long-term career development"[73]. In fact, in many countries, the reform effort can be described as moving "to and from" or even "forwards and backwards".

According to Meyer-Sahling "the large differences between the eight CEECs imply that the CEE region can by no means be seen as one world of civil service governance. Instead, we can identify different groups of countries in CEE that share broad characteristics, levels of fit with European principles of administration, and recent reform trajectories (...). It is more difficult to classify the CEE civil services with regard to some of the other major models of public administration, such as the classic Weberian model of bureaucracy and the new public management"[74].

The situation is different in Western and Northern Europe. Here, bureaucratic career systems were relatively effective and for a long time (in most cases until costs exploded in the 1980s). The first European country to deviate from a classical bureaucratic career system was the UK (after the Fulton report in 1968), followed by the Netherlands (after the so-called Pre-advies in 1982) and the reforms undertaken in Sweden (in the late eighties) and Italy (in 1993). Spain's public administration decidedly embraced the new "new wave of administrative reform" starting in 1989 with the publication of the so-called MAP (Reflexiones para la modernizacion de la administracion – MAP) which adopted some changes that were already taking place in Great Britain, Sweden and a number of other countries[75]. Less drastic, but also important, were the civil service reforms in Denmark, Finland, Portugal, Belgium, Germany and France. Today, almost all EU countries are in a process of de-bureaucratisation of their public services.

Today, it can be stated that while some bureaucratic features are not disappearing, they are nevertheless a subject of great reforms. Traditional government is transforming into "governance" and traditional administration into good admini-

---

73 A.J.G. Verheijen, Public Administration in Post-Communist States, in: Peters/Pierre (eds.), Handbook of Public Administration, op. cit., p. 491.

74 Meyer-Sahling, Sustainability of Civil Service Reforms in Central and Eastern Europe, op. cit., p. 75.

75 Joan Subirats, Public Administration and Administrative Science in Spain, in: Kickert/Stillman, The Modern State and its Study, op. cit., p. 141.

stration, although these concepts do not necessarily mean that we are taking a step forward towards solving problems and offering better solutions. Furthermore, the "evolving models of government are not intrinsically liberal or conservative, effective or not effective – they are simply different and new and thus require some careful thought on the part of those who care about good governance and well-functioning public administration"[76]. In the meantime it has become popular to define most models as post-bureaucratic or post-public service models. After the New Public Management euphoria it has also become popular to state that "post-bureaucratic forms of organisation perform less well than traditional bureaucracies..."[77] However, as it turns out, terms such as post-bureaucracy are as vague as the term New Public Management.

In "The Responsible Administrator" Cooper argues that "we are in a time of transition in which the modern heritage of public administration is increasingly in conflict with a postmodern model"[78]. The key phenomena of modernity are assumptions about universal values, absolute values, bureaucracy and rationality. Contrary to this postmodern is a term in which "fundamental assumptions are being discredited as final and absolute. Assumptions about some kind of objectively real and universal human nature, or natural law, or absolute values and ultimate truths (...) no longer hold..."[79]. "The homogeneity of traditional society, with its unifying and stabilising cultural bonds, has been broken (...). New forms of lifestyles have developed, and new ways of coping with a broad spectrum of lifestyles, diets, preferences, political philosophies, and modes of exchange have evolved"[80]. The implications of these changes for public administration are obvious: post-modern administrations tend to be much more diverse, less hierarchical, more flexible, diverse, representative and less separated from the citizenry. Whereas the term "bureaucracy" represents clear values ("hierarchy, formalism, standardisation, rationality, obedience etc.), the term "postmodernism" implies conflicting values and value dilemmas.

The problem with this description of the administration in the 21st century is obvious. Whereas the term "bureaucracy" or "modernity" can be defined and broken down into concrete contents, this is much less the case with the term "post-

---

76 Elaine Ciulla Kamarck, Public Servants for Twenty-First-Century Government, in: Donahue/ Nye (eds.), For the People, Can We Fix Public Service, op. cit., p. 134.

77 Christopher Politt, Bureaucracies Remember, Post-bureaucratic Organizations Forget? In: Public Administration, Volume 87, Number 2 June 2009, pp. 198-218.

78 Terry L. Cooper, The Responsible Administrator, Jossey Bass, 5th edition, 2006, p. 45.

79 Ibid., p. 46.

80 Ibid., p. 52.

modernity". The latter represents a fluid notion and neither offers a clear definition nor orientation. Although the term postmodernism may be an adequate description of the current change processes, it leaves those in charge of introducing change processes puzzled. The notion postmodern administration illustrates that we lack an understanding of what could be an (universal) alternative to the bureaucratic form of organisation. Mostly the terms postmodern, post-bureaucratic organisation or post-public service are nothing but negative "counter" definitions.

In 2005 Olsen published an article entitled "Maybe It Is Time to Rediscover Bureaucracy" [81]. In this article he questions the fashionable ideas that bureaucratic organisation is an obsolescent, undesirable, and non-viable form of administration and that there is an inevitable and irreversible paradigmatic shift towards market or network organisation. In contrast, the paper argues that contemporary democracies will again be involved in another round of ideological struggle over what desirable forms of administration and government are. Olsen's argument is not that bureaucratic organisation is the answer to all old and new challenges of public administration; rather that rediscovering Weber's analysis of bureaucratic organisation, enriches our understanding of public administration. This is particularly true when we look at the existing empirical facts in the different institutional contexts, and take into account the political context that bureaucracy is part of, not only the internal characteristics of "the bureau."[82]

When looking back in time we get an impression of what has changed. The boundaries between the civil services and the societies are further eroding. Modern technologies have changed communication styles. Public employees are better educated than ever and can now challenge the authority of their superiors. Line managers are given more individual responsibilities which threaten classical hierarchical decision-making procedures. Citizen orientation and principles of good administration are at the top of all administrative reform agendas.

In many Member States civil servants are recruited "on the market" and employed at mid-career levels. Everywhere, civil servants are required to be more mobile and flexible. Increasingly, civil servants are working on a part-time basis or making use of offers to work from home ("teleworking"). In the future, the internet and virtual social networks (e.g., Facebook, Wikipedia etc.) will also

---

81 Johan P. Olson, Maybe It Is Time to Rediscover Bureaucracy, in: Journal of Public Administration Research and Theory 2006, Vol. 16, No. 1, pp. 1-24.

82 Ibid.

challenge all post-bureaucratic concepts. According to Margetts, in the future traditional public organisations are changing into virtual organisations[83].

The ongoing and constantly changing *digitalisation* trend in our societies sets additional challenges to our conceptual understanding of work, structure and organisation in the public services. In the future, not only more public services but also classical civil service tasks (which involve the exercise of public powers) will be carried out at home, in social networks or on the street with the mobile IPhone. The digital era will further erode the boundaries between the civil service and the society, as well as between the public- and private sectors and between the professional and private sectors[84]. Because we have flexitime, improved information technologies and video phones, work is becoming less and less restricted by place and time. At the same time, work which was formerly carried out by state authorities is nowadays carried out by very different forms of public- or private organisations.

This blurring of boundaries between the different spheres is quite ironic as many traditional tasks and duties of the national civil services are not changing. Protecting the common good and ensuring liberty, freedom and human rights remain the prime goals of the public sector.

Another ironic fact is that – despite the many changes that have taken place and many reforms that have been introduced – one important part of the national public services, the civil service, is without doubt the section of the politico-administrative systems of the Member States of the European Union (EU), which has most been influenced by the respective national traditions and histories, and which for a long time was least affected by European integration. None of the present treaties therefore provided for any EU competences with respect to the regulation of the public service. The Treaty of Lisbon did not divert from this tradition either[85]. Thus, change has been taking place, not because of EU Membership, but rather because of other external and internal reform pressures.

---

83 Helen Margetts, Virtual Organisations, in: Ferlie/Lynn/Pollitt, The Oxford Handbook of Public Management, op. cit., pp. 305-326.

84 Dalton Conley, Elsewhere U.S.A., Pantheon, New York, 2008.

85 However, during the last few decades the European Union has decided upon a number of important legal instruments which are binding upon the Member States and which have an impact on the national public services, services of general interest and HR policies within the national public services. This is mostly the case in the field of anti-discrimination policies and to a lesser extent in the field of free movement of persons and working conditions and working time. In addition to this, the developments towards more international administrative cooperation, benchmarking, the identification

3. From monolithic concept to multiple providers

For many years, sociologists have been observing profound changes in our societies. For example, in *Elsewhere U.S.A.* Conley describes the change of the modern world "where modernist distinctions like home-office, work-leisure, public-private....no longer hold fast. In the twenty-first century, the boundary between work and home has largely disappeared, technological gadgets structure family life, business often intrudes on leisure...."[86]. Overall, traditional societal boundaries are fading and changing.

Contrary to this, public views about the definition, role and tasks of the public service are still very much grounded in the centralised and unified public administration which is clearly separated from the private sector. The civil service is still often seen as a closed and apolitical apparatus which is separated from the private sector. In fact, citizens, media and politicians often express dissatisfaction with the too big and costly public sector and with civil servants in general, as well as campaigning against the "bureaucrats" and the slow, inefficient, unresponsive and expensive bureaucracies. In the past, most public services were indeed carried out exclusively by state bodies. The "single employer concept was vital to the development of centralised public personnel systems... A government, rather than its individual agencies, was the employer. Accordingly, the employee was a career civil servant rather than a worker"[87].

Today the concept of public service has developed from a rather centralised to a decentralised and fragmented conception which includes a myriad of different services and providers from the public, semi-public and private sector. Public policies are also administered through increasingly complex networks, decentralised governance structures, public-private partnerships and cooperative ventures between NGOs, consultants and government. Many waves of externalisation, delegation and agencification have created a more complex picture of the national public services. Furthermore, most public administrations include or are closely linked to public institutions that are bodies which, for the execution of specific tasks, are relatively independent from government. These functional bodies, which are generally under indirect political control – for example they are nominated by a board – can be found in most Member States. Examples of these

---

of good practices, theories of good governance, common reform pressures and the growing impact of EU Legislation etc., all of these developments have – at least partially – led to a gradual "Europeanisation of Public Administrations".

86 Dalton Conley, Elsewhere U.S.A., op. cit., p. 8.

87 David H. Rosenbloom/Robert S. Kravchuk, Public Administration, Fifth Edition, New York, 2002, p. 594.

organisations include the non-governmental public bodies in the **United Kingdom**, *enti pubblici non-economici* in **Italy**, public establishments in **France** and **Greece**, *organismes d'intérêt public* in **Belgium** and independent administrative bodies (*Zelfstandige bestuursorganen*) in the **Netherlands**.

Even more complex is the situation in public organisations which recruit their employees under labour law (in France this concerned 172 900 people in 2006 who worked in the financial and social security sectors, but also in the wider commercial sector, i.e. in the Caisses nationales du régime général de la sécurité sociale, the établissements publics à caractère industriel ou commercial (Épic) etc.).

As a consequence of all of the abovementioned developments, the traditional concept of the public service as a single, unified employer is slowly disappearing. Today, civil service observers agree that the classical models and perceptions of public service and civil service were shaped in a world that no longer exists. This is the discrepancy between the monolithic and centralised 19th century roots and the fragmented and diverse (post-) modern realities we face at the beginning of the 21st century. The fragmentation of the public services, the decentralisation of responsibilities, outsourcing policies and private public partnerships make the public service a somewhat fragmented body.

Nowadays, more reform measures encourage the change, deconstruction and decentralisation of the public service and the civil service on all fronts. Beneath the simplistic image that public policy is a top-down matter between two participants – the State (and public authorities) and the private sector/citizens – lies a new and far more complex reality in which a growing number of actors (e.g., NGOs, citizens, lobbyists, Public-Private Partnerships, semi-public bodies) require an important decision-making role. Today, the term "Governance" describes this development.

The ongoing trend towards more decentralisation has important paradoxical consequences for our understanding of accountability and for the legitimacy of a specific civil service. While government is still held responsible for almost any "governmental failures", most public policies are nowadays carried out by mixed forms of public and private actors and authorities, or are even delegated to outside private organisations. Consequently, experts face growing difficulties in answering the question of who is carrying out public services and whether public services should be carried out by a specific group of public employees: the civil servants. Because of the speed of modernisation and the lack of clear strategies, there is no longer any common understanding of which services should be carried out by the public, by the private sector, or by combinations of state and private actors (e.g., public-private partnerships).

The definition of the term "public official", only because of a distinct legal status of public employees, no longer covers all employees who provide public services. In fact, there is a need to broaden the definition of the term "public employee" and to include also functional and economic criteria[88]. The alignment between the public service and the private sector and the blurring of the boundaries between the public and private sectors provoke additional confusion over the question of which tasks and positions should be carried out by civil servants with public status, and which by public employees, consultants, advisors and contractors.

4. Is public service reform a rational process?

4.1. Obstacles to a rational reform

Nobody denies the need to reform the public sector and to make it better; everybody wants the public sector to become more effective, efficient and transparent. Consequently, all reform projects are designed to reach these objectives. However, what are the problems in reaching these objectives? Is it at all possible to design administrative reform as rational processes? Is Human Resource Management reform a teleological and rational process?

The question of where reforms lead to is difficult to answer: "The question of what has resulted from the many reforms is obviously an absolutely fundamental one. Yet it is not at all simple. The label result can be applied to many different aspects, and may incorporate a variety of concepts (…). A full discussion of 'results' therefore embraces the wider question of 'results for whom, defined by whom, against what objectives?'"[89] Because of their rational approach to public management reforms in Europe, Pollitt and Bouckaert[90] wonder about the "large optimism about the potential of public sector reforms" and the results: tradeoffs, balances, limits, dilemmas and paradoxes[91]. Emery and Giauque also reveal several dilemmas and contradictions within public management reform[92]. One has to deal with the goal of motivating staff and the promotion of cultural change, while at the same time tenure is weakened and downsizing projects are going on.

88 Bundeskanzleramt Österreich, Das Personal des Bundes, Wien, 2009.
89 Pollitt/Bouckaert, Public Management Reform, 1st edition, op. cit., p. 97.
90 Ibid.
91 Ibid., p. 149.
92 Yves Emery/David Giauque, Dilemmes de la GRH publique, LEP, Lausanne, 2007.

They are also worried about the instability that seems to reign in public organisations, and point to several negative consequences of current reforms, especially the danger that they will destroy institutional memory as well as negatively affecting morale and trust.

Some decades ago, Lindblom suggested that "decisions within this political setting can never be wholly rational but (...) are of a bounded rational" nature. That is to say, instead of insisting on an optimal solution, the public policy maker must be satisfied with what is good enough, or as Lindbloom suggested, must "muddle through"[93].

A conceptual understanding of the reform process in public organisations inevitably leads back to the work of Herbert Simon. Simon did not deny the possibility of change processes as a result of rational processes. However, he showed that organisations never work purely rationally or perfectly: "We forget sometimes that an organisation is a group of people behaving. These people are not tools or machines. They have feelings, hopes, and fears. They get sick, hungry, angry, frustrated, happy, sad. Their behaviour is subject to a whole range of influences extending back to their births..."[94]. Very important "is the role that communication plays in the day-to-day work of every organisation. Without communication, not even the first steps can be taken toward human cooperation, and it is impossible to speak about organisational problems without speaking about communication..."[95]. At the root of public administration are continuous conflicts and communication blockages due to:

- Barriers of language (misinterpretation and misunderstanding)
- Differing frames of reference (different mental understanding of definitions)
- Geographical distance impeding the communication process (across units, countries, ministries)
- Status distance as a filtering process throughout hierarchical levels of organisation
- Self-protection (individuals tend to communicate more those things that are to their benefit)
- Pressure of work (people tend to overlook important matters)

---

93 Charles E. Lindblom, The Science of Muddling through, in Public Administration Review, 1959.

94 Herbert Simon, Public Administration, Alfred Knopf, New York, 1973, p. 55.

95 Herbert A. Simon, Donald W. Smitburg, Victor A. Thomas, The Communication Process, in: Richard, J. Stillman, Public Administration, Fourth Edition, Houghton Company, Boston, 1988, p. 254.

- Censorship (limitations on the flow of information by authority or force)

Changes in the public sector may also be a result of solving problems or of failure to address challenges (e.g., fighting unemployment). Solutions and reforms may contribute to improvements but – later on – to deteriorations. Reforms might therefore produce "waves" of different outcomes which are difficult to predict. There may be improvements in some policies, but – at the same time – deteriorations in other fields (e.g., advancing human rights and democracy, enhancing fairness, equality and non-discrimination, reducing crime, improving welfare, reforming public transport, guaranteeing peace and stability, protecting the environment, reducing disease and enhancing consumer protection, ensuring safe drinking water, promoting financial stability, increasing access to education, integrating minorities etc.[96]). In all these different dossiers, the civil service plays a crucial role and different ministries may produce different results.

The most important reason for this can be found in the lack of a coherent strategy in the field of HRM. Mostly, the final objective of HRM reform is not simply to "improve the quality and the performance of people", but to enhance efficiency, increase productivity, save resources and to serve political interests. Many critical observers even argue that the most important objectives of HRM reform are saving resources, increasing organisational performance and enhancing flexibility. They claim – as did Woodrow Wilson in 1887 – that public administration is a field of business. Others, however, are of the opinion that the public service is different to the private sector and that its specific characteristics (e.g., fairness, non-discrimination, equality, rule of law) will ensure that it remains so.

Indeed, fundamental questions as to the objectives of public sector reform were discussed more seriously in the past than in the present. For example, in the United States, at the beginning of the 20th century, the so-called Brownlow Committee stated: "in proceeding to the reorganisation of the government it is to keep prominently before us the ends of reorganisation. Too close a view of machinery most not cut off from sight the true purpose of efficient management. Economy is not the only objective, though reorganisation is the first step to savings; the elimination of duplication and contradictory policies is not the only objective, though the new organisation will be simple and symmetrical; higher salaries and better jobs are not the only objectives, though these are necessary; better business methods and fiscal controls are not the only objectives, though

96 Paul Light, Government's Greatest Achievements of the Past Half Century, in: Reform Watch, Brookings Institute, Vol. 2, November 2000.

these too are demanded. There is but one grand purpose, namely, to make democracy work today in our national government; that is, to make our government an up-to-date, efficient, and effective instrument for carrying out the will of the nation. It is for this purpose that the government needs thoroughly modern tools of management"[97].

Today, most modern reform concepts lack a coherent answer to the objective of HRM reform. The popular notion of "doing more with less" is such a concept. Prescriptions about how to structure organisations also tend to have their origins in reactions against failures (or perceived failures) of current institutions, rather than looking at what should be achieved instead. Consequently, programmes "for organisational success often amount to turning round what is seen as a recipe for disaster"[98]. "Slowly, however, the euphoria starts to wear off, then new heaven and new earth start to look all too much like the old ones, and the cycle of disappointment begins again" (Hood)[99].

4.2. The relationship between civil service reform and politics

The politico-administrative dichotomy became institutionalised after the Second World War and was seen as essential in order to yield the greatest efficiency. Today, the "idea that public administration can be separated from politics is odd. It was not at the founding, but later, of course, it became the cornerstone of the public administrative orthodoxy (…). Initially, the idea that governmental administration could and should be apolitical was widely opposed by entrenched politicians and their followers. Opponents wondered how apolitical administrations could be responsive to the people and be representative"[100]. Today, the widely noted crisis in public administration is related exactly to this "neglectedness": the failure and lack of understanding of the impact of political strategies on administrative thought.

The fact that the civil service and the "bureaucracy" is the frequent target of reform "bears witness to the central importance of personnel management to tech-

97 Louis Brownlow/Charles E. Merriam/Luther Gulik, Report of the President's Committee on Administrative Management (1937), in: Jay M. Shafritz/ Albert C. Hyde, Classics of Public Administration, The Dorsey Press, Chicago, Illinois, 2nd Edition, 1987, p. 94.

98 Hood, The Art of the State, op. cit., p. 23-24.

99 Ibid., p. 195.

100 David H. Rosenbloom, Administrative Theory, Political Power and Government Reform, in: Patricia W. Ingraham/ Barbara S. Romzek, New Paradigms for Government, Jossey Bass Publishers, San Francisco, 1994, p. 149.

nically and politically effective government operations (...). The challenge has always been to find a way to temper the control and flexibility that are required with appropriate levels of protection for public employees"[101]. One good example for this is the introduction of performance-related pay (PRP) in the public services of the EU Member States. While evidence was often lacking that PRP would enhance individual performance and individual motivation, politicians were enthusiastic about this instrument. In fact, many politicians supported the introduction of PRP throughout recent years because it supported the popular view that the "lazy bureaucrats" should perform better and PRP may work as a sort of performance incentive. Consequently, PRP became a political fashion although the effects of the instrument remain questionable.

In 1939 Pendleton was one of the first to underline that "law is not administered in a vacuum, but in an environment composed of all those who have an interest in the application or the non-enforcement of the statute. The official is surrounded by a web of interests..."[102]. In the field of implementation theory, Pressman and Wildavsky (1973) pointed to the fact that "the separation of policy design from implementation is fatal"[103]. Today, the best example for the validity of this thesis is certainly the policy-making process in the European Union. Today, everybody is aware of the important role of public officials in the formulation and decision-making process at the EU level. If civil servants in one Member State are not prepared for the "Regulatory competition" in Brussels, shortcomings in the implementation phase are almost inevitable.

As a body of thought and practice, public administration continues to overstate the extent to which it is concerned exclusively with execution and management. At the same time, public administration has to manage the rising confluence of executive, legislative, and judicial constitutional functions[104], while politicians find it appealing to criticise "bureaucrats" because it is widely accepted by voters responding to beliefs about the need to control bureaucrats. Politicians often

101 Edward Kellough/Lloyd G. Nigro (eds.), Civil Service Reform in the States – Personnel Policy and Politics at the Subnational Level, Suny Series in Public Administration, State University of New York Press, 2006, p. 2.

102 Herring E. Pendleton, Public Administration and the Public Interest (1936), in: Shafritz/Hyde, op. cit.

103 Jeffrey L. Pressman/Aaron Wildavsky, Implementation (1973), in: Shafritz/Hyde, op. cit., p. 487.

104 Rosenbloom, in: Ingraham/Romzek, op. cit., p. 151.

respond "to mythical beliefs about the poor performance of government and the reasons for it"[105].

Many still believe, however, that administrative reform can be separated not only from politics but also from power and interests. In reality, "attempts to solve administrative problems in isolation from the structure of power and purpose in the polity are bound to prove illusory" (Long, 1949)[106]. Administrative reforms are "embedded" in the context of power, scarce financial resources, conflicts, hierarchies, rules, attitudes, persons and traditions. In addition, Human Resource Management relates to feelings, emotions, communications, frustration, joy and experience. Because of these individual factors, every HR manager continues to ask the same question without getting a clear answer: "how can you manage what you can't even see?"[107]

The US administrative scientist Waldo (1948) argued that there can be no comprehensive public administrative theory that is not also political theory. "A variety of works came to support his conclusion, by showing that the core functions of public administration are laden with political questions: decision making (…), budgeting (…), organisation (…), personnel (…), and implementation (…). Failure to note the Waldo theorem is fatal for those seeking to reform government, although reformers and academic advocates of change frequently ignore that lesson"[108]. The problem of the bureaucracy is therefore not always attributable to the bureaucracy. The problem lies also with the political system. "In fact, the New Public Management (NPM) movement worldwide is not merely about administrative reform. It is really part of a wider debate about the proper role and scope of government. These are political decisions. Decisions about privatisation, for example, are also decisions about the proper role of government and who should be held accountable. If the public wants smaller government – and there is no clear indication that it generally does – those decisions should be made openly through the political process. What political leaders often want to do, however, is use the language of reinvention – with its emphasis on cost savings, job cuts, and elimination of red tape – to argue that they are cutting costs without cutting anything "basic". Blending together "works better, costs less" is at one level largely political theater – a way to look creative and justify cost

---

105 Hal G. Rainey, Facing Fundamental Challenges in Reforming Public Personnel Administration, in: Steven W. Hays/Richard C. Kearney (eds.), Public Personnel Administration, Fourth Edition, New Jersey, 2003.

106 N. E. Long, Power and Administration (1949), in: Shafritz/Hyde, op. cit., p. 212.

107 Harvard Business Review, Motivating People, Special Issue 2003, p. 8.

108 Rosenbloom, in: Ingraham/Romzek, op. cit., p. 145.

constraints in a highly political environment"[109]. In the United States, the Bush campaign won the presidential elections in 2000 with the promise to fight against the Washington Bureaucracy and to further reduce public employment. Three years later, the Bush administration employed more public employees than the Clinton administration did in 2000[110]. The paradox between rhetoric and reality in the USA showed that, administratively speaking, whilst public sector reform is about better rhetoric, it is also, politically speaking, about political or financial considerations. The "works better" is mostly a mere secondary consideration. It is relatively easy to determine whether government costs less[111]; it is more difficult, however, to see whether it works better.

All in all, the interrelationship between politics and public administration makes it very difficult – if not impossible – to engage in rational discourse about administrative reform trajectories which are based on sound theories, rational debates and hard facts.

4.3. How can you change what you cannot see? People, emotions and limitations of reforms

Often, people come to study civil service reform and HRM reforms and expect certainty and absolute knowledge. They expect to find detailed laws governing the behaviour of people, organisations and systems. These people will be disappointed! The study of people, organisations and civil service systems cannot be done with absolute predictivity since "the multiplicity of variables impinging on any one organisational situation is so great (...) that data on all of them sufficient to predict the precise outcome of that multiple interrelationship would never in practice be forthcoming"[112]. Therefore, studies on soft factors and emotional intelligence[113] have become popular although they, too, have clear limitations since they (often) fail to acknowledge the importance of legal principles and rational procedures in the national civil services.

Moreover, path-dependency and an institutionalist approach have their limitations when it comes to explaining why many reforms in Europe are taking a similar (or even the same) direction and why so many reforms go against established traditions and regulatory styles.

---

109 Aberbach/Rockman, op. cit., p. 186.

110 See the number of civilians employed in the US. http://opm.gov/feddata/ etmar03.pdf

111 See for example the Standard-Costs model in the field of Reducing Administrative Burdens.

112 Charles Handy, Understanding Organizations, Fourth Edition, London 1999, p. 13.

113 Daniel Goleman, Working with Emotional Intelligence, New York, 2000.

Here, the neo-institutional theory suggests that motivation differences, ethical foundations as well as reforms and their outcomes must also be seen in connection with institutional traditions, values, cultures and – societal – fashions. Moreover, researchers like Koselleck[114] or Lakoff[115] point to the importance of "reform language" and how much the political and public service reform discourse is dominated by fashionable linguistic trends, words and concepts (like "Flexibility", "Performance", "Reform", "Change", "Good Practice", "Benchmarking", "Competence", "Sustainability", "New Public Management"), which – despite their popularity – offer many explanations. Reform language mostly represents attempts to replace traditional concepts with more modern variants – "whatever "modernity" means in this context"[116].

On the other hand, the public itself perceives reforms differently and does not always follow the reform speed (and the many changes) that has taken place. For example, whereas many citizens maintain a rather traditional (and critical) attitude towards the national public services and its bureaucrats, recent studies show that a country can have a very traditional public service, a small public sector, decentralised HRM policies and participative management styles at the same time. This combination of factors may contradict (still prevailing) images that countries are either traditional bureaucratic, career-system countries or flexible position system countries.

Nevertheless, most reform projects in the field of HRM constitute legal, economic and political reforms that ignore psychological aspects, although there is massive evidence that individual behaviour is largely influenced by emotions and feelings, such as hope, fear, aspirations etc. At the end, many reforms do not produce expected outcomes, but instead, reform paradoxes and reform dilemmas[117].

For many years researchers such as Perry and Hondeghem[118] have studied the existence of motivational differences in the public sector. For example, Perry

---

114 Reinhart Kosselleck, Begriffsgeschichten, Suhrkamp, Frankfurt/M., 2006.

115 Georg Lakoff/Elisabeth Wehling, Auf leisen Sohlen ins Gehirn, Politische Sprache und ihre heimliche Macht, Carl-Auer, Heidelberg 2008.

116 Joachim Jens Hesse/Christopher Hood/B. Guy Peters, Paradoxes in Public Sector Reform – An International Comparison, Duncker/Humblot GmbH, Berlin, 2003.

117 Yves Emery/David Giauque, op. cit.

118 James Perry/Annie Hondeghem (eds.), Motivation in Public Management – The Call of Public Service, Oxford University Press, 2008.

(1996)[119] developed a measurement scale which consists of four dimensions: attraction to policy making; commitment to the public interest and civic duty; compassion; and self-sacrifice. The findings suggest that people who are attracted to working in the public services have unique motivational incentives that energise and direct their behaviour. Consequently, the motivational aspects of work in the public service cannot be fully explained by rational choice theories. In fact, the different dimension of work in the public service show that rational and egoistic motives are only two explanatory variables for work in the public service.

Although they have a lot in common, public motivation theories should not be mixed with public ethics theories. Both theories point to the likelihood of different values and motives in the public services. However, having different motivational values (than in the private sector) does not mean that public servants are "the better employees" and act more ethically. In fact, different forms of poor performance, unethical behaviour and corruption seem to exist as much in the public sector as in the private sector. Also in the public sector, many employees suffer from poor leadership, unethical behaviour (of colleagues), intimidation at work and bullying. In addition, far too little emphasis is placed on the relationship between organisational structure and personality or on the relationship between working conditions and personality. Furthermore, the high number of physical and psychological disorders (e.g., back pain, burn-out, stress) show that many "real issues" impact on work behaviour, individual and organisational performance and motivation (and possibly much more than the introduction of material incentives such as performance-related pay). Here, it does not matter very much whether we are turning our attention to the public or to the private sector.

For a long time, in many countries 'managing poor performance' has been a neglected issue as the focus was often on high performance. This poses a problem as there may be as many poor performers as high performers in an organisation and the impact of ongoing poor performance is rather high since poor performers:

- do not deliver required business outcomes or value for money;
- impair the standard, reputation and professionalism of the civil service;
- disrupt the flow of work and increase the workloads of their colleagues;
- cause resentment and lower morale; and
- set a bad example to those they manage.

---

119 James Perry, Measuring Public Service Motivation: An Assessment of Construct Reliability and Validity, in; Journal of Public Administration Research and Theory, Vol. 6, No. 1, 1996, pp. 5-22.

There is no doubt that staff becomes irrational, de-motivated and even cynical when poor performance is not dealt with. While inadequate recognition of good performance is often a cause of concern, the inability of an organisation to manage ineffectiveness and poor performance creates even stronger resentment and affects the credibility of the whole performance assessment system. There is also a difference between a short-term decline in performance and consecutive periods of poor performance. The longer that poor performance is allowed to linger, the greater the problem for the individuals and organisation when it is finally tackled.

A central challenge of managing poor performance results from the fact that many things, inside and outside the workplace can affect an individual's performance positively or negatively. Important reasons for poor performance may be a lack of incentives, unclear tasks and objectives, bad leadership, ability, skills and motivation, unethical behaviour from colleagues, misfit between job expectations and job tasks etc[120]. Managing poor performance consequently has to be understood as a key leadership task. A good manager will identify poor performance and discuss it with the person concerned to understand the reasons for poor performance and what can be done to improve the situation. In many cases training or coaching may be sufficient. Managers should also be sensitive to other factors such as stress, relationship problems and financial difficulties. Albeit managers cannot resolve such issues, they should do their best to bring performance back to an acceptable level.

Thus, changing behaviour is difficult and cannot be simply done by introducing performance management tools or asking for more public service ethos. Or, as Follett puts it in The Giving of Orders (1926[121]), you "cannot get people to do things most satisfactorily by ordering them or exhorting them; but also that even reasoning with them, even convincing them intellectually, may not be enough (...) For all our past life, our early training, our later experience, all our emotions, beliefs, prejudices, every desire that we have, have formed certain habits of mind ... Therefore it will do little good merely to get intellectual agreement; unless you change the habit pattern of people, you have not really changed your people".

---

120 Present HR literature sees that performance depends on two factors: motivation and ability. If either factor is missing, the outcome will be bad performance. See Edward Lawler III, Treat People Right! How Organizations and Individuals Can Propel Each Other into a Virtuous Spiral of Success, Jossey-Bass 2003, pp. 38-58.

121 Mary Parker Follett, The Giving of Orders (1926), in Shafritz/Hyde, op. cit., p. 65.

The reasons and motives for performing well or for under-performing can be described as an iceberg. Traditional HRM deals only with those aspects that "appear at the surface", or in other words, "hard facts and instruments". Consequently, HRM managers focus either on punitive measures or (mostly material) incentives to regulate individual performance and motivation. Because of this, it is at least questionable whether personnel management reform will advance if it does not also take into account the accumulated evidence of the so-called "soft sciences". Today, leadership training programmes cover the relationship between psychology and leadership, and leadership theories discuss the relationship between personality and psychology[122]. In addition, through coaching and mentoring programmes, psychological elements and communication as an important management tool have found their ways into training programmes. Unfortunately, those programmes are mostly only available to top officials (and are very expensive and – unfortunately – vary very much in quality). The problem is, as always, how to separate the "good" and high-quality from the "bad" and not very practical training programmes.

For example, in evaluating the impact of performance-related pay on individual performance, one should ideally evaluate the effectiveness of this instrument when placing it in the context of the "psychology" of the individual. Do material incentives make a difference to performance if employees are motivated to perform very well anyway, but for different reasons (e.g., seeking recognition, fear that colleagues are performing better, fear of being rewarded too little by the superior etc.)?

Generally, the role and importance of emotions at the workplace seems to be widely under-researched (apart from sexual harassment) and, sometimes is not even recognised in the public sector, despite the fact that emotions strongly determine performance and non-performance. Often, individuals act irrationally and emotionally (e.g., they are aggressive, get stressed very quickly, work too much rather than too little) and this behaviour cannot be changed and managed through the introduction of material incentives. Therefore, more and more consultancy firms are now also employing psychologists. However, in the public sector, personnel departments mostly employ Human Resource Managers and economists or experts from other disciplines, but only rarely psychologists.

122 Hans Jung, Personalwirtschaft, München/Wien, 3. Edition, 1999, p. 402.

IV. DEFINITION OF CIVIL SERVICE

1. Public administration, public service and civil service

In this study there is no space to discuss the various existing definitions of public management and public administration and the various terminological shifts over time as regards the use of these concepts. According to Hood, many authors vary with regard to the definition of the term, and most of the standard definitions of public management refer to "the study and practice of design and operation of arrangements for the provision of public services and executive government"[123].

By *public administration* we refer to organisations which are directly subordinated to political power and which are at the service of the executive in the policy-design, policy-making and in the policy-implementation and enforcement process. Therefore, public administration is the system of bodies, services and staff of the State and of other public bodies that regularly and constantly meet public needs. In a more material sense, public administration is the work carried out by these bodies, services and staff. Another more academic definition stems from Rosenbloom et al: "Public administration does involve activity, it is concerned with politics and policy making, it tends to be concentrated in the executive branch of government, it does differ from private administration, and it is concerned with implementing the law. We can be much more specific by offering our own definition: public administration is the use of managerial, political, and legal theories and processes to fulfil legislative, executive, and judicial mandates for the provision of governmental regulatory and service functions"[124].

Much more than in the case of defining public administration, different linguistic meanings play an important role when defining *public services*. For example, the term 'public service' is to be more broadly understood in the UK than in Germany. Whereas in the UK it also encompasses voluntary and honorary services for the public, this is not the case in Germany[125]. Until today, terms like *power*, *state*, *services of general interest* and *civil servant* have a different meaning for the French people than for the Scandinavians. In addition, the image of the public service is very different from country to country.

---

123 Christopher Hood, The Word, the Movement, the Science, in: Ferlie/Lynn/Pollitt, The Oxford Handbook of Public Management, op. cit., pp.7-27.

124 David H. Rosenbloom/Robert S. Kravchuk/Richard M. Clerkin, Public Administration – Understanding Management, Politics, and Law in the Public Sector, 7th edition, Mc Grawhill, Singapore 2009, p. 5.

125 Christoph Reichard/Eckhard Schröter, Der Öffentliche Dienst im Wandel der Zeit: Tradierte Probleme, aktuelle Herausforderungen und künftige Reformperspektiven, in: Der moderne Staat, No 1/2009, pp. 17-37.

Table 3: Subnational governments in OECD countries

Federal States	Municipal tier	Second tier	Federated States
Australia	694 local governing bodies[1]		6 States and 2 Territories
Austria	2,359 municipalities		9 Länder
Belgium	589 municipalities	10 provinces	3 Regions and 3 Communities
Canada	ca. 4,000 local governing bodies[1]		10 Provinces and 3 Territories
Germany	13,854 municipalities	323 districts	16 Länder , including 3 "City-States"
Mexico	2,438 municipalities		31 States and 1 Federal District
Switzerland[2]	2,470 territorial communes		26 Cantons
United States[3]	35,992 local governing bodies	2,975 counties	50 States and 1 District

Unitary States	Municipal tier	Second tier	Third tier
Czech Republic	6,258 municipalities	14 regions	
Denmark	98 municipalities	5 counties	
Finland	432 municipalities	6 provinces	
France	36,684 municipalities (including 114 in the overseas departments)	100 departments, including: 1 city department and 4 overseas departments	26 regions, including 1 special status authority and 4 overseas regions
Greece	1,031 municipalities including 901 towns and 130 rural municipalise	50 departments	
Hungary	3,158 municipalities	19 departments	
Iceland	79 municipalities	23 counties[4]	
Ireland	85 municipalities	29 counties	8 regions
Italy	8,100 municipalities	104 provinces	20 regions, including 5 "special status"
Japan	659 cities, 1,991 towns, 567 villages	47 prefectures	
Korea	72 cities, 94 counties and 69 districts	9 provinces and 7 metropolitan cities	

Luxembourg	118 municipalities		
Netherlands	467 municipalities	12 provinces	
Norway	434 municipalities	19 counties	
New Zealand	16 city councils and 57 district councils (4 of these are also regional councils)	16 regional councils and 1 territory	
Poland	2,489 municipalities	373 departments	16 regions
Portugal	278 municipalities (4,257 parishes[5])		
Slovakia	2,920 municipalities	8 regions	
Spain	8,106 municipalities	50 provinces	17 autonomous communities
Sweden	289 municipalities	21 counties, of which 2 are designated as "regions"	
Turkey	923 districts	81 provinces	
United Kingdom	36 metropolitan districts	34 counties	
England	238 districts 47 unitary authorities		
London	1 Greater London Authority +32 London Boroughs	London Assembly	
Scotland	32 unitary authorities	Scottish Parliament	
Northern Ireland	26 districts	Northern Ireland Assembly	
Wales	22 unitary authorities	National Assembly for Wales	

Notes:

1 The generic names of Australian and Canadian local governments vary across states/provinces/territories
2 Switzerland is formally a Confederation
3 The organisation and generic names of US local governments vary across states
4 Iceland's 8 regions are merely used for statistical purposes
5 Portuguese parishes are infra-municipal authorities.

Source: OECD, Challenges of Human Resources Management for Multi-level Government, Paris, 21. November 2008, pp. 10-11

In fact, state structures have a considerable impact on the organisation of the public administration and the public service and the wide variety of state structures is one of the characteristic features of European public administration. Each of the Member States has a unique state structure, but one can also see common structural elements.

In each of the Member States, there is at least one but usually two or three layers of government below the central government (see Table 3). There are local governments in all Member States, mostly in the form of municipalities or communes. With regard to the government layers situated between the central level and the local levels, one can distinguish between a regional layer of government – in some Member States, enjoying legislative competences – a provincial layer of government (or *département* or county) and a form of inter-municipal cooperation.

The Member States of the European Union can be subdivided into (quasi-) federal states, decentralised unitary states and unitary states. The federal states of the European Union are **Belgium**, **Germany** and **Austria**. The Regions and Communities in **Belgium** and the *Länder* in **Germany** and **Austria** have legislative powers. **Spain,** and to a lesser degree **Italy,** can be described as quasi-federal states. The Spanish Constitution recognises and guarantees the right of self-government of its national groups and regions which comprise the kingdom. In practice, the Autonomous Communities are largely self-determining. In the event of a contradiction between the laws of the state and those of the Autonomous Communities, however, the former take precedence over the latter. **Italy** is a state which is difficult to place in the classification of state structures. It is neither a federal nor a decentralised unitary state. Its unique status is due to the existence of five "special" regions with a "special" statute, as well as the creation of 15 "ordinary" regions in 1970. The five special regions have a status defined in special legislation with constitutional force. The legislative power of the "ordinary" regions is more limited and moreover under stricter government control.

Table 4: Legislative power of regions or Länder to regulate their civil service systems, by state structure

(Frequencies in parenthesis)

		Wide legislative powers	In-between	No legislative power	Total
Type of state structure	Federal or quasi-federal state	60 (3)	20 (1)	20 (1)	100 (5)
	Decentralised unitary state	29 (2)	0 (0)	71 (5)	100 (7)
	Unitary state	0 (0)	7 (1)	93 (14)	100 (15)
	Total	19 (5)	7 (2)	74 (20)	100 (27)

Regions in Austria, Belgium, Germany and Spain enjoy their own legislative powers in the field of civil service. Italy has a more centralised system. In **Austria**, legislation produced by the Regions/Communities and the *Länder* is not subordinate to legislation produced by the federal government. In **Germany**, all Länder have their own legal competences in the field of civil service (except for the regulation of the legal status of civil servants which is still regulated centrally at the federal level).

In **Belgium**, "the federalisation process has involved increasing autonomy to Regions and Communities in Belgium for the organisation of their own government. Originally with a rather rigid career-based system imposed by the Camus Statute, Regions and Communities are now free to organise their human resource management systems within the general principles established in the Royal Decree on General Principles (22 December 2000). A revised Camus Statute is still in force at the federal level.

Nevertheless, over the past decades, all governments in Belgium have started to review regulations in the HRM field (new codes, new job classification, rationalisation of ranks and grades, new pay scales), to simplify some rules in some areas of HRM, to introduce or implement competency-based and performance-based management, and to give a special role to a reformed senior management. These HRM reforms have been implemented within the framework of wider management reforms (balanced scorecards, satisfaction surveys, process reengineering, performance measures, etc.)[126].

126 OECD Reviews of Human Resource Management in Government, Executive Summary, Paris, 2007.

The decentralised unitary states of the European Union are **Czech Republic, Denmark, Finland, France, Netherlands, Sweden** and **United Kingdom**. Of these, **France** has a total of four government layers. Besides central government, these are regions, *départements* and communes. **The Netherlands**, **Denmark** and **Sweden** each have three government layers, while **Finland** has only two. The **French** regions were only established as a fully democratic government layer by means of the territorial decentralisation process established in the early years of the Mitterrand Presidency in the early 1980s. **Denmark** and **Sweden** each have a system of counties, which form the intermediate level of government and municipalities. In these two countries, the counties are largely devoted to health care activities. In **Finland,** municipalities form the second and most important layer of government. However, several forms of inter-municipal co-operation have *de facto* established an intermediate level of administration (not government) between central and local government. The **Netherlands** is subdivided into provinces and municipalities.

The unitary states of the European Union are **Cyprus, Estonia, Greece**, **Hungary, Ireland**, **Latvia, Lithuania, Luxembourg, Malta, Portugal** and **Slovakia**. In these countries, central government is by far the most dominant government layer. In **Ireland**, **Luxembourg** and **Portugal** (with the exception of the two autonomous regions of Azores and Madeira) there are only two layers of government. In **Portugal**, a referendum held in 1998 – on whether to establish administrative regions with executive competencies – failed to generate support. In **Greece**, there are three layers of government. In 1994, the then prefectures were transformed into "prefectoral self governments" based on democratic principles.

In the **European Commission** "agencification" and "externalisation" is still on the reform agenda. It is based on the assumption that agencies are more efficient and effective in policy implementation when they have acquired a sufficient degree of independence in financial and personnel matters. The ideas behind these changes have largely been developed in the new public management literature which has had extensive repercussions on thinking about public administration and public management in general.

One should also distinguish between Member States in which agencies are relatively new and Member States in which agencification is almost an old tradition. The most typical example in this second category is **Sweden**, which has had a system of agencies since 1809[127] and where 98% of all central government staff

127 Torbjörn Larsson, Governing Sweden, Statskontoret, Stockholm, 1995, p. 64.

works within an agency. This tradition of agencification contrasts with the classical hierarchical ministerial models.

2. Civil service

2.1. The public law status and the constitutional role of civil servants

For a long time, European societies believed that civil servants were linked to the authority of the state and could not be compared to other public employees or employees in the private sector. Civil Servants were offered a public law status in order to bind them to the state and not to an individual interest. From what is known, the public law status has its origin in the French revolution and aimed to establish and guarantee a democratic society based on the principles of the French Revolution. In Germany, the introduction of the public law status was inspired by the German philosopher Friedrich Hegel. Hegel's idea of the civil servant (and the state as such) was conceptualised as a "Leviathan" which stood above the society and citizens. Its main role was to protect the society, to achieve fairness by rules and to balance the diverging egoistic interests within the society.

Since its origins in the late 18th century, the public law status has survived in almost all national civil service systems. In this way it would be fair to say that this traditional element of a classical civil service is one of the few traditional principles which has endured over time (and differently to other established principles like for example the prohibition to go on strike, the career principle and the life-time principle).
According to the definition of the World Bank[128] "several criteria continue to distinguish civil servant status from other employment arrangements. These criteria can be summarised as follows:

1. Civil servants are appointed by decision of an authorised public institution in accordance with the civil service law. A decision by a representative of the State to appoint a civil servant must conform with established rules that structure the hiring process.

2. Once appointed, there are many constraints on dismissal. This is because civil servants are not simply employees of the state; they also have a constitutional role. The intent of civil service legislation is to balance the requirement that these employees are responsive to the government of the

128 http://www1.worldbank.org/publicsector/civilservice/civilservicelaw.htm (last time checked on 25 November 2009).

day, with the parallel requirement that they respect and maintain state institutions over time. In other words, additional job security is provided in order to prevent short-term political pressures from leading to inappropriate personnel changes.

3. There are more constraints on the actions of civil servants than on other groups. Again, this is because of the strategic and constitutional role of civil servants. The Labour Relations (Public Service) Convention, 1982 (No. 151) provides details of the fundamental labour rights of civil servants (the right to organise, to participate in consultations or negotiations in relation to their terms of employment and to settlement of disputes). Article 1 of the Convention states that its provisions apply to "all persons employed by public authorities" but permits exemptions for "high-level employees whose functions are normally considered as policy-making or managerial, or ... employees whose duties are of a highly confidential nature."
4. The employees concerned are within civilian central government or subnational government. There are many other employment arrangements in the public sector that provide something akin to civil servant status, under judicial career laws etc. However, common usage requires that civil servant status refers to employees within civilian central government, or subnational government. The judiciary can often be employed under arrangements that also provide constitutionally-based constraints on dismissal, but are rarely known as civil servants[129].

All EU countries still employ civil servants under a public law status. The three countries lacking public law status are the Czech Republic, Sweden and the United Kingdom. However, a civil servant statute is under discussion in the United Kingdom and the Czech Republic. The Swedish situation is somewhat specific as at least some elements of the working conditions of Swedish civil servants are regulated under public law.

---

129 http://web.worldbank.org/WBSITE/EXTERNAL/TOPICS/EXTPUBLICSECTORANDGOVERNANCE/EXTADMINISTRATIVEANDCIVILSERVICEREFORM/0,,contentMDK:20133489~menuPK:286372~pagePK:148956~piPK:216618~theSitePK:286367,00.html

Table 5: Civil servants' legal status by type of civil service structure

(Frequencies in parenthesis)

		Public law status	Civil law status	Total
Type of civil service structure	Career structure	100 (18)	0 (0)	100 (18)
	Non-career structure	67 (6)	33 (3)	100 (9)
	Total	89 (24)	11 (3)	100 (27)

Staff employed on a public law basis are generally appointed by means of a unilateral official act on the part of the administration. Private law based employees are generally employed on the basis of a contract of employment between the administration and the employee concerned. However, in eight EU countries public employees are also offered a public law status, i.e. in Cyprus, Estonia, France, Hungary, Luxembourg, Malta, Poland and Portugal

Table 6: Public employees' legal status by type of civil service structure

(Frequencies in parenthesis)

		Public law status	Civil law status	Total
Type of civil service structure	Career structure	41 (7)	59 (10)	100 (17)
	Non-career structure	13 (1)	87 (7)	100 (8)
	Total	32 (8)	68 (17)	100 (25)

N.B.: Information on Italy and the Netherlands is missing, as they do not have public employees but only civil servants.

The relative importance of these two groups varies a lot from one Member State to another. As analysed later on, the distinction between these two groups of staff is an essential characteristic of the civil service in most countries. In **Greece**, **Spain**, **Romania** and (on the federal level) in **Belgium** the primacy of public-status employment is even laid down in the constitutions. In practice, however, this stipulation is rarely applied in these countries. In an increasing number of Member States it is official policy to employ most staff on the basis of common labour law.

In contrast, in the other Member States, a clear preference for posts under public statutes can be seen. This is evident in the **Netherlands, Finland, France, Slovenia etc.** where almost all civil service staff are employed on the basis of a public law statute. In countries like **France** and **Belgium**, where the official policy has been that civil servants are normally employed in accordance with public law, one can also observe that this official policy is not successful in practice. In **France**, for example, 82% of all civil service staff are established civil servants who have tenure (*fonctionnaire titulaire*), but within the civil service (especially the civil service in local and regional authorities and the hospital sector), non-established staff are also employed in both public-law and private-law based employment patterns, such as unestablished civil servants (without tenure), and auxiliary and temporary staff. In **Belgium**, especially in Regional and Community administrations, a large number of contractual staff are employed. The same is true in **Spain** at the level of the Autonomous Communities and in the local administrations.

If a global comparison is to be made of the respective forms of public-status and private-contract posts, there is a clear overall tendency for private contracts to be given much greater scope at the local authority level than at the state level. In several countries, this special status covers a large proportion of central government employees[130]. In several Member States, the differences between publicly and privately employed staff are still very marked in terms of rights and obligations. For example, the case of Germany shows that these differences may be even more accentuated in some more areas (see Table 7).

In many other countries however, differences between working conditions of civil servants, public employees and private employees are much less accentuated. This is the case in the **Netherlands, Sweden, the United Kingdom, Finland, Latvia, Estonia, Austria,** (greater parts of the Civil service in**) Portugal and Denmark.** However, important differences exist amongst these countries. For example, the Netherlands and Sweden differ very much with regard to the legal status of civil servants, the degree of decentralisation of HR responsibilities, the pay system, the role and status of agencies, job security of civil servants and many other issues.

---

130 L. Bordogna, Industrial Relations in the Public Sector, European Foundation for the Improvement of Living and Working Conditions, Dublin, 2007.

Table 7: Differences between civil servants employed under public law and employees under private law contract in German public administration

Civil servants	Public employees
Public law (Civil Servants Act)	Private law
Official announcement (Ernennung durch Hoheitsakt)	Common labour law
Regulation through law	Regulation through contract and labour legislation
“Obligation to provide welfare rights” principle (Alimentationsprinzip)	Mutual exchange principle (Gegenleis-tungsprinzip)
No right to strike	Right to strike, sometimes restricted for some categories of staff
Loyalty and neutrality	No obligations set by law
Job for life	Unlimited contract or limited Contract
Career system	System with other organisational characteristics
Special pension schemes	General pension scheme

2.2. Definitions of civil services in national law

It seems strange for many ‘western’ observers, but the adoption of a civil service law “was one of the most important and most discussed elements of EU policy in the wider area of administrative reform in the pre-accession period. With respect to European principles of administration, a civil service law provides the basic mechanism for protecting the impartiality and promoting the professionalism of civil servants that is necessary to guarantee legal certainty as well as accountability of civil servants as individuals exercising state authority. EU policy therefore required the existence of a civil service law, stability of the law over time, full implementation of the law, and a clear definition of boundaries of the civil service vis-à-vis politics, private sector employment and potentially other forms of public sector employment.

At first sight, the CEE countries demonstrate a good fit with European principles of administration in this area of civil service governance"[131]. However, in some of the central- and Eastern European countries "the legal basis is subject to several flaws and the trend since accession has been negative in several countries (....) First, civil service laws are not always fully implemented or there are gaps that are not covered by the legal basis. Second, the legal basis has been subject to a high degree of instability, in that all civil service laws have been amended often or even very often. (...). The legal accountability, legal predictability and political neutrality of the civil service must therefore often be called into question. (....). At the end of 2007, the Slovak civil service law had already been amended 23 times since 2002 and 13 times since accession in 2004. Similarly, the Lithuanian law was amended 36 times between 1999 and the end of 2007 (eight times since 2004). Even the Czech civil service law, most of which is not in force, has been amended several times since 2004 (...). In other words, the formal rules governing civil services in Central and Eastern Europe are very unstable and, as a consequence, the predictability of civil service management is seriously undermined and arbitrary management may develop. Third, the definition of the scope of civil service laws is not always without problems. It has been a general trend that CEE governments have opted for narrow definitions of the civil service, as the scope of the civil service law is largely restricted to officials who exercise state authority. By contrast, employees in the wider public sector – for example, in education, health, and the armed forces – are subject to separate legislation. However, the scope of the various civil service systems is subject to ambiguities in several countries, such as Slovenia and Poland. The Polish situation is noteworthy, as the law distinguishes tenured, nominated civil servants and "civil service employees", who are within the scope of the civil service law but otherwise subject to ordinary labour law contracts. Yet the number of nominated and thus full-fledged civil servants stands currently at five per cent of the overall civil service. This means that legal accountability of the civil service is ensured but that man many of the management regulations to be discussed below apply to only a very small proportion of officials"[132].

The amount of regulation also differs amongst the EU Member States. For example in **Germany** civil servants are regulated by a combined total of 30 laws and regulations. All German Länder have their own civil service laws (and regulate on their own all civil service matters, excluding the legal status of civil servants, which is regulated at the federal level for all German officials). Other

---

131 Jan-Hinrik Meyer-Sahling, Sustainability of Civil Service reforms in Central and Eastern Europe, op. cit., p. 18.

132 Ibid, p. 18 and 20.

countries have only one civil service law which is applicable to all civil servants in the whole country.

Despite these differences, in all Member States civil servants, whether referred to as *fonctionnaire*, *ambtenaar* or *Beamte*, are responsible for carrying out public policies whilst ensuring public efficiency, legal certainty, independence, and stability. Moreover, in all Member States the legitimation for the creation of a civil service is the need to have a specific group of public employees who carry out important government policies. Moreover, professional civil servants should be doing more than merely fulfilling functions in the field of exercising state powers and safeguarding the general interest of the state. They should exercise their role with a certain sense of integrity – a public service ethos.

The term *civil service* is mostly defined more narrowly than the term *public service*. Broadly speaking, it concerns the collective administrative personnel of the government which is employed under a distinctive legal regime or statute. Despite this common understanding, the following national examples illustrate that different definitions of the term civil service still apply when analyzing the situation in detail. For example, some Member States apply a unified approach to the term civil service (all public employees can be considered as civil servants), whereas other Member States apply a fragmented civil service definition (the civil service law applies only to a part of the public workforce or even only to the federal or regional civil servants etc.). Again, other Member States define the tasks of civil servants more broadly than others.

A case for a broad definition is the Romanian definition in Art. 2 of the Romanian Civil service Law no. 188 from 08/12/1999. According to the law "the civil position represents the entirety of duties and responsibilities settled by the law, in view of fulfilling the prerogatives of public power by the central public administration, by the local public administration and by the autonomous administrative authorities. (...) The civil servant is the person nominated, as per the law, in a public position. The person who was released of the public position and is now in the reserve body of civil servants preserves the quality of civil servant". Another case for a broad definition is the Slovakian definition according to which the civil service, shall be the performance of state administration tasks or the performance of state affairs in the scope of activity laid down by special regulations), carried out by a civil servant at a Service Office (§ 7) in the relevant sector, if such performance of his/her tasks includes

a) management
b) decision making
c) inspection

d) professional preparation of decisions

e) professional preparation of legislation drafts and other generally binding legal regulations including professional activities related to discussion and approval of the above or

f) professional preparation of requirements for the performance of state affairs.

Much shorter but equally broad is the **Finnish** definition in the Finnish Civil Service Act, which defines a civil service relationship as an employment relationship under public law in which the State is the employer and a civil servant the employee. This definition looks similar to the French definition ("An official in the civil service works in a public organisation in an administrative capacity in which the recruitment is based on public law")[133]: both countries apply a broad definition. Most public employees have a public law status. However, the differences come to the fore when comparing the working conditions, recruitment procedures and organisational features of both systems. Whereas the Finnish system is very much aligned to labour law practices, the French system is very specific in many ways and differs from the private sector.

In **Cyprus**, according to the Public Service Law of 1990 to 2008, the term "civil service" means service under the Republic other than the judicial service[134] of the Republic, service in the armed or security forces of the Republic, service in the office of the Attorney-General of the Republic, the Auditor-General or their Deputies, the Accountant-General or his Deputies, service in any office in respect of which other provisions are made by law (e.g., educational service, armed forces etc.), service of workers/labourers or of persons whose remuneration is calculated on a daily basis or service by persons who are employed on a casual basis in accordance with "Employment of Casual Officers" (Public and Educational Service) Laws.

Ireland and **Poland** may be considered as the opposite systems to the above-presented cases in Romania, Finland, Slovakia and France. Each of these countries applies a very narrow definition of civil service. In **Ireland**, the Civil Service consists of the staff serving in the Department of the Taoiseach (Prime Minister) and a number of Departments of State.

133 Fonction Publique Française, Rapport Annuel 2007-2008, p. 247 http://www.fonction-publique.gouv.fr/article1488.html

134 Here the term 'Judicial Service' refers to the number of Judges of the Supreme Court and other Courts.

In **Poland**, the new act on the Civil Service entered into force on 24 March 2009. This new piece of legislation has introduced important and far-reaching changes in the Polish system of the civil service. Nevertheless, the two groups of civil service corps members have been maintained: civil servants, employed on the basis of nomination, and civil service employees, employed on the basis of employment contract. Thus, in the Polish civil service corps there are two groups of civil servants: 1) civil servants and 2) civil service employees. The term "civil service corps members" is not another group or status – it is merely the term that is used in the Law for both groups. Thus, the term 'civil service corps member' can refer to both a civil servant and a civil service employee. The police, defence forces, the university sector, primary and secondary education, and the hospital sector are part of the wider public service. Administrative support services for the Courts Service are provided by the civil service. Judges are appointed by the Government but are independent in the exercise of their judicial duties and are not classed as civil servants. In Poland (because of the narrow definition of the appointed civil service) the percentage of civil servants in the civil service is comparably very low (5.5% - 6 153 civil servants and some 104 000 civil service employees).

Some countries are difficult to classify. For example **Portugal** combines several conceptions. The law n° 12-A/2008, of 27 February states that appointments as civil servants are only effective for posts in some few and very well defined services: some groups in the military, the Foreign Office; State security information; criminal investigation; public security; inspection activities. The judiciary, diplomatic service, police, military, education and university staff are subject to specific rules, rights and duties, and are integrated in specific career systems. With regard to hospitals, in the last few years, the majority of them have obtained public cooperation status, thus are outside the scope of application of framing Portuguese civil service law (12-A/2008, of 27 February). In Portugal the civil service rules are centrally defined and are being applied with some adaptations to local and regional administrations. However, regional administrations may apply other rules regarding some features of the civil service system. All specific system careers in Portugal are under a process of revision. All other public employees have been offered employment contracts which introduced new rules, rights and duties but, in spite of being influenced by private labour law, they still maintain public law contracts. Thus, as of 1 January 2009 there are now three forms of public law employment contracts in the Portuguese public administration: currently, only appointed staff maintains the former rules and rights.

- Public servants with an appointment:
    - lifetime tenure (permanent post);
    - transitional appointment (fixed term post);

- Employment contracts in public functions:
  - for an indefinite period of time;
  - contract for a fixed or unfixed term;
- Employment contracts with a limited executive tenure
  - performance of posts not integrated into careers, namely managers and other situations, such as attendance at a specific training course

All of the above-mentioned definitions differ from the German definition according to which – from a legal point of view – civil servants cannot be considered as employees. In Germany, only one third of all public employees can be considered as civil servants. The latter is important since a number of European directives in the field of European labour and social law are applicable to employees in the public and private sector.

In the **United Kingdom** the civil service has a dual meaning. "First as a government institution the term is applied generally to the civilian officials of the Central Government. Secondly it stands for a spirit of vocational service to the State, of dedication to the service of the community"[135]. In the United Kingdom a civil servant may be defined as a "servant of the Crown (not being the holder of a political or judicial office) who is employed in a civil capacity and whose remuneration is wholly paid out of monies provided by Parliament"[136]. In the United Kingdom, the legal regime of civil servants is regulated by a number of codes. There exists no civil service law (only a draft which was proposed in 2008). Thus, the United Kingdom is the only country in the EU where civil servants are not regulated in a public law frame.

This short illustration illustrates the possibility and – at the same time – impossibility to define the term civil service. It all depends on the methodological approach; whereas a political definition is possible, a European-wide legal definition of the term is problematic.

2.3. Civil servants and the allocation of specific state tasks

The definition of who should be a civil servant has always been linked to the question of the special nature of the duties and the specific tasks concerned. Whereas some Member States have clearly defined provisions for which tasks

---

135 Gladden, Civil Services, op. cit., p. 1.
136 Ibid., p. 3.

should be carried out by civil servants, other national laws and regulations only provide for general provisions.

In terms of a case for broad provisions, the German civil service law states that the nomination to become a civil servant is only allowed in order to exercise powers conferred by public law and in order to safeguard the general interest of the state and the public. However, the law does not enumerate which tasks and functions are included.

Other countries offer a much more detailed task description. For example, the **Romanian** law lists a number of tasks and duties which should be reserved to civil servants. Art. 3 states that the activities performed by the civil servants that involve the exercise of public power prerogatives are the following:

- the execution of laws and other norms;
- the issuance of norms and other rules specific to public authorities or bodies, and providing for their approval;
- the issuance of projects of policies and strategies, of programmes, of studies, of analyses and statistics required for the execution and implementation of public policies as of the documentation required for law execution, with the purpose of achieving the competence of the public authority or body;
- the counselling, the control and the internal public audit;
- the management of human and financial resources;
- the collection of budgetary liabilities;
- the representation of the interests of the public authority or body in its relations with natural or juridical persons of public or private right, inside or abroad, within the limit of competence established by the manager of the public authority or body, as the representation in justice of the public authority or body where the activity is being performed;
- the performance of activities according to the strategy of computerisation of the public administration.

Also in **Slovakia** Art. 3 of the civil service law states that civil servants tasks include

- management;
- decision making;
- inspection;
- professional preparation of decisions;
- professional preparation of legislation drafts and other generally binding legal regulations including professional activities related to discussion and approval of the above; or
- professional preparation of requirements for the performance of state affairs.

In **Belgium** the Law of 22 July 1993 (M.B. of 14.8.1993, *portant certaines mesures en matière de fonction publique*) stipulates that civil servants with a public law status (Art. 3) should be recruited in clearly defined areas and organisations. Similarly to the situation in **Belgium**, in **Poland** the Civil Service Act of 21 November 2008 defines in detail which sectors and professions belong to the civil service corps. The official positions in the Chancellery of the Prime Minister are the offices of Ministers and Chairpersons of Committees (incl. The offices of central agencies), the offices of the voivodships and other offices which are part of the local government apparatus (and which is subordinated to the central Government administration), inspections and guards, the heads of the poviat services, the office of registration of Medical Products, Medical Devices and Bioproducts as well as the Forest Production Bureau.

At EU level, the principle of free movement of workers in Art. 39 ECT can be restricted for certain tasks (and positions) which may be reserved for nationals (and civil servants). The logic is exactly the same as in some Member States where the exercise of public powers may be reserved for civil servants. According to the case law of the ECJ, the exercise of specific public posts can be reserved for nationals. At least indirectly, European Law (or at least the interpretation of Art. 39 4 ECT by the ECJ) hints as to how Member States may define their civil services (and which positions may be reserved to civil servants).

According to the case law of the European Court of Justice, the ECJ worked out two criteria and made an exception of free movement only for those posts in the civil service which involve direct or indirect participation in the exercise of powers conferred by public law and duties designed to safeguard the general interest of the state or of other public authorities. It is obvious that both criteria (the exercise of powers conferred by public law, and the responsibility for safeguarding the general interest of the state or other public bodies), together (meaning "and" instead of "or"[137]) determine whether posts fall within the scope of 39.4 EC. According to the European Court of Justice the exception laid down in paragraph 4 has to be interpreted "very strictly". [138]

By case law, the following jobs do not fall within the scope of the public service exception: postal services: workers[139]; railways: shunters, loaders, drivers, platelayers, signalmen, office cleaners, painter's assistants, assistant furnishers, battery services, coil winders, armature services, night-watchmen, cleaners, canteen staff, workshop hands;[140] municipal councils: joiners, gardens hands, hospital nurses, children's nurses, electricians, plumbers[141]; state hospitals: male and female nurses[142]; state education: trainee teachers[143], secondary school teachers[144], foreign language assistants in universities[145]; civil research: researchers[146].

The European Commission decided in 1988 to implement a strategy for the elimination of restrictions on grounds of nationality on the basis of Communication 88/C 72/02: Freedom of movement of workers and access to employment in the public service of the Member States[147]. The commission considered that the derogation of Article 39.4 EC covered specific functions of the state and similar bodies in the following categories: the armed forces, the police and other law enforcement bodies, the judiciary, the tax authorities, and the diplomatic corps. Furthermore, the public service exception covers jobs in the state ministries, the regional authorities, the local authorities, the central banks, and other public bodies where the duties of the post in question involve the exercise of state authority such as the preparation of legal acts, their implementation and the monitoring of their application and the supervision of subordinate bodies. The position of the Commission as regards the interpretation of Art. 39 4 EC has devel-

---

137 This is our interpretation of the case law of the ECJ and the word "and". We have seen no case yet where the ECJ has used the word "or". See for example Case 307/84 Commission vs. France, paragraph 12; Case 66/85 paragraph 27.

138 Case 66/85 Lawrie-Blum vs. Land Baden-Wuertemberg.

139 Case 152/73 Sotgiu, paragraph 4.

140 Case 149/79 Commission vs. Belgium.

141 Ibid.

142 Case 307/84 Commission vs. France.

143 Case 66/85 Lawrie-Blum.

144 Case 4/91 Bleis.

145 Case 33/88 Allue vs. Coonan.

146 Case 225/85 Commission vs. Italy.

147 Communication 88/c72/02 Freedom of movement of workers and access to employment in the public service of the Member States. Commission action in respect of the application of article 39.4 of the EC Treaty OJ 1988 C72/2.

oped since 1988. Today, the interpretation is certainly stricter and more precise than it was in 1988.

Table 8: Public service employment within the scope of article 39.4 EC

Definition by the European Court of Justice Jobs which involve a) the exercise of powers conferred by public law, and b) responsibility for safeguarding the general interests of the state or other public bodies.
Interpretation by the European Commission Armed forces Police and other law enforcement bodies Judiciary Tax authorities Diplomatic corps Jobs in the state ministries (restricted) Regional authorities (very restricted) Local authorities (very restricted) Central banks (very restricted) Other public bodies where the duties of the post involve the exercise of state authority

In its communication on "Free Movement of Workers – achieving the full benefits and potential", the European Commission has also made it clear that not all jobs in state ministries, regional authorities, local authorities and in the central banks fall within the scope of Art.39.4[148]. For example, all technical, administrative or secretarial jobs would fall beyond the scope of Art. 39 4 EC. In addition, it is important to note that not all posts that involve the exercise of public authority and responsibility for safeguarding the general interest shall be restricted to nationals. For example, "the post of an official who helps prepare decisions on granting planning permission should not be restricted to nationals of the host Member State"[149].

---

148 European Commission, Communication from the Commission, COM (2002) 694 final, 11.12.2002.

149 Communication, op. cit., p. 19.

The importance of the EU case law on Art. 39 4 ECT can be seen when looking at how it is implemented into national law. For example, Art 39 4 ECT is interpreted in the Finnish legislation as follows:

Only a Finnish citizen may be appointed to the following offices:

1) the offices of Chancellor of Justice and Assistant Chancellor of Justice, Secretary General and Referendary Counsellor in the office of the Chancellor of Justice when the latter holds the office of Head of Department (176/2003);
2) the office of State Secretary, Permanent State Secretary, Permanent Secretary, Head of Department and Head of Unit, as well as any similar or higher office (176/2003);
3) an office in the foreign affairs administration;
4) an office of judge;
5) an office of head of a Government agency, however not that of principal of a university;
6) an office of Provincial Governor, of Head of Department of a Provincial Government, as well as of Provincial Readiness Director;
7) an office involving the duties of public prosecutor or enforcement officer;
8) an office of police officer referred to in the Police Act (493/1995);
9) an office in which the appointee is a member of the board of directors of a prison;
10) an office with the Ministry of Defence, the Defence Forces and the Frontier Guard;
11) an office with the Finnish Security Police, other than a police officer;
12) an office with the Customs Administration, which involves the authority to make arrests and an office, which involves participation in the supervision and the defence of Finland's territorial integrity, or which involves criminal investigation and supervision;
13) the office of head of the public authority department of Finavia, the Finnish Civil Aviation Administration;
14) the office of Maritime Security Director with the Finnish Maritime Administration.

Of course one may wonder why the many public employees fall under the free movement criteria although they exercise important powers and decide on the fundamental rights of citizens and take decisions which may impact on the fundamental rights of all citizens. On the other hand, only few positions may be restricted although not all of them exercise important powers.

In the meantime, the justification for art. 39 4 ECT becomes even more problematic. At the EU level it is challenged by concepts such as European citizenship, the emergence of dual citizenship and dual nationality[150], trends towards multiculturalism, globalisation and administrative cooperation. At the national level the term civil service is applied in many different ways. Moreover notions like “public employment”, “government organisations”, “the public sector” or “public services" vary across countries, depending on countries’ own definitions of what “public” or “government” means. Data on “public” employment available in the different countries reflect those differences as to what “public” means, and are thus meaningless to compare across[151] countries.

2.4. Specific duties and obligations

Traditionally, the special status of a bureaucrat and specific duties and obligations should both guarantee the neutrality of the civil servant and make him a loyal server of the state. In “Politik and Beruf” Weber suggested that civil servants should administer without fight, passion and emotion. Communication should be “dehumanised” by eliminating feelings like hate and other irrational and emotional elements. The civil servant should not do the task of a politician: fighting![152] Instead, one of the most important obligations of civil servants is to exercise their functions impartially.

Consequently, civil servants have different (and often, stricter) duties and obligations than private sector employees. Still, all national civil service laws contain a number of detailed and specific duties and obligations for civil servants and also of the employers. One good example is the civil servants act in **Slovenia** which regulates a number of important principles such as the principle of equal access (in Article 7), the principle of legality (in Article 8), the principle of professional conduct (in Article 9), the principle of honourable conduct (Art. 10), the principle on the restriction and duties in respect of the acceptance of gifts (Art. 11) and the principle of confidentiality (Art. 12).

---

150 Devorah Kalekin-Fishman/Pirkko Pitkänen (eds.), An Emerging Institution? Multiple Citizenship in Europe – Views of Officials, Peter Lang, Bern, 2008.

151 OECD, Employment in Government in the Perspective of the Production Costs of Goods and Services in the Public Domain, Paris, January 2008, p. 4.

152 Max Weber, Politik als Beruf, Reclam, Stuttgart 1999, p. 32.

In some Member States, specific obligations are even laid down in the respective constitutions or may be otherwise directly derived from them. Article 103, para. III of the **Spanish** Constitution, for example, cites the safeguarding of the impartiality of civil servants in exercising their functions; according to Article 98 of the **Italian** Constitution, civil servants only serve the nation; and Article 269, para. I of the **Portuguese** Constitution commits civil servants to ensuring the common good. In **Germany** the obligation of neutrality is one of the central principles on which the civil service is founded and is constitutionally enshrined in Article 33, para. IV of the Constitution. An indirect expression of the obligation of neutrality is given in Article 103, para. I of the **Greek** Constitution, according to which civil servants are to execute the will of the state and serve the people. In **Luxembourg**, the duty of civil servants to observe neutrality can be indirectly derived from the oath, which Article 110 requires they swear. The general obligation to perform tasks in a neutral fashion is expressed in concrete form in the various individual duties of the official. The neutrality of the public servant is safeguarded on the one hand against financial influence, and against political influence on the other. Measures relating to the former include bans on the taking of bribes and the acceptance of gifts. More and more, rules and regulations are also increasing in the field of conflicts of interests, post-employment, ancillary activities and multiple employment etc. Overall, in the field of ethics, Holders of public office and civil servants are regulated much more strictly than other public and private employees.

The focus in most Member States, however, is not only on the neutrality of the public employee with respect to financial influence, but also with respect to political influence – the aim being to safeguard the stability of the administration and provide a shield to the political forces that shape the life of the state. For example, in the past years many Member States have been particularly active in the field of regulating post-employment issues.

Despite all the differences that exist, all Member States agree that traditional principles (principle of impartiality, principle of legality etc.) and specific ethics rules and standards are necessary for civil servants. Justifications for specific principles and rules are the same in all EU countries: More so than other employees, civil servants are exposed to a number of (specific) conflicts of interest. They exercise important positions of power and influence, interact regularly with the private sector, take important decisions which have a financial impact, hold (often) important functions in boards, agencies or committees, possess information about important issues, allocate grants of public funds, make appointments to positions etc. In addition, civil servants introduce measures to decentralise public services, enhance public-private partnerships, improve customer and citizen orientation, promote outsourcing policies and enhance mobility between the public and private sector.

The most important principle in all Member States is the duty to respect the law and to serve the common good (and the principle of democracy). Civil Servants shall fulfil their tasks in an impartial and fair manner, and take into consideration the common interest. Other European-wide principles concern rules as regards the acceptance of gifts, the duty to take an oath, duties to treat certain issues as confidential or secret, duties to declare income, assets etc.

In most Member States of the EU there is furthermore a duty of good faith or loyalty on the part of an employee of the civil service towards their employer; however, the importance of this varies among the different Member States. This is particularly true with regard to loyalty to the constitution, which is more far-reaching in **Germany** than anywhere else. In contrast, the duty of obedience with respect to official instructions was for a long time incumbent on public employees in all EU Member States, and essentially served to highlight their subordination to instructions. How far that subordination extends today, however, is not clear in all Member States. In some, the threshold is the point at which a public employee is instructed to commit a punishable offence.

Other additional rules with regard to duties and obligations differ from country to country. For example, in the **German** Civil Service Law, 26 paragraphs deal with specific rights and obligations. These range from notifications to the media ("the Director of the institution decides who should provide information to the media"), the acceptance of gifts, specific references relating to clothing, the choice of an apartment (which should be not to far way from the place of work), the duty to take an oath and many other issues. Many of these duties and obligations do not exist in other Member States. For example, paragraph 78 regarding the Fürsorgepflicht des Dienstherrn (Duty of the Employer or Superior to take care of the civil servant). This paragraph obliges the superior/employer to take care of the civil servant and his family even after the end of their career in the civil service. According to this philosophy, the civil servant is not an ordinary state employee, but remains a civil servant – for their whole life. Consequently, it is expected that a civil servant is acting faithfully to the state and – in exchange – the State takes care of the civil servant: "*the link between a civil servant and the state (...) is different in nature to that of an employee and a private company. This link cannot simply be described by the concept of "life-time employment" (France prefers the expression "civil service career system" which is less negative) (...). This link continues throughout the entire active working life (..) and entails some obligations for the civil servant (...) but also explains the rights from which the civil servant benefits...*"

As the answers to this study show, many traditional (bureaucratic) principles, standards and ethical obligations are still in place. Moreover, traditional principles like the German *Fuersorgepflicht* or *Alimentationsprinzip* have never been changed. This is remarkable given the enormous changes that have taken place in other areas during the last years. In fact, the trend towards post-bureaucratic structure may even lead to the adoption of more rules and obligations that govern the behaviour of civil servants. Thus, despite all ongoing reform trends in the past and efforts to deregulate HRM policies, specific rules as regards duties and obligations have become more numerous in the field. Instead, it is a field of re-regulation and mostly in the field of ethics, conflicts of interests, anti-discrimination, diversity, accountability, performance management, transparency and citizen orientation.

3. Civil servants and other public employees

3.1. Distinction between civil servants and other public employees

In almost all Member States, the subdivision into different categories of staff with different legal statuses is an essential characteristic of the official organisation of the national public services. Often, the Member States employ two or more different categories of public employees. Just a small minority of countries employ only one category of staff, i.e. public law civil servants. Despite this common characteristic, the differences remain considerable. Recent developments in public employment make it even more difficult to separate the concept of public employment and civil service employment. The reasons for this are many: the possibility to employ, both, public employees and civil servants in the same positions, the alignment of working conditions, the application of EU directives to civil servants and also to public employees, shifting trends in public employment, ongoing reforms in civil service laws which lead to a shift from public law to labour law approaches as regards certain sectors (e.g., the University sector in Finland as of 1.1.2010), unclear definitions of civil service and public tasks etc.

A European-wide comparison of judges, politicians, top-officials or others shows a very diverse picture. In **France**, for example, judges are civil servants, even though they are governed by a special statute. In **Italy**, **Spain**, and **Denmark**, similar provisions apply. However, in **Germany** judges are not classified as civil servants. They do, however, have a special legally regulated public-contract status. **In addition, in Germany, the State Secretaries can either be Civil Servants or Political State Secretaries who do not belong to the Civil service.** In **Greece**, ministers and State Secretaries (who are deputy ministers) are excluded from the civil service since, as members of the government, they are subject to constitutional regulations and not to general civil service law. The same is true of **France**, where government office is incompatible with any civil service role. In the **Netherlands**, State Secretaries are classed as politicians whose job it is to represent ministers in accordance with the latter's instructions and who may, as is the case in **Greece**, be described as deputy ministers. In **Portugal**, ministers have public-contract status. They are subject to instruction and thus are not part of the civil service, but of its leadership[153].

Germany provides one example of a civil service system where throughout the three government levels – federal, *Länder* and local (*Kreise*, *Gemeinden*) – staff with different legal statuses often work together within the same organisations and in the same offices. The two staff categories are the public-law based professional civil servants (*Beamte*), and private-law based employees (*Angestellte*). Historical development has led to statutory and working conditions becoming almost identical, except that civil servants remain the elite and retain a symbolic supremacy over public sector employees. The Basic Law states the principle of the unity of civil servants' status, whether they serve the federation, the Länder or local government. Today, the federation is competent in defining the status of its own civil servants, but also in enacting framework provisions concerning the status of all German civil servants. These provisions ensure a certain level of homogeneity between the different statuses. However, important issues such as pay or pensions may be regulated differently on the federal and the Länder level.

A similar distinction between these categories of staff throughout the civil service applies for Austria (and also in Luxemburg). In **Austria** the Federal law foresees two different types of public employees:

- Tenured civil servants based on the public-law system regulated by the Civil Servants Act (Beamten-Dienstrechtsgesetz 1979)
- Contract agents based on the civil-law system regulated by the Contract Agents Act (Vertragsbedienstetengesetz 1948)

The status of civil servants in the Länder and municipalities is governed by a specific law in each state. In the Austrian public sector, there are two main types of employees: career public servants (*Beamte*) and contract public employees (*Vertragsbedienstete*). This corresponds with two types of employment relationships. In the case of career public servants this is a public-law relationship, whereas contract public employees are under a private-law relationship. Both

153 See Niedobitek, in: Magiera/Siedentopf, op. cit., p. 14.

types of employees have special service regulations (*Dienstrecht*) which are laid down in detail by statute. According to prevailing legal opinion, the state may assign sovereign functions (*hoheitliche Funktionen*) to either type of employee. Nevertheless, sovereign functions are usually performed by career public servants. The difference between the two types of employees lies mainly in the fact that a career public servant is appointed and as a matter of principle remains in the service of the state for life. This is the basis of the so-called *Pragmatisierung* – the career public servant's permanent tenure which carries absolute protection against dismissal. When they reach pensionable age, career public servants do not leave the public sector but are transferred into a retirement relationship. By contrast, contract public employees are engaged under a private-law contract of employment and may be dismissed under certain circumstances. When they reach pensionable age, they receive a pension under the statutory scheme provided for according to the General Social Insurance Act (*Allgemeines Sozialversicherungsgesetz*, ASVG) in exactly the same way as private-sector employees.

However, in practice the differences between the two types of employees are not that significant, since the contract public employees also enjoy very strong protection against dismissal; furthermore, other terms and conditions are very similar to those laid down by statute for career public servants. Thus, in Austria (and similarly to Germany), the distinction between civil servants and public employees has been blurred within recent years. Yet, important differences remain amongst both systems. For example, whereas in Germany any attempt to "align" the working conditions between civil servants and public employees must be in accordance with the principles set by the German Constitution and the Federal Constitutional Court, this is much less the case in Austria. Consequently, any reform of the Austrian Civil service is "easier" than in Germany.

In **Luxemburg** the national administrative law distinguishes between different categories of personnel. The State civil servants have a status regulated by the *amended laws of 22 June 1963 and 16 April 1979.* Public sector clerical employees have a status defined by a set of alternative or additional rules to the civil servants' status, which covers certain points such as continuous training or allowances. Finally, State manual workers are covered by a collective bargaining agreement. Local government officers have a status regulated by the *amended law of 24 December 1985.*

In **Belgium** the status of State employees is stipulated by the *Royal Decree of 2 October 1937* which has been revised on many occasions (principally by the Royal Decree of 4 August 2004). Statutory employees have permanent tenure and a grade or a class. The **Bulgarian** administration has two types of personnel (civil servants (47.1%), whose status is governed by the *law of July 1999 and* which has been amended several times) and contract employees (52.9%), under general employment law. In **Cyprus** the *Public Service Law of 1990-2006* defines the notion of public service and the different categories and grades of public posts. Officials in the Judicial Service, Educational service as well as in the Service of the Armed or Security Forces are subject to specific laws. Employees in semi-governmental organisations and local authorities have their own status.

In the **Czech Republic** there are two groups of public sector employees: civil servants (who are working in central administrations and are governed by the *2006 Labour Code*, as the civil service law of 2002, providing the framework for the working conditions and pay of State employees, has not yet come into effect), and civil servants of the territorial self-governing units (municipalities and regions) whose status is defined in Act No.312/2002 Coll. on civil servants in territorial self-governing units. The general labour legislation (Labour Code) does not apply to security forces personnel. The employment of persons serving in the security forces (Police of the Czech Republic, Fire Rescue Service, Customs Administration, Prison Service, Security Information Service and Office for Foreign Relations and Information) is governed by a special act. The legislation also awards a special status to staff of territorial self-governing units. As far as pay is concerned, the salaries of judges and state prosecutors is subject to special legislation

In **Denmark**, there are **three** categories of public sector staff, namely civil servants, employees employed on the basis of collective agreements and staff with individualised contracts of employment. The majority of staff working in the state sector are employed as employees under a collective agreement. In addition, a number of staff are employed on civil servant-like conditions and a small number according to regulations or on individual contracts.

Similarly to Germany, **Spain** applies a decentralised system with some central elements (which are described in the general framework of the Basic Statute of the Public Employee). In the Spanish public sector a distinction needs to be made between the following categories:

1. Career civil servants
2. Interim civil servants
3. Non-civil service staff
4. Fixed-term workers
5. Management staff
6. Others

Career civil servants are those who have passed a public examination; they have permanent contracts and develop their career within the public administration. Selection and mobility are based on performance of the tasks assigned to each employee. Interim civil servants carry out tasks proper to career civil servants, providing that there is no one to occupy the post and in cases of temporary replacement or temporary programmes. They also go through a public procedure, but their job ends when the reason for their recruitment ends. Non-civil service staff are all contracted staff who are in paid employment in the public administrations. They may have permanent or fixed-term contracts. Fixed-term staff are persons of trust who carry out qualified tasks or provide special advice. They are freely appointed and dismissed. The management staff carry out professional management tasks and are appointed according to advertised criteria of suitability.

In **Estonia** the *public service law of 25 January 1995* specifies three categories of public sector employees:

- officials: staff elected or appointed in an administrative department. A distinction is made between State employees and local government employees.
- support staff: office staff employed in the administrative departments on individual private law work contracts.
- non-staff civil servants: employees recruited for a limited period on individual private-law contracts

The **Finnish** state administration has two categories of public sector employees, civil servants and public employees. The civil servants (83%) are governed by the *State Civil Servants' Act*. and public employees (17%) by the Employment Contracts Act. The rules which apply to them are quite similar to each other; collective agreements are applied to both categories.

France has three branches of the civil service (central government, local government and hospital). Together, these branches employ 5.2 million people. Nearly half are employed by the central government civil service, 31% by the local government civil service and 20% by the hospital civil service. Each branch is governed by a specific set of provisions, which are applied nationwide. The General Regulations for all three branches were unified by the Law of 13 July 1983 (Title I – General Regulations), which defined and maintained the specificities of each branch. Judges and members of the military are governed by special regulations.

The **Greek** administration has three categories of public sector employees. The civil servants' status is defined in the *Civil Service Code (law 3528/2007)* which is governed by public law (constitutional, legislative and regulatory rules). Public employees are governed by private law (*general labour code*) and some special rules (*presidential order 410/1988*) and also have permanent contracts. Other contractual employees are recruited on a temporary basis for limited periods to cover special requirements and emergencies.

There are several categories of public sector employees in **Hungary**, each governed by a specific statute. *Law no. XXIII of 1992* defines the status of the 105 000 civil servants. *Law no. XXXIII of 1992* defines the status of public employees.

Ireland also distinguishes between a (small) group of civil servants and public employees. Employment in the Civil Service is governed by the Civil Regulation Acts 1956-2005 and by the Public Service Management (Recruitment and Appointments) Act 2004. The Irish Minister for Finance has responsibility for the Irish Civil Service. Responsibility for the wider public service such as the health and education sectors; the police and the defence forces and other State agencies rests with the appropriate Minister.

Italy is a specific case and applies a different system of civil service employment. Italy has been running a vast programme to contractualise the civil service since 1993. The civil service reform of February 1993 instituted contract-based relations between public employees and the State (this process is also known as the "privatisation of public employment") leaving plenty of scope for collective bargaining. With the exception of diplomats, magistrates, members of the prefectural body, armed forces and the police force, civil servants now sign a private contract. These contracts are in line with those of the private sector. They are signed for a period of four years and salaries are negotiated every two years. As a result, civil servants are governed by private labour laws and disputes in which they are involved are mainly settled by ordinary judges. Some categories of personnel have not been privatised in order to guarantee their independence (sitting judges, public prosecutors, university professors, military personnel and police officers, diplomats and prefects). These categories have civil servant status, as defined by *the decree n. 165 of 30 March 2001*. However, only 15% of public sector employees come under this status; the rest are contractual staff governed by private law. Their status, working conditions and any specific details (salary increases, leaves, working time and flexitime, professional content, relation with union, recruitment via competitive exam, incompatibility with other jobs etc.) are set out in collective agreements.

In **Latvia** there are **two** categories of public sector employees in state administration. Civil servants are governed by the *State Civil Service Law of 2001* (which applies only to 116 State administration institutions (ministries, agencies, etc.) and public employees who are working on job contracts and are governed by common labour law. In Latvia the civil service status is not introduced in local governments who autonomously determine the status of employees.

In **Lithuania**, a legal status of civil servants is defined by special Law on Civil Service (LCS). In this law, civil servants are divided into:

- Career civil servants,
- Civil servants of political (personal) confidence,
- Statutory civil servants,
- Public managers.

In Lithuania about 27 000 employees are career civil servants with the legal status governed by the Law on Civil Service, civil servants of political confidence and heads of institutions. About 25 000 statutory civil servants (i.e. diplomats, police, customs officers, etc.) have a specific legal status governed. The absolute majority of ministry employees (approx. 90%) are career civil servants. A career civil servant means a civil servant admitted to the service for an indefinite term, and with an opportunity to seek a higher position in the civil service. In addition, a small share of ministry employees are civil servants of political (personal) confidence (i.e. civil servants admitted to the service for the term coinciding with the term of powers of state politicians or collegial state agency who have chosen them, or for the term specified in other laws) and employees admitted to the service under employment contracts.

In **Malta** 41 000 persons are employed in the public sector. These employees are divided into two categories:

- 70% of public sector employees work for the central administration. Their status is regulated by a collective bargaining agreement which sets the salary level and employment conditions.
- About 30% of public sector employees work for government agencies or other public law entities. Each entity defines the employment conditions of its staff based on a collective bargaining agreement.

Efforts are currently being made to harmonise conditions at central level to avoid excessive disparities between the statuses of employees in these entities. Within the public sector there exist categories of employees who, due to the position they occupy, are granted special status. Furthermore special status is granted to public officers on scale four or higher. Special status is also granted to employees who have been in the civil service since before 1979.

In the **Netherlands** the employment relationship of the vast majority of public employees is first and foremost regulated by the Law on Civil Servants (*Ambtenarenwet*). In a material sense, most of the arrangements can be found in the General Rules on Civil Servants in the Central Government (*Algemeen Rijksambtenarenreglement*, ARAR). The ARAR covers recruitment procedures, appointment and dismissal. The ARAR also to a large extent covers subjects such as pay and working time. With regard to working time, the normal rules for employees (which can be found in the Law on working time, *Arbeidstijdenwet*) also apply to civil servants. The same is true for legislation with regard to the right to adapt the duration of working hours and legislation on work and care. Despite these rules, it would be misleading to define the Dutch system as a centralised civil service system. In reality, the government sector has been divided into sectors (of which central government is one), and each sector having its own collective agreement.

Theoretically, there are two categories of public sector employees. Most public sector employees in the Netherlands have the status of civil servant. Their employment conditions are very similar to those of private-law employees. This situation is the result of a policy aimed at bringing the status of public sector employees into line with the general conditions prevailing on the labour market. This is referred to as "normalisation". Indeed, civil servants do not have tenure and have no entitlements in terms of becoming career civil servants in the administration. The contractual employees work on contracts governed by private law. This type of contract was stopped in 1993, meaning that this category of employee will eventually disappear.

In **Poland** the centralised public administration includes ministries, special government administrations and deconcentrated government offices in the 16 regions (voivodships). The voivodships constitute the delegated government administration headed by a Voivode, a representative of the Council of Ministers in a given region. The local government, which includes municipalities (*gminas*), self-governing districts (*powiats*) and self-governing voivodships (marshal offices) is not part of the central public administration. Employees in the fields of education and healthcare are basically submitted to the labour law. In Poland, the public sector workforce has three different employment regimes. A first distinction can be made between nominated statutory civil servants and (civil service) public employees who have employment contracts: both types of staff are part of the civil service corps. The civil service corps comprises some 117 796 (2008) members employed in official positions such as the Chancellery of the

Prime Minister, Offices of Ministers, Chairpersons of committees, offices of central agencies, voivodeships offices, inspectorate and registration offices. Among the civil service corps, only 5046 (2008; 6153 in 2009) employees are appointed statutory civil servants, who have either passed a qualification procedure or who are graduates from the National School of Public Administration. There is, however, a trend to further increase the number of appointed civil servants. Appointed civil servants and (civil service) public employees are subject to the civil service law (Act on the Civil Service of 21 November 2008).

Besides the civil service corps members, the Polish public sector consists of 4.3 million employees. Outside the civil service corps, public employment covers staff working in schools, hospitals, universities, in the judiciary, in the armed forces or also fire fighters, policemen, self (local) government administration etc.; they either have their specific statutes, or their employment status is regulated by a specific law or by labour law.

In **Portugal** as of 1 January 2009 there are three forms of legal public employment. The first category represents the appointed civil servants (lifetime tenure or fixed-term post); the second includes civil servants under an employment contract (for an indefinite period and on a contract for a fixed or unfixed term); and the third form comprises civil servants with limited executive tenure (for posts which are not integrated into careers, namely managers and other situations such as attendance at a specific training course). The new law lays down that appointed civil servants may only be recruited in a few well-defined services:

- The Military (generic and specific missions of Armed Forces in permanent establishment plans);
- The Foreign Office;
- State Security Information;
- Criminal Investigation;
- Public Security;
- Inspection Activities.

The specific feature of the Portuguese situation is that all these different categories of civil servants are under employed under public law.

There are three employee categories in **Romania**. The civil servants status is defined by the *law of 8 December 1999* (which was revised by the law of 4 July 2006). In addition, the Romanian administration employs contract employees, whose status is governed by the labour code, and healthcare and education employees who are public sector employees under the general labour code.

In **Slovakia** Civil servants are governed by *Civil Service Law no. 312/2001* and partially by the Labour Code. Public employees are governed under the *law no. 552/2003, the law no. 553/2003* and also under the Labour Code. Some State public servants such as police, armed forces or customs personnel come under a special status and are regulated separately. The public employees are employed on private-law contracts.

Slovenia's civil service is characterised by the fact that general employment conditions in the public sector, as in the private sector, are determined by the law on labour relations which has been in effect since 1 January 2003. Most public sector employees are therefore recruited on permanent private-law contracts. However, the state employees, local government and public-law body employees are recruited on civil service employee law *of 11 June 2002* and the *civil service salary system law of 26 April 2002*. Article 23 of the civil servants act establishes two types of civil servants (officials and professional-technical civil servants). To this should be added all other public sector employees.
In **Sweden**, there is no specific civil servant status. However, a *1994 civil service law* lays down a minimum of specific rules for public employees and processes for handling misbehaviour and disciplinary action. In Sweden the conditions of employment in the civil service are governed by collective agreements concluded between the Swedish Agency for Government Employers on one side, and union organisations on the other. Most agreements defining the direct working conditions of central government employees are signed at decentralised level within the framework of central discretionary agreements. The rules applicable to public sector employees are nearly identical to those applicable to private-law employees.

In the **United Kingdom**, the number of people employed in the public sector was 5.8 million (in 2005). Public employees are usually classified into three main groups: central government, local government and public corporations.
2.5 million staff work in central government. This category comprises all administrative departments of government and therefore strictly includes the National Health Service (NHS). The NHS is the largest component with an estimated 1.5 million employees. It also includes the civil service which comprises civil servants engaged mainly in providing services to the public (e.g., social security benefits and employment services) with a small group of senior staff providing information and advice to government ministers in support of policy development. The civil service comprised approx. 550 000 civil servants in 2005. 2.9 million staff are employed by local authorities. These are organisations with

elected leaders who have some powers to raise funds through levies and taxes, and are responsible for the provision of education (schools), social services, police, fire and other services. 380 000 staff are employed in publicly owned and controlled corporations which nevertheless have substantial freedom to conduct their activities along business lines. These companies receive more than half of their income from sales of goods and services in the market place. For example, the Royal Mail is included in this category.

The allocation of functions between these three main groups is partly an accident of history and has altered over time. Employment regulation in the civil service, as in many other European countries, retained some distinguishing features that set it apart from the two other public sector groups, although these differences have declined over time. In the United Kingdom, strictly speaking, only those working for the ministries or their executive agencies are civil servants. They represent about 9% of public sector employees. Until very recently, the rules governing their status were based on tradition and there was no actual civil service code. The working conditions in the civil service and the rules regarding human resources management were codified in the Civil Service Management Code in 1996. Most public sector employees or "public servants" are employed on a contractual basis and are subject to general labour code legislation. Employment conditions vary considerably between public employers

As this overview shows, only a small number of countries have a relatively uniform and homogenous civil service law, as is the case in the Netherlands, France, Greece and Finland (where almost all public employees are employed under a public law contract). On the other hand, Italy also offers a relatively homogenous legal regime for most of its civil servants. However, unlike the Netherlands, France and Finland, Italy provides for a system under labour law. Italy's public service system is regulated according to sectors. France provides for a special case: although almost 80% of all French public employees have the status of a tenured civil service, the French system consists of three state *fonctions publiques* (under a general statute). All other EU countries have a dual system and provide for different employment regimes in the national public service. The United Kingdom falls somewhat outside since it is the only country in the EU without a public civil service law.

3.2. Civil service employment - which sectors employ civil servants?

What is true for the concepts and definitions of the term civil service is also true for the different employment categories. There is no European-wide conception and definition as to the employment of public employees or the employment of civil servants. Although some general patterns exist, the Member States employ public employees and/or civil servants in many different sectors, functions, jobs, areas etc. Furthermore, the term public employee and civil servant can mean many things. Civil service jobs range from street sweeping to the exploration of outer space, where both persons could be employed as a civil servant or as a public employee with an employment contract. In many cases, the selected employment status lacks clear logic.

According to the World Bank, civil service legislation always covers the permanent employees of civilian central government and, in some settings, subnational government. Often teachers, health professionals, and the police are excluded.

- Employment in the education sector is also generally regulated by specific legislation.
- The health sector workforce, which usually comprises a significant element within the total public sector workforce, may be either directly employed by the public sector health system, or work in public-funded agencies or organisations (e.g., social insurance funded). In many countries healthcare will also be delivered by organisations in the private sector and by voluntary organisations.
- Subnational government employment often represents a substantial portion of the total public sector workforce – frequently over 50% in federal counties. However, subnational government employment is considered a separate, legally defined civil service in many countries. In most continental European countries, military and law enforcement personnel (e.g., police, customs, etc.) have their own specific legislation as the basis for employment. However, more often than not, the police are considered civil servants.
- Employees of state owned enterprises may be subject to specific, but different legislation, or may be subject to the general labor law that governs employment contracts in the private sector"[154].

After the examination of the national responses to our study, the civil service employment pattern showed the following characteristics. Civil servants in the central ministries, police staff, judges, diplomats and soldiers have a specific, yet often also a special status.

---

154 http://web.worldbank.org/WBSITE/EXTERNAL/TOPICS/EXTPUBLICSECTORANDGOVERNANCE/EXTADMINISTRATIVEANDCIVILSERVICEREFORM/0,,contentMDK:20133489~menuPK:286372~pagePK:148956~piPK:216618~theSitePK:286367,00.html

In almost half of all EU Member States, teachers, professors and health professionals are excluded from having a specific status. However, employment in the education sector is also regulated by specific legislation in some Member States. The health sector workforce, which usually comprises a significant element within the total public sector workforce, may be employed directly by the public sector health system or work in public-funded agencies or organisations, e.g., social insurance funded. In many countries healthcare is also be provided by organisations in the private sector and by voluntary organisations.

Table 9: Do these administrative sectors belong to central civil service or do they have their own civil service systems?

(Frequencies in parenthesis)

Administrative sector	Central civil service	Specific civil service	Not part of civil service	Total
Central Government	100 (27)	0 (0)	0 (0)	100 (27)
Government agencies	85 (22)	0 (0)	15 (4)	100 (26)
Diplomatic service	59 (16)	41 (11)	0 (0)	100 (27)
Judiciary	48 (13)	33 (9)	19 (5)	100 (27)
Police	41 (11)	44 (12)	15 (4)	100 (27)
Military	37 (10)	37 (10)	26 (7)	100 (27)
Education	19 (5)	30 (8)	52 (14)	100 (27)
University	19 (5)	26 (7)	56 (15)	100 (27)
Hospitals	19 (5)	26 (7)	56 (15)	100 (27)

Subnational government employment often represents a substantial portion of the total public sector workforce – frequently over 50% in decentralised or federal counties, but also in Scandinavian countries. In some Member States, subnational government employment is often not part of the civil service (Poland, Ireland) or is considered a separate, legally defined civil service. For example, in the Scandinavian countries the term civil service is usually defined as the state level. Local authorities and municipalities in these countries are distinct from the central state level. However, (in Finland and Denmark) they also employ local civil servants. For example, Finland employs more than 80% of all public employees as civil servants at the state level but only approx. 40% of all public employees on the local level have a civil service status.

In **Estonia,** according to the Public Service Act, public servants are employed by central government institutions (ministries, administrative agencies, boards and inspectorates, constitutional institutions, county governments) and local governments (227 towns and rural municipalities). Certain groups within the public service are regulated by special legislation (e.g., the diplomatic corps, the police, the judiciary and the military).The public service system does not cover medical staff, teachers and academic staff.

For example, in **Romania** the Civil service Law No. 188 (r2) from 08/12/1999 is applicable to all civil servants of the government, local public administration, autonomous administrative authorities, public authorities and bodies of central and local public administration. In **France,** the public administration is organised on the basis of the general rules governing the civil service (Law of 13 July 1983) as well as three other laws[155] which determine the legal position of civil servants of the state (*Fonction publique d'Etat*), the civil services of the territorial governments (*Fonction publique territoriale*) (municipalities, *départements* and regions) and the hospital service (*Fonction publique hospitalière*)[156], each comprising numerous "*corps*" or *cadres d'emplois* (regional and local level). Lastly, special rules apply to magistrates, the armed forces and civil servants in parliamentary assemblies[157].

The **United Kingdom** is a special case; for a long time, it was a unitary state where all legislative competencies were vested in Westminster. However, in recent times this has changed dramatically. The devolution processes in Wales and especially Scotland have led to the creation of a Welsh assembly and a Scottish parliament with legislative competences. This devolution, as well as the establishment of the Northern Ireland assembly and its executive committee of ministers, has changed the unitary character of the United Kingdom. The civil service and the military are both directly under the central government. Local government comprises, amongst other things, education, social services and the police force. In the **United Kingdom**, the civil service is limited to the staff of the ministries and the numerous agencies[158].

---

155 Law of 11 January 1984, Law of 26 February 1984, and Law of 9 January 1986.

156 This enumeration does not mean that three forms of the civil service cover the whole public sector. See Ministère de la Fonction Publique de l'Etat, La fonction publique de l'Etat, Paris 1999.

157 Law of 13 July 1972 concerning the armed forces (including the Gendarmerie), Decree of 22 December 1958 relating to judges, and Decree of 17 November 1958 on parliamentary staff.

158 Next Steps: Agencies in Government, Review 1994, HMSO, London; Barberis, Next Steps: Consequences for the Core and Central Departments, in: Barry J.

The distinction between government levels is also very relevant in the cases of **Sweden, Finland** and **Denmark.** In **Sweden**, there is a distinction between the central civil service, the civil service of the counties and the local civil service, while in **Finland** the distinction is between central government and local government. Generally, in all Scandinavian countries the decentralised authorities enjoy wide discretionary powers with regard to the management of their civil services. **Danish** civil servants are employed by the state, the counties and the municipalities. The legal status of the civil servants is determined by the Civil Service Act 1969. The legal status of county and municipal civil servants is determined by regulations passed by the regional and local authorities. The main provisions of the Civil Service Act and the regional and local regulations are, however, identical. Public employees are employed on the basis of a collective agreement, and are governed by ordinary labour law.

Again, different to the above-mentioned models are those countries that have a civil service which is divided according to sectors. The public administrations in which the subdivision into functional sectors is the main characteristic in terms of organisation include **Ireland**, **Italy** and the **Netherlands**. In **Ireland**, the different sectors are the civil service (which encompasses the staff of central government ministries only), the police, defence, education, non-commercial public enterprises, the health service and local government. In **Italy**, one can distinguish between the sectors belonging to the state and the other sectors of public administration. To these other sectors belong the *enti pubblici non economici*, regional and local entities, the national health service and research entities and institutions[159]. The **Dutch** civil service has been subdivided into eight sectors since 1993: the civil service of central government, the judiciary, the police, education and science, the military, the provinces, the municipalities and water agencies (*waterschappen*).

Things become more diverse when looking at the employment in the so-called grey areas, e.g., prisons, nuclear power stations, inspectorates, risk prevention etc. A comparative study by Demmke (2006)[160] revealed that the EU Member States apply a very different definition of the term "status". Some Member States even employ different categories of public law civil servants. In addition, they even employ, both, civil servants and private employees in the same sectors

---

O'Toole/Grant Jordan (eds.) Next Steps, Improving Management in Government, Dartmouth, Aldershot, 1995, pp. 99-118.

159 Presidenza del Consiglio dei Ministri (Prime Minister's Office) (1998-1999) Relazione sullo stato della pubblica amministrazione.

160 Christoph Demmke, Are Civil Servants Different Because They Are Civil Servants? EIPA, Maastricht, 2006.

or positions. Logic behind this is difficult to find, thus, the Member States do not only differ with regard to the employment of different categories of public employees in different sectors. In fact, the Member States also apply different concepts of the term civil service. These concepts range from broad and centralised to very narrow and decentralised concepts.

Table 10: Public employment by sector and country[161]

Central banks	
Yes, most employees are civil servants or specific categories of staff	Cyprus, Czech Republic, Finland, Ireland, Italy, Luxembourg, Spain
No, mostly employees under labour law	Austria, Belgium, Denmark, Estonia, France, Germany, Greece, Hungary, Latvia, Lithuania, Malta, Netherlands, Poland, Portugal, Slovakia, Slovenia
Comments	In many Member States, senior managers are appointed at political level.
Diplomatic sector	
Yes, most employees are civil servants or specific categories of staff	Austria, Belgium, Cyprus, Czech Republic, Estonia, Finland, France, Germany, Greece, Ireland, Italy, Latvia, Lithuania, Luxembourg, Malta, Netherlands, Poland, Portugal, Slovakia, Slovenia, Spain
No, mostly employees under labour law	Denmark
Comments	
Universities (professors)	
Yes, most employees are civil servants or specific categories of	Belgium, Cyprus, Czech Republic, France, Germany, Greece, Hungary, Ireland, Italy, Netherlands, Poland, Portugal, Slovakia, Slovenia, Spain (60.96%)[162]

161 In Sweden and the UK, a distinction is difficult. In Sweden, the same overall labour law applies in principle to the public sector as to other sectors in the labour market. However, some groups enjoy greater employment security, e.g., judges. Consequently, most public employees do not fall within the definition of civil servant used in this survey, even though they are referred to as civil servants in Sweden. In the UK, there is no distinction between public and private law in employment. However, a new civil service bill is being planned.

162 Ministerio de Administraciones Públicas, Civil Service in Spain, Madrid 2002, p. 48.

staff	
No, mostly employees under labour law	Austria, Denmark, Estonia, Finland, Italy, Latvia, Lithuania, Luxembourg, Malta, Spain (39.04%)[163]
Comments	In many Member States, professors at public universities have public-law status, whereas professors of private universities have private-law status.
Inspectorates (food control, health and safety)	
Yes, most employees are civil servants or specific categories of staff	Austria, Cyprus, Czech Republic, Estonia, Finland, France, Greece, Hungary, Ireland, Italy, Lithuania, Luxembourg, Malta, Netherlands, Poland, Portugal, Slovakia, Slovenia, Spain,
No, mostly employees under labour law	Denmark, Germany, Latvia, Lithuania
Comments	
Hospitals (nurses, doctors)	
Yes, most employees are civil servants or specific categories of staff	Cyprus, Czech Republic, Finland, France, Greece, Hungary, Ireland, Italy, Malta, Portugal, Spain, Slovenia
No, mostly employees under labour law	Austria, Belgium, Czech Republic, Denmark, Estonia, Germany, Italy, Latvia, Lithuania, Luxembourg, Netherlands, Poland, Portugal, Slovakia, Spain
Comments	In many Member States, there are private as well as public hospitals.
Border control (customs) and aviation (air traffic control)	
Yes, most employees are civil servants or specific categories of staff	Austria, Belgium, Cyprus, Czech Republic, Estonia, Finland, France, Germany, Greece, Hungary, Ireland, Italy, Latvia, Lithuania, Luxembourg, Malta, Netherlands, Poland, Portugal, Spain, Slovakia, Slovenia
No, mostly employees under labour law	Austria (air traffic control), Denmark, Germany, Netherlands, Poland, Portugal
Comments	In some Member States, such as Austria, Germany, Netherlands, Poland, Portugal and Spain, a distinction is made between border control (customs) and air traffic control, with civil servants or specific cate-

163 Ibid.

	gories of staff mostly being employed in customs, and private employees mostly being employed in air traffic control. In Poland, the Civil Aviation Office is responsible for providing and maintaining safe air services to, from and within Poland. Staff are subject to civil service law. In Spain, air traffic is handled by the "Spanish Airports and Aerial Navigation (AENA)", an Entrepreneurial Public Agency with a special legal framework. Employees used to be civil servants, but became subject to common labour law in the 1990s. In Slovenia, approx. 80% are civil servants.
Risk management/environmental inspection and control	
Yes, most employees are civil servants or specific categories of staff	Austria, Belgium, Cyprus, Czech Republic, Estonia, Finland, France, Greece, Hungary, Ireland, Italy, Latvia, Lithuania, Netherlands, Poland, Portugal, Spain, Slovakia, Slovenia
No, mostly employees under labour law	Denmark, Germany, Latvia, Malta
Comments	In Slovenia, approx. 80% are civil servants.
Water sector	
Yes, most employees are civil servants or specific categories of staff	Austria, Cyprus, Ireland, Italy, Luxembourg, Slovenia
No, mostly employees under labour law	Belgium, Czech Republic, Denmark, Estonia, Finland, France, Germany, Greece, Hungary, Italy, Latvia, Malta, Netherlands, Poland, Portugal, Slovakia, Spain
Comments	The regulation of this sector is subject to EU law. However, the status of employees varies according to specific functions and situations in the water sector.
Nuclear Power Stations	
Yes, most employees are civil servants or specific categories of staff	Czech Republic, Greece, Italy, Slovenia
No, mostly employees under labour law	Belgium, Finland, France, Germany, Hungary, Latvia, Lithuania, Netherlands, Spain, Slovakia, Sweden

Comments	A number of Member States do not have nuclear power stations.
Prison service	
Yes, most employees are civil servants or specific categories of staff	Austria, Cyprus, Czech Republic, Denmark, Estonia, Finland, France, Germany, Greece, Hungary, Ireland, Italy, Latvia, Lithuania, Luxembourg, Malta, Netherlands, Poland, Portugal, Slovakia, Slovenia, Spain
No, mostly employees under labour law	
Comments	In the UK, prison officers are civil servants. In Austria, contractual employment is not possible from a legal point of view. Since 1993, prison officers in Italy may be recruited under a special private law status.
Other (Energy, Postal Services, Transport, Telecommunication)	
Yes, most employees are civil servants or specific categories of staff	
No, mostly employees under labour law	
Comments	These sectors are subject to EU Regulation. However, some Member States also employ civil servants in these sectors.

N.B.: The matrix shows the legal status that the **majority** of employees of the indicated Member State have in the various sectors. However, this does not mean that there might not be a minority of employees having also the opposite legal status. This study does not show the situation in the post and telecom sectors as most of these services have been privatised.

Source: Christoph Demmke, Are Civil Servants different because they are Civil Servants? EIPA, Maastricht, 2006

3.3. The size of the civil service and public employment

Although the image of a civil servant is still influenced by the perception of a ministerial bureaucrat, in reality functions, ranks and positions reflect a much wider picture. According to the Austrian report *Das Personal des Bundes* a lot of work is no longer carried out in offices. Instead, civil servants work in schools, in the judicial services, police, military, as well as in many technical agencies. Only one third of the personnel belong to the administrative service (*Verwaltungsdienst*). Consequently, the report states that the federal employees are not at all a homogeneous group[164].

With regard to their education, civil servants may have a broad educational background. Only few countries still apply a so-called *Juristenmonopol* which stems from times when it was seen as essential to ensure that civil servants have a thorough education and knowledge in administrative law. Today, civil servants in all Member States are increasingly well-educated professionals, who are at the forefront of their fields of specialisation. On the other hand, also public employees who are employed under labour law are better educated than ever, and are now drawing up policies that have a nationwide impact and may benefit millions of people. On the other hand, some civil servants work in areas where they have virtually no responsibility for policy making. In both cases these include "doctors, lawyers, scientists, engineers, accountants, budgeters, policy analysts, personnel officers, managers, clerks, keyboarders, and manual labourers"[165].

Mostly, civil service employment represents only a fraction of total public employment. For example Sweden, with almost 30% of public employees among the economically active population has almost three times more public employees than Germany and Ireland (both countries with only 11-12% public employees amongst of the active population), but almost all public officials are employed under legal provisions and/or rules which do not differ very much from those working under labour law. Greece has a relatively small public sector (approximately 14% of the active population) but a high percentage of civil servants among all public employees (approximately 80%). This can be explained by the fact that the Greek constitution and/or civil service law generally requires the recruitment of civil servants.

---

164 Österreichisches Bundeskanzleramt, Das Personal des Bundes, op. cit., p. 18.
165 Rosenbloom/Kravchuk, op. cit., p. 4.

Figure 1: Employment in general government as a percentage of the labour force (1995 and 2005)

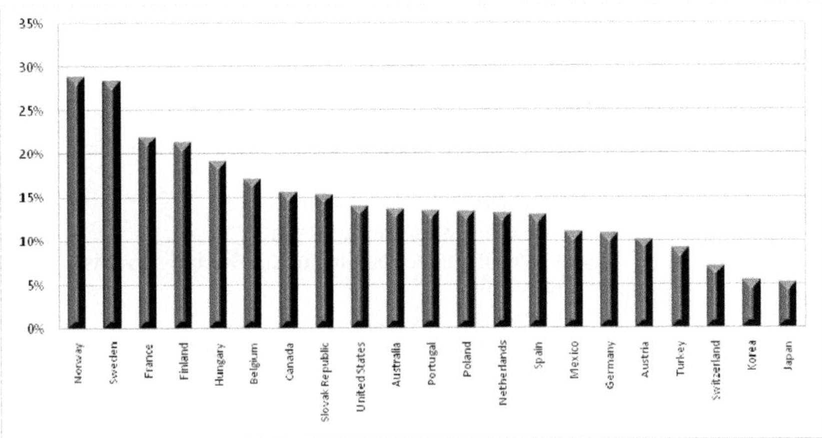

Source: OECD, Government at a Glance, Paris, 2009, p. 67

In the EU Member States, the percentage of civil servants amongst all public employees varies enormously from approximately 0.5% (judges and military officials in Sweden) to almost 100% (Netherlands)[166]. In Estonia, for example, most public employees are defined as civil servants under national law. Also in Ireland almost all public employees are civil servants as long as the civil service is defined narrowly. Contrary to this, Greece, the Netherlands, Finland and France apply a much broader definition of the term Civil Service and employ between 75% and 100% of the public workforce as civil servants. In France approx. 4.2 million people are employed as "*fonctionnaires titulaire ou militaire*" amongst the approx. 5 million public employees.

166 European Commission has 68% civil servants, 6% temporary agents, 17% contract agents, 8% local agents, 1% special advisers

Table 11: Percentage of civil servants and other employees by Member State

Member state	Percentage of civil servants and other employees
Czech Republic	0% civil servants, 62% public employees, 38% officials in territorial self-governmental units
Sweden	1% statutory civil servants, 99% contractual employees
Latvia	6% civil servants, 94% public employees
Poland	6% civil servants, 94% civil service employees
Romania	6% civil servants, 1% specific civil servants, 93% public employees
United Kingdom	10% civil service, 90% wider public sector
Ireland	13% civil servants, 87% public servants (*)
Italy	15% civil servants (under public law), 85% civil servants (under labour law)
Hungary	25% civil servants, 75% public employees
Cyprus	28% civil service, 17% education, 15% security, 14% craftsmen and labourers, 20% semi-government organisations, 6% local authorities
Slovenia	34 % civil servants, 66% public employees
Denmark	36% civil servants, 66% public employees
Germany	37% civil servants, 59% employees 59%, 4% soldiers
Bulgaria	48% civil servants, 52% contractual staff
Spain (**)	59% civil servants, 27% contracted personnel 14% other types of staff (regional and local level excluded)
Austria (**)	61% civil servants, 39% contractual staff
Lithuania	67% civil servants, 28% employees under labour contract, 5% other
Malta	67% civil servants, 33% public sector employees
France	73% civil servants, 15% contract agents, 12% other specific staff
Greece	74% civil servants, 26% contractual personnel
Belgium (**)	75% civil servants, 25% contractual employees
Luxembourg	77% civil servants , 23% public employees
Finland	83% civil servants, 17% public employees (regional and local level excluded)
Slovakia	85% civil servants, 10% public employees, 5% contractual employees
Estonia	90% public servants, 7% support staff, 3% non-staff public servants
Portugal	100% civil servants
Netherlands	100% civil servants

(*) In Ireland only those who work for the ministries are called civil servants, others are public servants.

(**) These figures concern only the federal level administration (in Spain the regional level).

In Austria and Spain, the figures for officials have gone down to roughly 60%. Germany has approx. 37% of civil servants in the national public service. In Denmark, approx. 36% of all public employees are civil servants (and the number is decreasing), and in Hungary 25%. In the United Kingdom the term civil service is narrowly defined and includes the 500 000 or so Crown Civil servants amongst the 5 million public sector workforce. In Latvia and Poland, less than 6% of the public workforce is employed as nominated civil servants.

It is also important to compare civil service employment at the central governmental level and also on the horizontal level (amongst the different ministries). For example, in Germany approximately 68% of all employees at federal level are civil servants. In France the figure is approx. 85% of all employees of the state (Fonction Publique d'Etat) who have a civil servant status. However, the figures are even more diverse when looking at the sectoral level. For example, in Austria all judges and prosecutors have the status of a civil servant. However, only 47.0% (61.1% of all men and 34.1% of all women) of all employees in the federal executive service (*Verwaltungsdienst*) and 41.5% of all teachers are civil servants[167]. In Denmark civil service varies between 2% and approx. 84% in the different ministries.

All of these figures demonstrate one thing: civil service structures and civil servant employment vary sharply amongst the Member States.

4. Specific organisational structures

At the beginning of the 20th century Max Weber believed that a bureaucracy would be the most efficient and rational form of a public or private organisation. However, Weber was also concerned as to the negative effects of the rationalisation process in the European societies in the beginning of the 20th century and the negative impact of the bureaucratic structure on the personality on those who work in these organisations.

Often, public organisations are seen as hierarchical, formalised, rule bound and inflexible. A widespread image is that public organisations are different from private sector organisations. This may be true to some extent – mostly public organisations tend to have a higher degree of rule orientation and formalism. On the other hand, many big private sector companies may be just as bureaucratic as public organisations.

---

167 Österreichisches Bundeskanzleramt, Das Personal des Bundes, Wien 2009.

According to the classical description of Weber a bureaucracy possesses the following specific organisational features:

1. There is a clear hierarchy of offices,
2. There is a career structure,
3. Promotion is by seniority and merit,
4. The whole organisation is rule governed.

When applying this classical description of bureaucratic organisational structures, almost all national civil services can still be considered as organisational systems with – at least – some common and traditional organisational structures. Most civil services apply one or more of these classical features of bureaucracy in their administrations. At least parts of the classical elements of the bureaucratic career system also exist in countries which are often classified as post-bureaucratic countries. In particular, the organisation of the military, the customs service or the police do not differ too much amongst the different countries. In addition, seniority still plays a role in many countries, although it is gradually seen as being in conflict with the principle of anti-discrimination, experience and merit which should become the dominant feature of career development policies. Thus, no new universal alternative model of civil service organisation is likely to replace the bureaucratic model.

On the other hand, the classical bureaucratic career model has probably seen its best times. Initially designed as an instrument against politicisation, our study shows many Member States are keeping only certain skeleton elements and discarding those aspects which they consider too inflexible, too hierarchical, too slow or too unresponsive. Today, all Member States seem to take the position that at the beginning of the 21st century, pure bureaucratic models are no longer adapted to the needs of a modern society since they are too hierarchical and inflexible, not transparent enough, decision-making procedures are too formalised and slow, managers lack motivation due to too little own responsibilities and decision-making discretion etc. Overall, public organisations are seen to focus too much on standardisation and equality and too little on autonomy and performance.

Therefore, contrary to Weber's perception, bureaucracies are no longer seen as more efficient and effective than other forms of organisations, although it is not clear as to where the starting point of criticism against bureaucratic structures is. Criticism mostly related to the observed poor performance is very broad and lacks analytical power. Another problem is the object of comparison: to whom should public organisations be compared?

Still, it seems much easier to criticise what is well known. The specific characteristics (and especially the lack of flexibility) of the traditional model no longer fit modern requirements for flexibility, individualism, performance, adaptation and more variety. Today most observers of civil service reforms believe that the traditional bureaucratic features have produced as many benefits as damage. For example, the focus on impersonal treatment as a principle has led several public organisations to develop into extremely dehumanised, anonymous, hierarchical and impersonal machines. The principle of seniority has de-motivated (and almost discriminated) younger, talented officials. The principle of stability has led to inflexible, almost closed-up organisations with very little contact to the wider (public and private) sector and limited mobility.

In addition, factors such as subordination, lack of transparency, and rigidity (in the sense of organising bureaucracies too strictly into careers and closing up public organisations from the private sector) conflict with demands for transparency, pluralism, flexibility, democracy and responsibility.

Better qualifications have led to civil servants who are more qualified, critical, flexible and self-confident and who would not simply accept the taking and giving of orders. Moreover, our modern, conceptual understanding of bureaucracy is that it should serve the society and the citizens instead of controlling them. Consequently, public bureaucrats (just like bureaucratic organisations) face an increasing inherent tension between new values, the wish for individual flexibility (and discretion) and the need for legal correctness (and fairness). Or, to put it differently: between the need to serve individualism and the need to preserve the societies.

The answers to our study also show that some Member States have not only reduced but also completely abolished classical careers and career structures. According to Table 12, it seems that in general there are pressures to reform and reduce the career system. Six countries indicated that they are reducing the number of careers/corps, while two countries, Belgium and Portugal, are conducting major reorganisation of their career systems, which includes some reductions, abolishing as well as introducing new career structures. Three countries, Luxembourg, Poland and the United Kingdom, are going to introduce new careers. However, most of the EU-27 countries have no plans to modify present systems.

Table 12: Career system reforms by EU Member State

(Frequencies in parenthesis)

Introduce new careers/corps: LU, PL, UK (x)	11 (3)
Reduce the number of careers/corps: FR, DE, IT, SI, ES, SE (x)	22 (6)
Major reorganisation: BE, PT	7 (2)
No changes: AT, CZ (x), DK (x), FI (x), EL, HU, LV (x), LT, BG, CY, EE (x), IE, MT, NL (x), RO, SK (x)	59 (16)
Total	100 (27)

x = position system country

A typical fault of the traditional career system is seen in the fact that it inhibits too much inter-ministerial mobility and mobility between the public and private sector. From an organisational point of view, employees within a career system often face career bottlenecks and reach the highest position they could reasonably expect to achieve at around 50 years of age. After that they can only expect an automatic increase in step every two years. With further promotion improbable, the organisation fails to provide these employees (mostly older staff) with a good career development perspective. On the other hand, young, promising officials have a long way to go until they (theoretically) reach top positions, and older employees suffer from the lack of career perspectives. Another problem of the rigid career system is that it is often difficult to move between careers. Yet in an age of increased mobility, individualism and lifelong learning, such a rigid structure appears outdated. Moreover, the advance of IT has made the traditional lower grades largely superfluous.

Another popular criticism against a career system is the pay system which is regulated by law and pays officials according to experience and seniority, but less according to individual performance. In order to react to this criticism many Member states have started to introduce performance-related pay and abolish seniority automatisms.

As convincing as these arguments are, they lack a discussion about the potential strengths of a career-based organisation. How will career development be defined if careers are abolished? Will there be more and better or fewer and worse possibilities to develop the personal career? Will there be more or fewer possibilities for politicisation in the post-career age?

Answers to these questions may be known in a couple of years. As could be seen in our study some Member States have reformed their career systems. On the other hand, other countries were more reluctant. For them, at least some classical features still made sense. For example, countries like France or Germany considered whether a number of classical characteristics of the Weberian bureaucrat are really bad per se or whether they have been perverted by bureaucratic pathologies within the last decades. Moreover, careers are still seen as an organisational shield against politicisation and patronage. Despite these arguments, these countries, too, are reforming their careers. For example, since 2005 France has started an important process in order to fuse together and reduce the number of corps. Since 2005, a total of 320 corps have been abolished[168]. Due to its decentralised structure, Germany represents one of the most interesting laboratories of reform in the field of organisational reforms. Only recently, mostly at the Länder level, important career system reforms have been carried out. For example, Bavaria has implemented an important reform which led to a fusion of different careers in the Bavarian civil service. Future benchmarking exercises may show the advantageous and disadvantageous of the different systems in Europe.

Overall, the emergence of a new European-wide organisational model in the national civil services cannot be identified. One reason for this is it is the fact that it is much more difficult in the public sector (than in the private sector) to design alternative organisational models. Whereas in the private sector organisations need to be efficient and performing well, it is widely accepted that public sector organisations have multiple tasks and objectives.

Almost 30 years ago, Drucker stated that "public service institutions always have multiple objectives and often conflicting, if not incompatible, objectives"[169]. Such goals make it difficult for public organisations to develop per-

---

168 "L'architecture des corps de la fonction publique de l'État a connu, depuis 2005, une évolution d'une ampleur inédite. Sur la base de la mise en oeuvre du protocole Jacob, 440 corps ont en effet fait l'objet d'opérations de fusions, dont l'entrée en vigueur interviendra au plus tard en 2010, et permis la suppression de 320 corps. En 2005, 220 corps en voie d'extinction de fait ou de droit, et environ 700 corps vivants - c'est-à-dire des corps pour lesquels des recrutements interviennent de manière régulière et pour lesquels une commission administrative paritaire est constituée - étaient recensés. Le nombre des corps vivants a donc été ramené à 380 corps", See: Fonction Publique d'Etat, Rapport Annuel 2008/2009, Paris 2009, p. 30.

169 Peter Drucker, What Results Should You Expect? A User's Guide to MBO, in: Shafritz/Hyde, op. cit., p. 427.

formance standards to serve as a basis for effective incentive systems"[170]. Other problems in measuring the impact of reforms can also be found in the fragmentation of the public sector as such, and the difficulties of obtaining better data and information about performance across units, departments, sectors and countries. Moreover, it is extremely difficult to compare private and public organisations or New Public Management organisations with traditional "Weberian" organisations.

Therefore, it seems unlikely that a completely new universal organisational model will come into effect in the near future. Instead, the current development of organisational structures in the European civil service reflects the general tendency towards more differentiation and individualisation in society. This trend may also lead to more organisational diversity and less unity in the European civil services.

5. Specific working conditions

At the beginning of the 20th century, almost all European States were convinced that a bureaucratic civil service guaranteed a maximum of stability and efficiency. The development of specific civil service structures was the consequence of the theory that ethical behaviour is influenced by *work organisation* and the organisational structure[171]. In this conception, employment conditions and HR systems were very different in the public and private sectors. Civil servants were seen as the servants of the royals and enjoyed very different working conditions. At least until the 1980s, the development of bureaucratic organisations led to sophisticated and specific organisational features where civil servants had a specific status, civil servants were recruited in special hiring procedures, recruitment took place for a lifelong career, pay systems were adopted by law, remuneration systems were based on a common grading of posts and a common salary scale for each grade, the salary was not measured like a wage in terms of work done, but according to "status", that is, according to the kind of function (the "rank") and, in addition, possibly, according to the length of service, civil servants enjoyed many specific allowances, social security benefits and rights were different from those in the private sector, working time was

---

170 J. Norman Baldwin, Are We Really Lazy?, in: Review of Public Personnel Administration 4, Spring 1984, pp. 80-89.

171 Guurtje van Sloten, Work Organisation, Technology and Working Conditions, European Foundation for the Improvement of Living and Working Conditions, Dublin 2002.

fixed and not flexible[172], the "official is set for a "career" within the hierarchical order of the public service. He moves from the lower (...) to the higher positions"[173]. Civil servants were recruited for life at the bottom of the organisational hierarchy and then moved slowly forward. Consequently organisational features such as hierarchy, formalism, precision, speed, lack of ambiguity, knowledge of files, continuity, discretion, unity, strict subordination etc. should motivate the bureaucrats to act impartially and in a professional way. They should be bound to specific secrecy rules, supposed to stay within one organisation or in one ministry and recruited according to specific recruitment procedures. Thus, many civil servants enjoyed privileged but also relatively inflexible working conditions. However, the price for higher job security was a relatively low salary in many Member States.

Today, empirical studies on the degree of patronage and politicisation are still lacking. This is a pity since the whole legitimacy discussion for the need for specific working conditions is based on this link: specific working conditions are needed in order to avoid patronage and politicisation. The "function of security of tenure, pensions, incremental salaries and regularised procedures for promotion is to ensure the devoted performance of official duties. Its Independence should be legally guaranteed by tenure"[174].

Until today, nobody knows for sure whether there is a positive relationship between specific working conditions and impartiality – or not. And what is the dimension of political patronage and nepotism? Mostly, civil servants know that the problems are real; however, in most cases they cannot tell how important the phenomenon is and how frequently it occurs[175]. In fact, the present trend is clearly towards the alignment of working conditions between civil servants and other public employees and between the public and the private sector. The conviction seems to be growing that individual performance and ethical obligations can also be achieved under the condition of "aligned" working conditions. The

---

172 The purpose of this chapter is not to discuss organizational theories but to analyse organizational reforms within the context of their impact on civil service and HRM-reforms. The writings on organizational structures have been voluminous in the past decades. One of the most important has been Henry Mintzberg´s book The Structuring of Organizations, Prentice Hall, 1979. This 512 page volume illustrates how complex the term organisation is.

173 Max Weber, in: Shafritz/Hyde, op. cit., pp. 54-55; see also Max Weber, Wirtschaft und Gesellschaft, op. cit., p. 825.

174 Robert K. Merton, Bureaucratic Structure and Personality, in: Shafritz/Hyde, op. cit. p. 108.

175 Herbert Mandelartz, Sisyphos Lebt, Berliner Wissenschafts Verlag, Berlin, 2009, pp. 149-162.

answers from the Member States to our study show that nowadays many specific working conditions do not exist or are no longer required.

According to Table 13, civil servants and other public employees differ from each other in many respects. In Germany and Lithuania civil servants and other public employees are two clear-cut groups that have their own exclusive rules and standards. In these countries civil servants have, for example, different recruitment procedures, separate career and salary systems, as well as very restricted rights to strike. Overall, in most EU Member States, different rules apply to civil servants regarding their legal status, recruitment procedures, job security, career and salary systems. However, in terms of disciplinary rules, social dialogue, ethical rules, pension systems and right to strike, civil servants and other public employees have the same or similar rules. According to the data, in the UK and the Czech Republic there are no significant differences at all between the civil servants and the other public employees. Furthermore, position-based countries in general have less sharp differences than the career-based countries.

Today civil servants should no longer be persons who give and take orders and who should have specific working conditions that differ sharply with the existing practices in the private sector. Instead, the conviction is growing that, for example, the right to safe and healthy working conditions, the right to fair wages, the right to freedom of expression, the right to participate in the formulation of working conditions, the right to strike (not in all positions), equal treatment and diversity and working time issues should not vary too much between the public and private sectors, as should the right of line managers to take autonomous decisions in appraising, recruiting, training and in remunerating employees.

In the meantime, most Member States have abandoned the traditional lifetime tenure (today only 14 from 27 Member States offer a life-tenure), specific pension systems, the prohibition to strike, incremental salaries and standardised procedures for promotion. Salary is paid less in terms of status but for individual performance. Careers, hierarchy and formalism are subject to many changes. Most existing national surveys reveal that "civil servants" are satisfied with their work. They are well educated and ready to take over new responsibilities. They enjoy more job autonomy and job control. They receive more training and are managed according to specific "Competency Development" schemes. Moreover, Member States offer civil service positions on time and allow for the recruitment of external people.

Table 13: Main differences between civil servants and other public employees by issue and EU Member State

1 = yes, 2 = no

	Legal status	Recruit-ment	Job security	Careers	Salary	Disci-pline	Dialogue	Pension	Strike	%
Germany	1	1	1	1	1	1	1	1	1	100
Lithuania	1	1	1	1	1	1	1	1	1	100
Estonia	1	1	1	2	1	1	1	1	1	89
Hungary	1	1	1	1	1	1	1	2	1	89
Ireland	1	1	1	1	1	1	1	2	1	89
Romania	1	1	1	1	1	1	1	2	1	89
Cyprus	1	1	1	1	1	1	1	1	2	89
Slovakia	1	1	1	1	1	2	1	2	1	78
Belgium	1	2	1	1	1	1	1	1	2	78
France	1	1	1	1	1	2	1	1	2	78
Greece	1	1	1	1	1	2	1	1	2	78
Luxembourg	1	1	1	1	1	2	2	1	1	78
Spain	1	1	1	1	1	2	2	1	1	78
Italy	1	1	2	1	1	1	1	2	2	67
Poland	1	1	1	1	1	1	2	2	2	67
Austria	1	2	1	2	1	1	2	1	1	67
Malta	1	1	1	1	1	1	2	2	2	67
Portugal	1	2	1	1	2	2	1	2	1	56
Latvia	1	1	1	2	2	1	2	2	2	44
Netherlands	1	2	1	2	2	2	1	1	2	44
Slovenia	1	1	2	1	2	2	2	2	1	44
Bulgaria	1	1	2	1	2	1	2	2	2	44
Denmark	1	2	2	2	2	1	2	1	1	44
Sweden	2	1	1	1	2	2	2	2	2	33
Finland	1	1	2	2	2	2	2	2	2	22
Czech Republic	2	2	2	2	2	2	2	2	2	0
United Kingdom	2	2	2	2	2	2	2	2	2	0
%	89	74	74	70	63	56	52	44	48	

Today, the Member States have only maintained few traditional bureaucratic elements: enhanced job security, specific recruitment procedures and specific ethical requirements.

Table 14: HR policies in the new civil service in the 21st century

Civil service principles and procedures	General developments
Categories with a public law status	Yes, but restricted to a few categories (e.g., judges, police, military), nomination and oath only for these categories
Private law status	Large majority of employees in the public service, further alignment of working conditions and status with private sector
Administrative principles and ethical standards	Classical values (legality, impartiality) remain in place, ongoing trend towards more ethical rules, controls and accountability mechanisms, more ethical bureaucracy
Trends in public employment	Generally further slight reduction of employment, need for additional recruitment in certain sectors and in some countries, downsizing "fashion" stopped in many countries
Job security	Importance of job security recognised, however, relaxation of "lifetime tenure", dismissals possible also for reasons other than disciplinary
Bureaucratic career and post-bureaucratic systems	No trend towards a "best-practice" model, move away from "pure forms" and more diversity of different systems, overall still trend towards post-bureaucratic models
Principle of hierarchy	Remain important, however also trend towards more communication, participation and new organisational structures
Decentralisation of responsibilities	Still trend towards more decentralisation, growing awareness of the need for more consistency and coherence in standards, working conditions and HR policies
Mobility between the public and private sector	Further enhanced, difficult in some countries because of difficult competitive situation of the public sector
Leadership	Due to ongoing trends towards decentralisation of responsibilities and the changing nature of work leadership will further in-

	crease in importance. However, growing gap between leadership expectations and the leadership "reality"
Career development	More focus on individual development plans, competency management, lifelong learning, management of older employees more important, promotion policies remain a challenge
International mobility	Ongoing challenges as regards technical (coordination of pensions and tax issues), low cross-border mobility, legitimacy of Art. 39 4 ECT questioned by societal trends (multinational citizenship, EU citizenship etc.)
Anti-discrimination and diversity	Ongoing focus: more efforts in those countries that have neglected these issues in the past, greater focus on new areas (age discrimination)
Recruitment procedures, selection of top officials	Need for further reform: move away from recruitment to entry level as principle, more flexible recruitment (also at mid-career), open competitions for top managers
Pay according to performance	Ongoing popularity of PRP despite criticism, more differentiation and decentralisation in pay
Performance management and personnel appraisal	Increasing challenges, greater focus on communication and trust, need for better leadership in this policy area
Working conditions	Pressure on pay systems in some countries, need to combine private with professional working life, in some countries deterioration of working conditions; need to improve attractiveness in some Eastern European countries
Working time	Flexible working times, in some countries increase of weekly working time
Social dialogue and distribution of competence in HRM	Further decentralisation and fragmentation, local differentiation, informal SD at EU level
HRM and role of Personnel Department	Decentralisation of HRM Department, need for more coherence in HR management
Training	Ongoing trend towards more investments,

	lifelong learning, more focus on training for older officials
Specific pension system	Further alignment with private sector, increase of retirement age, early retirement more difficult, calculation not on basis of last salary, more old age poverty

However, the present reforms of working conditions do not only have positive effects. For example, although civil servants are generally very satisfied with their work, they are not happy with career development policies, performance assessment, performance management issues, pay policies and – to a lesser extent – their leaders[176]. Moreover, top managers have slightly different views than the lower ranking employees. Mostly, top officials are more optimistic about the effects of the reforms. Women may also have different perceptions than men. However, more research is also needed here to understand why women have – at least in certain fields – more positive attitudes than men.

In the end, the present developments create a highly ambivalent picture. Whereas some improvements can be noted (e.g., in the field of anti-discrimination, job responsibility, work-life balance, flexibilisation of working time, job content, ethics and diversity) other areas are not improving (poor performers policies, performance management, reward management etc.)[177]. Most reforms seem to have little effects on the development of public trust. However, the development of trust depends very much on the media attitudes and the right "marketing" of the public services. Generally the public services must do better and show the "real world" of the public services. In reality, many features are positive but less known than the critical developments. In particular, the media focus on the critical developments, scandals and failures.

As the study by Demmke, Henökl and Moilanen showed, overall the older Member States are more successful in fields such as anti-discrimination, equality and diversity policies. However, overall the Scandinavian countries are seen as more successful with regard to a number of individual HR policies. Generally, Eastern European States and the two new Member States face more challenges than the older Member States. Moreover, public employees in some of these countries are less satisfied and observe fewer improvements. At the same

176 Christoph Demmke/Thomas Henökl/Timo Moilanen, What are Public Services Good at?, Success of Public Services in the Field of Human Resource Management, Study for the Slovenian EU Presidency, May 2008 (in further citations quoted as Demmke/Henökl/Moilanen, Slovenian Study).

177 Demmke/Henökl/Moilanen, Slovenian Study, op. cit.

time – despite some important exceptions – many developments in these countries are also positive.

Overall, public service work is much less "dull and boring" than is commonly acknowledged. On the other hand, the public services still have some work to do in the field of "perception" management. Most public officials believe that HR policies are not competitive with those in the private sector. A totally different question is whether this is also the case in reality. At least public services are better than the perception.

6. Public service motivation and different values

Despite all changes, new evidence, scientific work, numerous publications, new developments and reforms, surprisingly little is still known about the relationship between organisational structure, personality and individual behaviour. Most experts have so far offered a number of explanations as to why the behaviour and performance of civil servants differ from other employees, e.g., too many rules, too little delegation and decentralisation, too much political influence, too little motivation, not enough performance incentives, no individualised development strategies and tools, decision-making procedures that are too slow. Another widely believed explanation is that public employees have too much protection against being laid off, too few incentives to perform, too little external pressure (from clients and citizens) and too many privileges. With their structures, the story goes, public employees do not have to work hard and well since it will be very difficult to dismiss or discipline them for poor performance. In this scenario, the public sector suffers from too many poor performers.

At the end of the 19th century Woodrow Wilson was the first to be become interested in the performance of civil servants and whether public service motivation would be specific as such. Not much later, Max Weber observed that there is a connection between organisational structure and personality. According to Weber, the individual becomes a cog in the machinery of modern bureaucracy. Despite the fact that he believed that no other organisational model is more efficient and powerful than private or public bureaucracies, he was also concerned about the impact of bureaucracies on the personality of those who work in it.

Max Weber would certainly have subscribed to the phrase of Winston Churchill's famous remark on democracy and turned it into "Bureaucracy is the worst form of organisation – except for all the rest". "We do not love bureaucracy, but we need it, at least until we devise workable alternative organisational schemes that permit us to retain the features of bureaucracy that we embrace eagerly – predictability and stability, rationality, reliance on expertise, equitable treatment

– while discarding the features we hate – rigidity, inability to deal with special needs, and a setting of barriers between officialdom and citizens."[178]

Merton (1940)[179] was actually the first scientist to analyse the connection between personality and bureaucratic structure. According to him "...the bureaucratic structure exerts a constant pressure upon the official to be methodical, prudent, disciplined (...). An effective bureaucracy demands reliability of response and strict devotion to regulations..."[180]. According to Merton, the bureaucrat's official life is structured in terms of a graded career, promotion by seniority, pensions, incremental salaries, etc., "all of which are designed to provide incentives for disciplined action and conformity to the official regulations (...). But these very devices (...) also lead to an over-concern with strict adherence to regulations which induces timidity, conservatism, and technicism". In fact, according in favour of the bureaucracy could also be turned around: the focus on rationality, hierarchy, rules and formalised and standardised treatment would become a goal in itself and lead to unethical behaviour. Moreover, he was convinced that strong hierarchy levels would lead to conformity with superiors and the political class, and red tape would reduce public service motivation.

Another feature of the traditional bureaucratic structure, "the stress on depersonalisation of relationships, (...), the dominant role of general, abstract rules, tend to produce conflict in the bureaucrat's contacts with the public or clientele (...). The impersonal treatment of affairs which are at times of great personal significance to the client gives rise to the charge of "arrogance"..."[181]. In fact, the process of alienation of the individual's personality starts with a demand for control by the organisation. This is implemented by an official through rule compliance, with an emphasis on correctness. As a consequence, individuals become defensive, rigid and reliable. Subsequently, this behaviour (rigidity, slowness, resistance to change, attachment to rules, excessive discipline, need to control) was called "bureaupathic" behaviour (Thompson)[182]. Merton demonstrated that certain bureaucratic structures indeed influence behaviour.

---

178 See Barry Bozeman, Bureaucracy and Red Tape, New Jersey, 2000, especially the preface and page 19.

179 Robert K. Merton, Bureaucratic Structure and Personality, in: Shafritz/Hyde, op. cit., p. 111.

180 Ibid., p. 112.

181 Ibid., p. 112.

182 Victor A. Thompson, Modern Organisation, Alfred A. Knopf, 1961.

- *Seniority and career*: "The career structure supports an over-concern with strict adherence to regulations."
- *Esprit de corps*: "There is a sense of common identity for all those who work together in a bureaucracy. They share the same interests and there is relatively little competition in so far as promotion is based on seniority, and group aggression is thus minimised. This esprit de corps may lead, however, to personnel defending their entrenched interests rather than assisting the higher officials or clients of the organisation."
- *Process of sanctification*: "There is a tendency for certain bureaucratic norms, originally introduced for technical reasons, to become rigidified and "sacred"."
- *Impersonality*: "The personality of the official is "nucleated" about the norm of impersonality. This, in association with the bureaucrat's tendency to categorise all matters of concern to the organisation, frequently causes the peculiarity of individual cases to be ignored. Since the client inevitably tends to be convinced of the special features of his own problem, he often objects to such treatment. This gives rise to charges of the bureaucrat being arrogant and haughty in his behaviour."

According to this concept, a traditional bureaucratic structure produces a bureaucratic personality which can be defined by the following:

- Subordination: a willingness to comply fully with the orders of the superior;
- Compartmentalisation: confidence in expert judgement and a need to restrict one's concerns to one's own area of specialisation;
- Impersonalisation: a preference for impersonal or formal relationships with other individuals;
- Rule conformity: a desire for adherence to rules, regulations and standard operating procedures.

Merton's explanations supported the view of the entrepreneur as an innovator and individualist and the civil servant as a conformist and someone avoiding innovation. At the same time, the notion of a bureaucratic personality and the belief that adult personality socialisation develops through work organisation emerged.

Another argument as to why public organisations produce certain types of personalities is related to the long and complicated hiring and recruitment procedures in national public services. These procedures were increasingly considered to interfere with the selection of highly motivated individuals who were easily lost to private organisations.

After the Second World War, however, more authors claimed that these traditional views were not correct and that civil servants and public organisations differ from each other and also show a high degree of flexibility. For example, Kohn (1971) found in his empirical analysis that officials were "more intellectually flexible, more open to new experience, and more self-directed in their values than are those who work in non-bureaucratic organisations."[183]

In the following, the traditional view of the rigid bureaucrat is increasingly called into question[184]. Allinson concluded in his study (1984) that the "traditional image of the bureaucrat, with his dissatisfaction and insecurities reflected in pathological behaviour patterns, is not generally applicable."[185] The rigid bureaucrat concept is a false image.[186] According to Allinson, the average bureaucrat is "probably engaged in non-managerial clerical work, relatively satisfied in his job, (…) well adjusted individual who has found his niche in the organisational world. He is amenable to a degree of autonomy and will use his discretion as long as he is given a clear indication of what is expected of him… He understands the need for rules, documentation, standard procedures and specialist skills, and may well be more capable of exercising the self-discipline necessary in their use than the most prone to criticising him (…). Thus the popular view of the modern bureaucrat may be an injustice."[187]

As in the case of Allinson, Goodsell revealed that "the empirical evidence reviewed to verify the "bureaucratic mentality" does very little to assure us that it actually exists. Bureaucrats have not shown to be less flexible and open-minded than non-bureaucrats, and they do not appear more rule oriented. Indeed, much evidence points to little difference between bureaucrats and ordinary people."[188] In his polemic "The Case for Bureaucracy", Goodsell presented interesting socio-demographic information and data about the average civil servant. He concluded that the average civil servant is in fact not much different to other citizens. In reality, average civil servants are middle aged, middle class, repre-

183 Christopher W. Allinson, Bureaucratic Personality and Organisation Structure, University of Leeds, 1984, p. 39.

184 Ibid., p. 40.

185 Ibid., p. 114.

186 Ibid., p. 39.

187 Ibid.

188 Charles E. Goodsell, The Case for Bureaucracy, A Public Administration Polemic, Third Edition, Chatham, New Jersey, 1994, p. 123.

sent different religions, political and educational backgrounds and include both males and females (but the composition of the sexes is different according to functions and positions/senior positions).

Goodsell concluded that "bureaucrats are ordinary people". They teach children, manage forests, program computers, chase speeders, arbitrate labour disputes, calculate benefit-cost ratios, inspect meat, enforce environmental permits, conduct research, negotiate contracts, prepare laws, fight wars, etc." Within a point or two, bureaucrats as a whole are identical with the general public in their concern about crime, drugs, the environment, welfare, and the condition of the cities. Their views are similar close on capital punishment, premarital sex, school bussing, and fundamentalist religion. Overall, comparability outweighs contrast…"[189]

Since some years many researchers have been studying the (non-)existence of motivational differences in the public sector. For example, Perry (1996)[190] developed a measurement scale which consists of four dimensions: attraction to policy making, commitment to the public interest and civic duty, compassion, and self-sacrifice. The findings suggest that people who are attracted to working in the public services have unique motivational incentives that energise and direct their behaviour. Consequently, the motivational aspects of work in the public service cannot be fully explained by rational and public choice theories. In fact, the different dimension of work in the public service show that rational and egoistic motives are only two explanatory variables for work in the public service[191]. Despite the fact that research in the field of public service motivation theory is expanding fast[192] "it is unclear what its relative importance is"[193].

---

189 Ibid., p. 114.

190 Perry, op. cit., pp. 5-23.

191 Gerhard Hammerschmid/Renate E. Meyer/Isabell Egger-Peitler, Das Konzept der Public Service Motivation – Status Quo der internationalen Diskussion und erste empirische Evidenzen für den deutschsprachigen Raum, in: Der moderne Staat, No. 1/2009, p. 73.

192 The latest publication is James L. Perry/Annie Hondeghem (eds.), Motivation in Public Management, op. cit.

193 Peter Leisink/Bram Steijn, Recruitment, Attraction and Selection, in: Perry/ Hondeghem, Motivation in Public Management, op. cit., p. 124.

Still, many questions remain unanswered[194]. Far too little research has been carried out so far on comparative public service motivation. Still, it is not yet clear as to whether and how motivation differs within the public service, civil service, different governmental levels and different categories of staff. It is also unclear as to whether and how public service motivation differs from the core governmental level, to agencies, semi-public bodies to public private partnerships (and also into the private sector). So far the concept has been applied far too homogenously and does not reflect the growing differentiation within the public service. Moreover, international research is only about to start. The concept as such was for a long time dominated by US approaches[195]. However, it may well be that different administrative cultures and public service systems have a different influence on public service motivation.

Another question is how ethics management correlates with public service motivation[196] since mostly a number of values are not included in the public service motivation concept (e.g., impartiality, integrity)[197]. Moreover, it is far from clear whether a strong public service motivation is something positive or whether it may also lead to unethical conduct[198]. Although they have a lot in common, public motivation theories should not be mixed with public ethics theories. Both theories point to the likelihood of different values and motives in the public services. However, having different motivational motives (than in the private sector) does not mean that public servants are "the better employees" or act more ethically[199].

---

194 Yves Eymery/Carole Wyser, Identities of Public Sector Employees as a Source of Inspiration for Differentiating HRM Practices: the Swiss case, Paper presented at the EGPA Conference, 2.-5 September 2009.

195 Pablo Alonso/Gregory Lewis, Public Service Motivation and Job Performance: Evidence from the Federal Sector, in: American Review of Public Administration,Vol. 31, No. 4, 2001, pp. 363-380; Gene A. Brewer/Sally Colman Selden/Rex L. Facer II, Individual Conceptions of Public Service Motivation, in: Public Administration Review, Vol. 60, No. 3, May/June 2000, pp. 254-264; David Houston, Public Service Motivation: A Multivariate Test, in: Journal of Public Administration Research and Theory, Vol. 10, No. 4, October 2000, pp. 713-727.

196 Jeroen Maesschalk, Zeger van der Wal/Leo Huberts, Public Service Motivation and Ethical Conduct, in: Perry/Hondeghem, Motivation in Public Management, op. cit., pp. 157-177.

197 Ibid, pp. 161-162.

198 Ibid, pp. 161-162.

199 Ibid, pp. 171.

In fact, many of today's public service reforms are implemented because more and more people believe that there is no longer any cogent reason to consider that public functions are of greater and of different value than those functions performed by the private sector[200]. They wonder that many civil servants "occupy positions similar to those in private enterprises with only one difference: public administration is a different branch of trade."[201] To this should be added the feeling that the values of public servants are about to change and match with values of private sector values. However, the latter cannot be confirmed as values continue to be relatively stable and specific (although they are also subject to constant changes and lead to a new mix of values). In some cases traditional values even seem to enjoy a new revival as the OECD study "Governance at a Glance" shows[202] (see Figure 2). Despite all changes and reforms, impartiality and legality have remained the top public service values over the past decades. "They are distinct from the private sector, which emphasises profitability and innovation"[203].

As it seems, the future will be dominated by more value conflicts and newly emerging values. For example, during the last ten years, "the number of countries identifying transparency as a core public service value almost doubled"[204]. Also, efficiency is seen as an increasingly important value. Thus, it may well be that in ten years time "privacy" or – alternatively – "risk protection" may become ever more important values. Moreover, some ethical problems may be resolved and others will emerge. Therefore, dilemma training for civil servants may become more important than in the past.

---

200 See Christoph Demmke, European Civil Services between Tradition and Reform, Maastricht, 2004, p. 94.

201 Ron Niessen, Legal Position of Civil Servants; the Process of Standardisation, in: Ministerie van Binnenlandse Zaken en Koningsrijksrelaties (ed.), the Dutch Civil Service, Kluwer, Netherlands, 2004, p. 27.

202 OECD, Governance at a Glance, op. cit.

203 Ibid., p. 40.

204 Ibid.

Figure 2: Frequently stated public service core values (2000 and 2009)

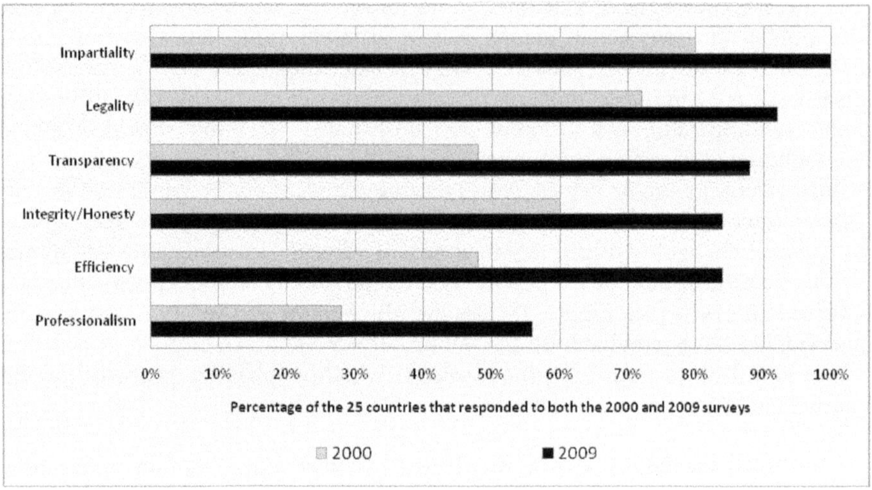

Source: OECD, Governance at a Glance, Paris, 2009, p. 40

There is less evidence that traditional public service values are getting lost, although the feeling of a loss of values is as old as mankind. For example, in his book "The Division of Labour in Society" (1893), Emile Durkheim, a French sociologist, introduced the concept of *anomie*. He used *anomie* to describe a condition that was occurring in society. This meant that rules on how people ought to behave towards one another were breaking down. *Anomie*, simply defined, is a state where norms are confused, unclear or absent. According to Durkheim, it is a situation of normlessness. *Anomie* therefore refers to a breakdown of social norms and it is a condition where norms no longer control the activities of members in society. Changing conditions as well as adjustment of life leads to dissatisfaction, conflict, and deviance. Durkheim observed that social periods of disruption, e.g., economic depression, brought about greater *anomie*. Durkheim felt that sudden societal change caused a state of anomie. A similar theory was presented later on in the USA by Robert Merton ("Social Structure and Anomie", 1938).

However, most value studies contrast to some degree at least with the popular stereotypes regarding an ongoing moral and ethical decline in our societies. In fact, it seems that citizens have clear attitudes but also support conflicting values about what they believe is accepted moral and ethical behaviour and what is not. For example, the acceptance of the rule of law, individual freedoms, e.g., the right to express an opinion, right to be protected against discrimination, right to vote, support for principle of democracy, etc. are very widely accepted among European citizens. In addition, voluntary engagement in religious, political or cultural organisations is not decreasing but remains quite stable. Furthermore, the growing individualism in our societies does not seem to lead to less voluntary social engagement. “Individualism is not the same as egoism”[205].

As the French sociologist Dubet demonstrates, the current trend is not necessarily towards the abolishment of values and principles. Rather it is a trend where different and changing values and principles pose constant dilemmas, conflicts and paradoxes. Whereas the public service was for too long dominated by values such as equality, standardisation and formalism, new values and principles such as performance, autonomy and individualism find their way into the public service. In the future, a too strong focus on performance, individualism and autonomy may automatically produce negative effects and people could call for more equality. Even a too strong focus on ethics and integrity may bounce back since awareness will grow that more integrity management and ethical rules are needed because civil servants are not ethical enough.

In the future, societal trends may tend to strive for a combination of different values and principles. Whereas the present trend is towards more autonomy, performance, risk avoidance and integrity, it is already causing growing inequalities, frustration, fear and distrust in our societies (and also in our public services). The best example for this may be the current trend in the field of pay reforms and the introduction of performance-related pay. Whilst people do not want to go back to the old standardised pay systems (which were based on the principle of automatic pay progression), they are starting to question the effects of new pay systems (which are based on performance related pay). Whilst many people accuse the traditional systems of being unfair (since they consider that they are based too much on the principle of equality and too little on the principle of performance) they are becoming frustrated once performance-related pay is introduced (since they consider that these systems are also unfair).

---

205 Sociaal en Cultureel Planbureau, De moraal in de publieke opinie, Den Hague, 2004, p. 81 (translation).

V. ORGANISATIONAL AND HR REFORM TRENDS

"Most of these strategies look good, sound great, and make sense – on paper. The problem lies in implementation. When it's time to turn these ideas into action, trouble begins"[206].

1. Reform trends and reform priorities

Civil service reforms are supposed to be the outcome of a rational decision-making process. In fact, they are embedded in a turbulent environment which makes it different to follow a clearly defined reform trajectory. This environment is characterised by changing and competing values and new reform priorities on the political agenda. Therefore, reforms are rarely the product of well designed and carefully implemented strategies.

In our study we asked the Member States to indicate their reform priorities and those reform topics which are of less importance. The outcome showed a great variety of reform priorities, but also similar trends. For example, in all of the Member States the need to reduce administrative burdens ranks very high on the reform agenda. On the other hand, issues such as the fight against corruption or the reform of civil service laws are only important for some Member States. In fact, the Member States of the EU respond differently to reform pressures since economic pressures, different political agendas, administrative structures and norms differ amongst the countries. As can be seen, Sweden does not regard most reform issues as reform priorities (mostly because many reforms have already been implemented), whereas Slovenia ranks many reform issues high on the national reform agenda.

Again, whereas some Member States rank some issues (such as diversity management) very high on the reform agenda, others focus on other reform priorities. Still, the results of our study also confirm that some reform trends and reform challenges are similar in all Member States. This observation is interesting (and important) as such since it illustrates one interesting conflicting trend: convergence and differentiation can go hand in hand. Consequently, benchmarking studies may be possible in one area whereas they are much more complicated in other areas.

---

206 Robert Kriegel/David Brandt, Sacred Cows Make the best Burgers, Harper Business, Australia 1996, p. 3.

Table 15: Various reform priorities by EU Member State (1=very important, 5=not important at all)

	A	B	C	D	E	F	G	H	I	J	K	L	M	N	O	P	Q	R	S	T	U	V	W	X	Y	Z	Ä	Ö
Slovenia	1	1	1	1	1	2	1	1	1	1	1	1	2	1	2	2	2	2	2	3	2	2	2	2	2	2	3	2
Hungary	1	1	1	2	2	1	2	1	1	1	2	2	1	2	2	2	1	2	2	2	2	2	2	2	2	2	3	2
Bulgaria	1	1	1	2	2	1	1	1	1	1	1	2	2	2	2	2	2	2	2	2	2	3	3	1	2	2	3	2
Portugal	1	1	2	1	1	1	1	2	1	2	1	1	1	1	1	3	2	2	1	3	2	3	3	3	3	1	3	2
Austria	1	1	1	1	1	1	1	1	1	1	2	1	1	3	1	3	1	2	3	3	2	3	3	3	2	3	3	2
Latvia	1	1	1	2	1	1	1	2	1	3	1	3	2	1	3	2	3	2	2	1	2	2	3	1	2	3	3	2
Denmark	1	1	2	1	1	3	1	2	2	1	2	4	1	3	1	1	1	3	3	1	2	3	1	2	3	3	1	3
Italy	1	1	1	2	2	1	1	1	1	2	2	1	2	2	3	3	2	3	1	2	3	2	3	3	2	2	1	3
Lithuania	1	1	2	1	2	2	1	1	2	2	1	1	3	2	3	2	3	2	2	2	1	2	3	2	2	2	2	3
Spain	1	1	1	2	1	1	1	1	1	2	2	2	1	2	2	3	2	2	2	3	2	2	3	2	2	1	3	5
Malta	1	2	1	1	2	1	2	1	3	2	2	2	2	3	3	3	2	2	2	2	3	2	1	1	2	3	2	3
Belgium	2	1	3	1	2	2	1	2	2	2	1	1	2	3	1	1	2	2	2	2	2	3	2	3	3	3	3	3
United Kingdom	1	1	1	1	1	4	1	1	1	1	1	2	1	1	1	2	1	1	3	3	3	3	3	4	5	3	4	4
Czech Republic	2	2	1	2	1	1	5	1	1	2	2	1	5	3	1	2	4	2	3	2	2	2	2	3	2	2	3	2
Poland	1	2	1	2	2	1	2	1	1	1	3	2	2	1	3	2	3	2	2	1	3	3	3	5	2	2	4	4
Greece	2	3	2	2	2	1	1	2	1	2	2	1	2	3	1	2	2	2	3	2	2	2	3	3	3	3	3	5
France	3	3	2	2	2	2	3	3	2	3	2	2	2	2	2	1	1	1	3	3	3	3	3	1	2	2	3	2
Estonia	2	2	1	2	2	1	2	2	2	2	2	2	2	1	3	2	3	2	2	3	3	2	3	3	3	4	4	3
Ireland	2	2	3	2	2	2	1	3	2	2	2	2	2	2	1	2	2	2	2	2	3	3	2	3	3	4	3	4
Finland	2	3	3	1	2	3	2	2	2	2	2	2	2	3	1	1	3	2	3	3	2	3	3	3	2	5	2	2
Germany	1	2	3	2	2	1	3	3	2	2	2	2	2	1	3	2	3	3	3	3	3	3	3	3	3	2	3	3
Netherlands	2	3	2	2	3	2	3	2	3	3	3	1	3	3	2	1	1	3	1	3	4	2	3	3	3	4	2	3
Cyprus	2	1	2	2	2	2	1	2	2	2	2	3	2	4	3	5	3	3	2	2	2	3	3	3	3	4	2	4
Romania	2	2	1	2	2	1	3	2	3	1	3	2	4	1	5	3	4	3	3	3	3	3	2	3	3	2	3	4
Slovakia	2	3	2	3	2	2	3	2	2	2	2	4	2	3	3	3	3	2	2	3	3	1	3	3	4	3	3	3
Luxembourg	2	2	2	3	2	2	2	2	2	1	2	4	3	2	3	2	3	4	3	3	4	3	3	4	4	2	4	4
Sweden	2	3	4	2	2	5	2	4	5	3	2	4	2	2	3	3	2	3	3	3	4	5	3	3	4	4	2	3

A = Reducing administrative burdens, B = Quality management, C = Ethics and fight against corruption, D = Leadership, E = Performance management, F= Reform of civil service law, G = Citizen orientation, H = Open government and transparency, I = Reform of principles of good administration/good governance, J = Training, K = Competency management, L = Reducing public personnel / savings policies, M = Equality, N = Salary reform, O = Anticipating demographic change, P = Measures to raise attractiveness of public service employment, Q = Diversity policies, R = Enhancing public-public mobility, S = Addressing poor performance, T = Reform of HR departments, U = Reform of working conditions, V = Alignment with the working conditions of other public sector employees, X = Deregulation of HR rules, Y = Decentralisation of HR competencies, Z = Enhancing international mobility, X = Career system reform, Ä = Working time reform, Ö = Enhancing public-private mobility

For example, almost all Member States believe that reducing administrative burdens is an important reform priority. Moreover, in most Member States public employees have similar opinions about successes and failures in civil service reforms. Whilst many respondents in most Member States believe that the whole field of anti-discrimination is booking progress, most people also agree that this is not the case in the field of managing poor performance. Here, it would be important to continue with more research in order to find out when and how the identification of good practices makes sense at all. The selection of reform priorities is not only linked to pressures and the outcome of the internal political decision-making process, lobbying and the role of the media. In fact, reforms are also closely connected with new fashions and the emergence of new norms and values.

Within the last twenty years many new values have been supplemented by new public management values and – later on – by post-bureaucratic values. The constant struggle has produced popular new models of emerging paradigms for public management[207]. According to Dubet ("Injustices. L'experience des inégalités au travail"[208]), the contemporary societies are based on three conflicting principles. They strive for freedom (autonomy), equality and performance at the same time. In fact, all existing organisational models in the private and in the public sectors are based on these principles. However, private sector organisations put more emphasis on freedom and performance (and less on equality); whilst public sector organisations focus on equality and freedom (and less on performance). Although this is changing, public organisations still focus on equality and autonomy and less on performance.

The attitude of the public towards this value struggle is contradictory. Whereas public organisations are criticised for their lack of individual performance orientation, managers in the financial sector are accused of being too egoistic and too "greedy". Value conflicts seem to be becoming increasingly complex. In the 21st century conflicts have emerged between fundamental values: individual performance and equality, political responsiveness and individual accountability, rule of law and customer flexibility, efficiency and effectiveness, individual motivation and budgetary constraints, customer rights and citizen rights, transpar-

---

207 Kellough/Lloyd, Civil Service Reform in the States, op. cit., p. 1.

208 Original title in French. We have used the German version. Francois Dubet, Ungerechtigkeiten, Hamburger Edition, 2008.

ency and human dignity, performance management and bureaucracy, fight against conflicts of interests and privacy[209].

In the field of HRM civil servants strive for more job control and job autonomy. In fact, more civil servants are given more responsibilities. Thus, the current trend towards more decentralisation of HR responsibilities means that leadership issues are becoming more important than ever. At the same time civil servants are also becoming more critical towards their leaders. In the future, poor leadership will be less tolerated. Hence, the issue of leadership is also becoming a reform issue of growing complexity.

1.1. The reform of administrative law and the importance of principles of good administration

Strangely enough, discussions on the importance of (administrative) law did not play a big role during the times of New Public Management euphoria. One reason for this may be that administrative law was mostly seen as a constraint that blocks policy choices and reform policies. Too much law as such was often seen as suspicious and an underlying reason for public sector inefficiencies. Consequently, traditional administrative behaviour was held to be rigid, rule bound, centralised and obsessed with dictating how things should be done – regulating the process, controlling the inputs – but ignoring the outcomes, the results. Old public administration thinking was also dismissed as neutral, hostile to discretion and flexibility, not focused on efficiency and concerned too little with citizen involvement[210]. Until today, new public management theories are dominated by economic-, political- and organisational theories.

This is strange as such since the commitment of the state and of the administration to the rule of law plays a key role in a modern constitutional state. In this concept, citizens should be protected from arbitrary (political and administrative) decisions, and individuals should be given rights to protect themselves against the state and the administration when necessary. The widespread nature of the "French Model" of administrative law is still important to understanding the current state of the national civil services, since it is part of the distinction between private law and public law. It is also important to recall the legitimacy

---

209 The original concept stems from Donald E. Klingner, Societal Values and Civil Service Systems in the United States, in: Kellough/Lloyd, Civil Services in the States, op. cit., p. 11.

210 L.E. Lynn Jr., The Myth of the Bureaucratic Paradigm: What Traditional Public Administration Really Stood For, in: Public Administration Review, March/April 2001, p. 144.

of administrative courts. In order to check "against arbitrary administrative actions, the Conseil d'Etat was established in the Constitution of 1799. Napoleon charged the Conseil with addressing complaints against civil servants, and the executive branch review of administrative actions was born"[211].

The rise of the European Union has seen the impetus of the creation of some common principles of administrative law across diverging systems[212]. Schwarze notes that doctrinal "convergence" has been achieved on several principles[213]. Also very important has been the growing importance of the Swedish model throughout the last years. Ziller suggests that "Sweden can be easily defined as the country of origin of three rather successful waves of institutional export"[214]. The first wave was that of the ombudsman, first exported to Denmark in 1954, later to the United Kingdom, France (with the creation of the Médiateur) and then to Portugal, Spain, the Netherlands and – finally – to the European Union. The second wave was the "export" of the concept of open government to the decision-making process within the EU: from closed machinery to a relatively transparent and open bureaucracy. And the third wave was an adaptation of the Swedish model in many countries: that of executive agencies and decentralised management practices. "A deeper look into these experiences shows, however, how different the constitutional bases and institutional context may be. All three waves have in common that, when imported, Swedish institutions are transformed in order to adapt to the local context"[215].

Today, discussions about the importance of administrative law and principles of good administration have been revived. In the context of new governance, many national public sector reform programmes include proposals towards good administration and more citizen orientation and citizen rights. Consequently, Member States have started to introduce a number of reforms in order to reduce administrative burdens for citizens, strengthen their rights against the administration and speed up administrative procedures. However, despite these positive developments, it remains unclear whether the importance of administrative law, standardised treatment and due procedures are also highlighted.

This dichotomy in the public reform discussion reveals the question of how these four can be reconciled in the future: reducing administrative burdens, cut-

---

211 Anthony M. Bertelli, Public Management and the Law, in: Ferlie/Lynn/Pollitt, The Oxford Handbook of Public Management, op. cit., p. 140.

212 Ibid., p. 143.

213 Jürgen Schwarze, European Administrative Law, Sweet & Maxwell Ltd., 2000.

214 Ziller, European Models of Government, op. cit., p.105.

215 Ibid.

ting public budgets, enhancing citizen rights and maintaining classical administrative law principles.

Is it possible to continue with the introduction of reform measures that implicitly challenge classical public administration and aim at de-regulation, reducing administrative burdens, responsibilisation, individualisation and more flexibility, while at the same time promoting the importance of administrative law? Despite all positive intentions and rhetoric it remains at least doubtful whether modern governance and management reform exhibits more respect for democratic rules, law, politics and citizens than traditional theories did on public administration. Measuring the impact of reforms on (economic) performance is easier than measuring the impact on the actualisation of public services, citizen rights and democratic values[216].

Here, dilemmas seem to arise from the gap which separates the traditional conception of law, its implementation and enforcement (by courts and citizens) from new governance mechanisms. "Thus, for example, whereas a traditional conception of law looks for a unitary source of ultimate authority, new governance is predicated upon a dispersal and fragmentation of authority, and rests upon fluid systems of power sharing. Whereas a traditional conception of law posits hierarchies, and places courts at the centre of systems of accountability, new governance posits heterarchy, and often looks outside of the courts in seeking to secure real accountability. A traditional conception of law appears to rest upon a clear distinction between rule making on the one hand, and rule application and implementation on the other"[217]. The characteristics of new governance (participation, power sharing, diversity, decentralisation, flexibility, benchmarking, non-binding rule-making) on the contrary, accepts that this distinction must break down, as indeterminate and flexible rules are adapted to meet new challenges and resolve unexpected problems.

Although there are many good reasons to criticise the focus on rules, traditional administrative practices were designed to assure standardised and fair treatment. Today this is no longer seen as sufficient to legitimise the authority of an administration. Instead, an administration is required to be efficient, fast, citizen-oriented, respectful towards minorities, diverse in its own structure, effective and competent. It should serve both, the commercial as well as the individual interests. Yet, can this be possible in times of budgetary constraints?

---

216 J.J.,Kirlin, Big Question for a Significant Public Administration, in: Public Administration Review, No. 2, 2001, p. 142.

217 Joanne Scott/David M. Trubek, Mind the Gap: Law and New Approaches to Governance in the European Union, in: European Law Journal, Vol.8, No. 1, 2002, p. 8.

1.2. Civil services between de-regulation and re-regulation

As we have seen earlier in this chapter, Public discussions on civil service reforms are full of interesting paradoxes. Whereas people demand more efficient and better performing public services, they allow for the emergence of a new performance management bureaucracy. While people place higher demands on the national public services, they agree to public budgets being reduced. While observers pledge for administrative simplification, they also favour the introduction of new complex concepts (e.g., sustainable public administration) even if it is difficult to implement these concepts in practice. Today many civil service reformers call for administrative simplification, deregulation and the reduction of administrative burdens, while constantly asking for new laws and rules (e.g., in the fight against terrorism, data protection, climate change etc.).

Also in the field of civil service law, reforms are challenging the need for overly complex laws. In fact, civil service laws are indeed highly regulated instruments. For example, German civil servants are regulated by approximately 30 different civil service laws (e.g., the Bundesbeamtengesetz) and regulations (e.g., the Bundeslaufbahnverordnung). They contain an impressive number of principles such as the Public law principle, Life time Principle, Public ethos Principle, Impartiality Principle, the Career Principle, the *Alimentationsprinzip* etc. Many of them are so complicated that they pose an easy target for public criticism. On the other hand, few people criticise the constant call for new laws and rules in the field of the regulation of corruption, conflicts of interests, citizen rights, anti-discrimination, intrusion into privacy rights etc. There is also a continuous new demand for new investments in new management concepts and new hot topics: Value Management, Sustainable Administration, etc.

Another interesting paradoxical feature of the current reform discussion is the discrepancy between the reform speed in many areas on the one hand and the reform inertia in other areas on the other hand. Today, it is interesting to look at which principles are subject to reforms and which are still seen as sacrosanct principles which seem to *survive* all reform discourses. For example, the public law status belongs to those principles that have survived all reforms in the Member States of the European Union. However, there is almost no public discussion taking place on why civil servants still enjoy a special legal status. Nonetheless, the old-fashioned *Alimentationsprinzip* in the German and French interpretation has never been abolished.

Today, most civil servants perceive the salary as an exchange for the work they are doing. Only few civil servants consider themselves as state officials who receive “Alimente” because they dedicate “their full personality” to the state.

Moreover, only a few remember that the public law status is a product of the French Revolution. Already at the beginning of the 19th century the German Philosopher Hegel argued that a public service status (*Amtsverhältnis*) is clearly different to a contractual status (*Vertragsverhältnis*). It was introduced in order to protect the civil servant against the political influence. Thus, as such it stems from the belief that a public law principle should better protect a civil servant in carrying out his (neutral) duties.

Today, it seems that some very old civil service principles seem to escape all reform discourses, whereas almost everything else is questioned in the world of civil service reforms.

1.3. The new importance of administrative principles

Traditionally the function of rule orientation of the civil service is relatively simple. In fact, the purpose of rule orientation is to allocate rights and to limit arbitrary decisions serving positive objectives, e.g., the protection of citizens against arbitrary decisions of the administration and the protection of civil servants against arbitrary political decisions.

As members of the European Union, all EU Member States have adopted specific administrative law principles and principles of good administration[218]. The principle of lawfulness definitely belongs to the core principles in European administrative law, constitutionally guaranteed in almost every Member State of the EU. In some countries, such as Austria for instance, it is explicitly linked to public administration. Article 18, subsection 1 of The Austria Constitution states that: "The entire public administration shall be based on law".

The importance of rule oriented, good and citizen oriented administration is frequently stressed by politicians, civil servants and the media. However, as a concept it often lacks definition or at least clarity as to its content. At a minimal level, administration may be considered 'good' if it achieves the implementation of the policy goals of the Government of the day. Thus what constitutes good administration may change as the requirements of Government and the role of the State changes. Good administration in the context of the Welfare State may be different from good administration in the context of reducing administrative burdens or enhancing citizen orientation.

---

218 Statskontoret, Principles of Good Administration, Stockholm, 2005.

As a legal principle, the right to good administration as well as the right of access to documents was included in the Charter of Fundamental Rights of the European Union. Article 41 contains the right to good administration:

1. Every person has the right to have his or her affairs handled impartially, fairly and within a reasonable time by the institutions, bodies, offices and agencies of the Union.
2. This right includes:
   - The right of every person to be heard, before any individual measure which would affect him or her adversely is taken;
   - The right of every person to have access to his or her file, while respecting the legitimate interests of confidentiality and of professional and business secrecy;
   - The obligation of the administration to give reasons for its decisions.
3. Every person has the right to have the Union make good any damage caused by its institutions or by its servants in the performance of their duties, in accordance with the general principles common to the laws of the Member States.
4. Every person may write to the institutions of the Union in one of the languages of the Constitution and must have an answer in the same language.

This minimalist view of what constitutes good administration is based on the premise that its main purpose is to support the executive and the political process. However, this approach would seem to confuse the role and tasks of the civil service with the principles that govern its operation and which support the legal position of civil servants as non-partisan servants. This requires the adherence to principles which ensure the legality of administrative action and protect public servants from political interference and corruption. These principles also provide a base line or blueprint for the way in which decisions are made and services delivered to the citizens.

As already discussed earlier, the importance of administrative principles and administrative law seems to be widely underestimated despite the growing importance of concepts such as the concept of good administration. As such, knowing the basic principles of Administrative law is just as important for civil servants who are bound to base their decisions on administrative law principles, as it is for citizens who should know their rights regarding the administrations. The principles of administrative law are to protect the individual and the wider public from an arbitrary exercise of power by the executive and by civil servants. Indeed, it could be argued that what constitutes good administration is about the executive. In fact, the principle relates directly to the daily work of civil servants and the daily interests of citizens.

In many Member States the constitution very often defines basic rules which are applicable to the public administration and the wider civil service, complemented by a multitude of acts and regulations which form a disparate set of rules. On top of these general rules, there are often specific rules concerning certain categories of staff. Whereas in some countries, the constitution contains only references to general principles on the organisation of the public administration applicable to statutory civil servants, in Germany the Basic Law and the jurisdiction of the *Bundesverfassungsgericht* (Federal Constitutional Court) have established a set of detailed *hergebrachte Grundsätze des Beamtentums* (established principles of Civil servants) which could only be changed by changing the German Basic Law.

Regardless of how it is formulated in the Constitution, the principle of lawfulness is usually also expressed in the respective Administrative Procedure Acts in the Member States. The principle of non-discrimination is also constitutionally guaranteed in almost every Member State. Some Member States state that everyone is equal before the law and that no one shall be treated differently from other persons.

In most Member States, civil service laws and/or regulations require that the main difference between the civil servant and any other citizen is that the civil servant has been entrusted with the preparation and execution of the Government's programme. This position gives rise to special rights and duties and professional requirements which differ from those of an employment relationship in the private sector. For example, the duty to enforce laws and maintain the rule of law requires at least some knowledge of constitutional and administrative law. In many countries with a bureaucratic career system, therefore, the civil service contains a particularly high number of lawyers (although the number of lawyers seems to have decreased – at least in some European countries). However, the importance of knowing administrative law is decreasing. Often, the concept of Competency Management does not list Administrative Law as a core competence. Therefore, Rosenbloom suggests that – once again – it will become more important in the future to train and to teach public employees about administrative law[219]. If public administrations are supposed to become more citizen friendly, one precondition will be to continue to train administrators in the field

---

219 Rosenbloom, Administrative Law, op. cit.

of administrative law AND to inform citizen (better) about the importance of administrative law principles (and their rights).

1.4. Too many rules and burdens? The challenges of deregulation

Still, in all Member States the national civil services and the HRM policies within the civil services are subject to more and special rules, which are sometimes stipulated in the constitution, by parliamentary acts, government decrees or regulations and in some cases by collective agreements. Often, regulations and administrative circulars deal with all kinds of aspects including the official legal status of civil servants, recruitment procedures, diversity issues, anti-discrimination matters, career development policies, pecuniary entitlements, pay increases and pension rights as well as other rights and obligations. Because of the high degree of regulation, national civil service HRM policies are often seen as rigid and not very innovative (and not easy to reform). Consequently, reducing administrative burdens is nowadays seen as an important top-priority reform in this area.

The absence in any reform discussion about the pros and cons of the traditional civil service principles is striking. Instead, European-wide discussions on de-regulation, re-regulation, codification and simplification started in the eighties and have never stopped since then[220]. One of the most common complaints by businesses, citizens and civil servants is the excessive rules, paperwork, formalism and reporting requirements. This would even threaten the rule of law and put a negative burden on the European economies. In response to these complaints (and also in the framework of the Lisbon process), the national public services have started to review, to reduce, to simplify, codify and to deregulate administrative burdens and red tape. At the EU level an ambitious Action Programme was launched in order to reduce the administrative burden of existing regulation in the EU (reduction of 25% by 2012).

The private sector in particular complains that these administrative burdens are costly. However, many national studies have started to illustrate that administrative burdens also represent a significant cost (and burden) for citizens. Therefore, many Member States have introduced interesting programmes that aim at the reduction of notification requirements[221]. However, the partial successes in the field of reducing administrative burdens have not been matched in the field of reducing bureaucracy (in general) and reducing red tape. One reason may be

---

220 See also the various contributions in Der Moderne Staat, No. 1/2008, pp. 29-121.

221 See for example www.whatarelief.eu

that – while reducing administrative burdens is mostly welcomed and supported by all involved actors (Government, private sector, citizens, administrations) – reducing red tape is a field where many conflicting interests clash.

As Hugh Heclo wrote more than 20 years ago, the term *civil service* has come to mean cumbersome personnel rules rather than civic institutions. An abundance of research has shown that public organisations seem to have more extensive formal, written rules for employment, which reflects the stronger tendencies for such provisions in public service systems[222].

To most people, rules and red tape have entirely negative meanings (the term 'red tape' derives from the nineteenth century British Government practice of binding official governments in red tape). In addition, bureaucratic rules and procedures are often criticised because they necessarily imply the image of a slow-moving bureaucracy, control and standardisation (although in many respects, the expectation of standard treatment should also be considered as a great advantage and strength). All of these are unsatisfying to individuals because "People are unique. Routine or disinterested treatment is not generally what we wish. If we have to stand in line for thirty minutes to obtain an automobile registration we find little consolation in the fact that others must stand in line for the same period"[223].

Yet, one may distinguish between red tape, rules and formalisation of procedures. In fact, many rules and procedures are necessary and provide benefits in terms of control, accountability, equality, public safety, security and non-discrimination. Like this, one may distinguish between rules and procedures which are necessary and beneficial, and unnecessary red tape. Experts in the area also differ between red tape (excessive und unduly expensive rules) and formalisation (important and necessary rules and procedures). Or as Bozeman does, one may differentiate between red tape and red tape as pathology. The OECD also applies a distinction between red tape and smart tape[224].
According to Bozeman, "Much of the pathologies of bureaucracy are of the "too much of a good thing" sort (…). Control is useful for coordination, but over control is pathological; standardisation can be highly destructive; rules, regulations, and procedures are part and parcel of every bureaucracy, but dysfunctional ones

---

222 Robert Maranto, A Brief Against Tenure in the U.S. Civil Service, Praising Civil Service but not Bureaucracy, in: Review of Public Personnel Administration, Vol. 22, No. 3 Fall 2002, pp. 175-192.

223 Bozeman, Bureaucracy and Red Tape, op. cit., p. 1.

224 OECD Observer, Policy Brief, From Red Tape to Smart Tape: Administrative Simplification in OECD Countries, June 2003.

waste considerable energy to no one's benefits. But how is one to determine differences among control and over control, standardisation and rigidity, necessary and useful rules…?.What is normal?"[225] It is also well known that many managers complain about the adverse effects of the complex web of controls, procedures and regulations in the field of recruitment, promotion and the determination of pay. Research on red tape also supports the view that public organisations are more strongly regulated than private organisations.

A study by the Brooking Institutions (2000) explains different performance levels in public organisations. It is not the people that are the problem but the organisations. "Government is filled with good people trapped in bad systems: budget systems, personnel systems, financial management, and information systems. People are not the problem (...)[226]". "Bad systems may discourage the full use of the considerable talents that may be available. Or inadequate resources and outside pressures may keep quality administrators from delivering the kinds of services they and the citizenry would like"[227].

Table 16: Popular explanations of why civil servants are behaving differently in public organisations

- Too many rules
- Too much centralisation
- Too much job protection and too little performance incentives
- Slow decision-making procedures
- Bad leadership
- Processes and structures influence personality
- Bad systems discourage innovation
- Inadequate resources
- Negative effects of downsizing
- Personnel management differs

Source: Christoph Demmke, Are Civil Servants Different?, op. cit.

Many studies have indeed shown that – not the individuals but instead - too much red tape and a too high degree of formalisation may lead to reduced workplace autonomy, the feeling of powerlessness and reduce the inherent meaningfulness of work. "Red tape (…) may inhibit self-expression and the ability to positively affect clientele (…) and suppress natural desires for self-expression,

225 Bozeman, Red Tape and Bureaucracy, op. cit., p. 35.
226 Aberbach/Rockman, op. cit., p. 58.
227 Ibid., p. 86.

responsibility, growth, and achievement"[228]. Also, "centralised decision-making mechanisms, in and of themselves, reduce organisational commitment and job satisfaction"[229], and may lower morale of public managers. "Most important, when surveys have asked government and business managers about the extent of red tape in their organisations, the public managers have consistently reported higher levels than the business managers"[230].

More concretely, higher rules in public organisations tend to concentrate on the area of personnel management. Bozeman and Rainey (1998)[231] report that managers in government, compared to business managers, would prefer their organisations to have fewer rules. This contradicts the view that managers in government generate excessive rules[232]. As Rainey and Han Chung note, there is substantial evidence of greater concerns among public managers, compared to their counterparts in business firms, about complex administrative rules and red tape. The public managers perceive, for example, more problems with personnel administration, such as complexities in the rules about pay and discipline"[233]. The results show that the "attractiveness" criteria differ very little from those in the public sector, so public sector employers would have at least the same chances to compete with private sector employers as long as they can and are willing to show that they offer attractive jobs. Rainey (2003)[234] concludes that public organisations generally tend towards higher levels of internal complexity, centralisation, and formalization – especially in such areas as personnel and purchasing – than private organisations[235]. "Government organisations may not have more formalised and elaborate rules than private organisations of similar size, but they often have more centralised, formalised rules for functions such as personnel and procurement"[236].

228 DeHart-Davis/Pandey, Red Tape and Public Employees: Does Perceived Rule Dysfunction Alienate Managers, in: Journal of Public Administration Research and Theory, Vol. 15, No. 1, 2005, p. 136.

229 Ibid., p. 144.

230 Hal Rainey, Understanding and Managing Public Organizations, San Francisco, 2003, pp. 206-207.

231 Barry Bozeman/Hal Rainey, Organizational Rules and the "Bureaucractic Personality", in: American Journal of Political Science, Vol. 42, No 1, January 1998.

232 Rainey, Understanding and Managing, op. cit., p. 208.

233 H. Rainey/Y. Han Chung, Public and Private Management Compared, in: Ferlie/Lynn/Politt, op. cit., p. 91.

234 Rainey, Understanding and Managing, op. cit., p. 210.

235 Ibid.

236 Ibid., p. 210.

If this analysis is correct the situation in the EU-Member states seems to be characterised by taking one step forward and one step back. As we will see later on in this study many experts believe (with the exception of some experts in the Eastern European countries) that the public services have become less rule-oriented and less bureaucratic and that the rules in the field of HRM have become clearer and more transparent. However, they do not believe that the number of rules as such has decreased. Thus, whereas the regulatory culture could be "relaxed" and more transparency introduced, the number of rules has not decreased. However, this seems to be much more of a problem for the career-system countries than for the position-system countries. Mostly respondents from Austria, France, Germany, Belgium and Luxemburg agreed that the number of rules in the field of HRM have not decreased. Moreover, the highest percentage of respondents who fully disagree stems from the continental career-system countries. The situation seems to be much different in the Scandinavian countries. Here, most respondents are of the opinion that HR rules have decreased[237].

The topic as it is remains a highly discussed and contentious issue. Nevertheless, discussions on rules consist too often of simple "denunciations of what are regarded as the inefficient and malevolent workings of government". It is time to take the topic to a more serious level of analysis. One should not forget that one person's red tape is another's due process[238].

2. Performance management

One reform topic ranks high on the reform agenda in all Member States: Performance Management. The call for better performance has become stronger throughout the last few years because "it is commonly argued that as the public sector is not exposed to market imposed disciplines there is a tendency for inefficiencies to arise..."[239]. Consequently "a wide array of measures has been introduced to public sector management to try and overcome the inherent tendency to inefficiency, including value for money audits, policy reviews, performance indicators, evaluations, appraisals, output statements, consumer surveys, regulation, outsourcing, privatisation, procurement skills, devolved budgets, autonomous accountable agencies, stress budget methods and better accounting, finan-

237 Demmke/Henökl/Moilanen, Slovenian Study, op. cit., p. 55.

238 Charles T. Goodsell, Red Tape and a Theory of Bureaucratic Rules (Review of the Book by Bozeman), in: Public Administration Review, July/August 2000, Vol. 60, No. 4, p. 373.

239 Ibid.

cial and budget management systems and skills. Despite these new systems and techniques it remains very difficult to measure the output of the public service..."[240].

Performance management is a complex issue. On the one hand, "it is commonly accepted that an effective and appropriately sized public service is essential for economic progress and social cohesion. Education, health, regulation, security, utilities and other public services produce both desirable and essential outputs for society and economy"[241]. On the other hand, it "is not enough that public services are delivered efficiently and are effective, they must also be affordable" and the level of taxation should not cause problems for other objectives. It is also difficult to balance the desired level of tax and the desired level of services. The natural preference is for the lowest level of tax and the highest level of public services"[242].

Although governmental, organisational and individual performance are different concepts they are often not treated separately. Performance is very difficult to manage as the underlying reasons for poor performance may be very complex. Many "of the indicators used in public discussions to comment on public sector efficiency do not give direct information on efficiency. The size or growth of the public sector in the absence of output measures tells us nothing about productivity and efficiency"[243]. Moreover, the actual size and cost structure is due to a combination of the following; additional new services and costs for fulfilling new tasks and duties (fight against terrorism), increased costs for increased quality standards (e.g., lower class size in schools), increased demand for existing services (increased health costs due to the ageing of our societies), costs of inputs (personnel costs), balanced costs for outsourcing (pay bill is reduced but purchases expenditures remain).

Moreover, it is difficult to link bureaucratic structures to performance and to measure whether bureaucratic systems are performing better or worse than post-bureaucratic systems. Whereas in the past years many experts claimed that bureaucratic systems are performing worse than post-bureaucratic systems, more recent studies are more cautious. For example, Pollitt maintains that bureaucratic systems outperform post-bureaucratic systems[244].

---

240 Foley, op. cit., p. 74.
241 Ibid., p. 71.
242 Ibid., p. 74.
243 Ibid., p. 99.
244 Politt, Bureaucracies Remember, Post-bureaucratic Organizations Forget?, op. cit., p. 198.

The discussion of what has been achieved throughout the last decades is the most controversial and the most difficult issue of all. In his historical analysis of performance measurement, Van Dooren[245] identifies 14 movements since the 19th century that have promoted performance management and measurement in government. Looking back, Van Dooren comes to the conclusion that "change is not the path of glory which is often portrayed"[246]. Yet criticisms against traditional features of public services were not at all useless. Rather, the criticism transformed over time and became more systematic, specialised, professionalised and institutionalised. However, the concept as such lacks clarity. In fact, performance management includes many different concepts, ideas and approaches[247].

Many experts feel strongly with regard to what to conclude about performance and public services failures, but less about achievements and objectives. However, public criticism as to the role and performance of public services is not new, is not an Anglo-Saxon invention and did not come only from the private sector. Already in 1887 the later President of the USA Woodrow Wilson stated that "it is the object of administrative study to discover, first, what government can properly and successfully do, and secondly, how it can do these proper things with the utmost possible efficiency and at the least possible cost either of money or of energy"[248]

The Scientific Management movement promoted the detailed analysis of workers' tasks with the objective of maximising efficiency by processes according to a mathematical and logical formula (Frederick Taylor, 1911). "First-generation performance measurement was concerned with measuring government activities that were eventually to be defined in terms of service delivery"[249].

A next generation of performance measurement activity emerged after the Second World War. This resulted in the development of tools and planning, programming and budgeting instruments. This focus on budgeting and planning provoked new doubts in the discipline. Already in 1953 Waldo pointed to the fact that "while the idea of efficiency remains, for most students, at the center of administrative study as the goal of measure of achievement, there has arisen

---

245 Wouter van Dooren, Performance Measurement in the Flemish Public Sector: A Supply and Demand Approach, University of Leuven, 2006.

246 Ibid., p. 227.

247 Bouckaert/Halligan, op. cit.

248 Woodrow Wilson, The Study of Administration, in: Dwight Waldo (ed.), Ideas and Issues in Public Administration, Greenwood Press, Westport, 1953, p. 65.

249 Bouckaert/Halligan, op. cit., p. 46.

considerable doubt as to what, precisely, efficiency is, and about how- and even whether – it can be measured in human affairs"[250].

In the 1970s, more scholars (especially in USA) started to concentrate their research efforts on monitoring policy effectiveness. Many of these so-called implementation studies showed that performance fell short of policy expectations and concern shifted from the "what?" of policy outcomes to the "why?" of policy failures. At the time, Implementation Theory as a concept became famous when Pressman and Wildavsky subtitled their classic implementation study "How great expectations in Washington are dashed in Oakland; or Why it's amazing that Federal Programs Work at all" (1984). Parallel to the emergence of implementation as a theory, the Management by Objectives approach (MBO) departed from scientific management theories. In "What Results Should You Expect? A User's Guide to MBO" (1976), Peter Drucker defined several preconditions for an effective public management system. According to Drucker, the ultimate result of management by objectives is decision. "Filling out forms, no matter how well designed, is not management by objectives and self-control. The results are!"[251] This was a direct assault against the traditional bureaucratic career system, with its focus on rules and procedures rather than outcomes.

However, the limitations of the MBO approach became more and more evident when researchers like Thompson pointed to the fact that a "system contains more variables than we can comprehend at one time, or that some variables are subject to influences we cannot control or predict"[252] In addition, many MBO systems failed because they were too rigid and not able to take account of human factors (e.g., they failed to recognise the limitations of formal systems in influencing employees' motivation). From here, multi-dimensional and quality-focused systems such as the Balanced-Scorecard and Total Quality Management Systems and other quality measurement systems (such as the Common Assessment Framework - CAF) were developed for public sector organisations.

Despite all the performance management theories, until the 1990s the tasks of most states expanded further (especially in the social and education sectors) and more and more people were recruited as public employees. Consequently, personnel costs and public sector budgets reached a new peak at the beginning of the 1990s. This expansion of the public services and the increasing (personnel)

---

250 Waldo (ed.), Ideas and issues in Public Administration, op. cit., p. 407.

251 Drucker, op. cit., p. 436.

252 Carolyn Heinrich, Measuring Public Sector Performance and Effectiveness, in: B. Guy Peters/Jon Pierre (eds.), Handbook of Public Administration, Sage Publication, London, Thousand Oaks, New Delhi, 2003, p. 28.

costs for the public services have not necessarily improved their image. On the contrary, citizens, media and politicians have expressed more and more dissatisfaction with the costly public sector and campaigned against the bureaucrats and their expensive, slow, inefficient, and unresponsive bureaucracies. Widespread public scepticism about a state sector which is too big and too costly, and numerous clichés about the poor performance of civil servants and public organisations, also implied sharp differences between public and private organisations.

When Osborne and Gaebler published "Reinventing Government" (1992) they insisted that this publication would not present original ideas. However, their suggestions for improving public organisations became very popular and were later defined as the "New Public Management Movement". Parallel to the emergence of the New Public Management, Implementation Theory lost much of its importance, since more people believed that the New Public Management would automatically lead to better and more effective public services. The call for privatisation of public services and criticism of traditional bureaucratic organisational structures led to a new wave of "bureaucracy bashing". Public organisations were seen as inefficient and ineffective *per se* and private sector organisations as superior and role models for the public sector. Consequently, privatisation, delegation, decentralisation, outsourcing and public-private partnerships were recommended as the best strategies for increasing organisational performance and as solutions for solving the "efficiency" and "performance" crisis of public sector organisations. The New Public Management hype reached its peak after the fall of the Berlin Wall, when many observers called for quick privatisation, outsourcing, delegation and decentralisation of the highly rigid, hierarchical and ineffective public services in Central and Eastern Europe. All of these recommended reforms had a strong "efficiency" focus and aimed at "doing more with less".

The discussions about governmental and public sector performance changed abruptly after the terrorist attacks in New York, Madrid, London and – later – the natural disasters in New Orleans, Southeast-Asia and Haiti. Also, new global security threats and new risks (e.g., bird flu), have triggered renewed discussions about the need for strong public services and the protection of populations. In the United States, two conclusions were drawn from the September 11 attacks. First, that "the public sector" is important and "government workways are important, and indeed critical, for the nation's well-being; and second, that defects in government operations are most readily discovered in events of crisis or scandal – all too often after the damage has been done"[253]. Since the early 1990s new

253 Roger H. Davidson (ed.), Workways of Governance, The Brookings Institution, Washington D.C., 2000, p. 2.

discussions about the negative effects of radical downsizing policies in the public sector added to the growing criticism as regards NPM approaches.

In Europe, discussions about public sector performance moved slowly away from "doing more with less" to the demand for better services. In particular, concerns about capacity problems and staff shortages in the health and education sectors, about inefficiencies and programme failures as a consequence of privatisation, outsourcing and downsizing policies, and about the state's responsibility in fighting increasing levels of poverty and growing income differences between rich and poor played an important role in the shift of the public management debate.

With the changing focus in the public performance debate, there was also a change in assumptions of what instruments and measures are likely to induce better performance. At the beginning of the 21st century, the public discourse on both sides of the Atlantic is becoming less ideological and more pragmatic. Experts and citizens are no longer asking for "less state involvement" but for better services, more effectiveness and efficiency, respect for equity and non-discrimination issues, diversity management, the rule of law, democracy, fairness and dignity. It does not matter whether these services are delivered by the public or the private sector, public-private partnerships or new governance structures. When Milton Friedman was asked in 2001 what the former Communist states should do in order to increase the efficiency of the public sector, he replied. "Ten years ago, I would have said "Privatise, Privatise, Privatise. But I was wrong. The rule of law is much more important than privatisation"[254].

This example illustrates that the debates about public performance have become less ideological and have left room for important new reflections. For example: why are certain countries with a big and costly public service more efficient and effective than countries with a small public sector? The outcome of this discussion has resulted in more evidence about the need for good management, political stability, high integrity, adherence to the rule of law, and powerful public bodies in the context of effective public institutions.

Today, more observers agree that the reasons for organisational and individual poor performance are almost always very complex. A Dutch study on "*Bewijzen van goede dienstverlening*" (evidence of good services) showed that organisational performance is very different from sector to sector. Whereas the media

---

254 Quoted from: Francis Fukuyama, State Building Governance and World Order in the 21st Century, Ithaca, New York, Cornell University Press, 2004.

mostly debates problems with waiting lists in hospitals, poor school education systems, inefficiencies in social security systems, failures in security, cases of corruption, waste of money in construction etc., the successes and cases of good performance of public organisations are only rarely discussed (e.g., successes in the fields of public health, life expectancy, social security, women rights). According to the study, organisational performance is very much the result of good networking, effective accountability systems, powerful instruments, efficient coordination mechanisms, realistic public perceptions and expectations, the quality of monitoring and control systems, institutional capacities, legal certainty and the competence of personnel.

According to an expert report to the United Nations[255], important dimensions of improving public sector performance and effectiveness now include:

- Responsiveness to public needs
- Equity – e.g., ensuring greater equity in the distribution of services
- Quantity – ensuring that the proper quantity of services is provided
- Quality – enhancing the quality of services
- Efficiency – enhancing the cost-effectiveness and efficiency of the provision of services
- Provision – enhancing the equity, accessibility, speed and reliability of services
- Reducing economic impediments – reducing the extent to which costs, procedures and processes impede economic and social progress
- Transparency – providing timely, relevant and complete information
- Integrity – ensuring ethical behaviour

Despite this multidimensional approach, in many countries the issue of performance is still dominated by "black and white" discussions although the perceptions in the media and the population about the role and tasks of the public service are slowly changing after the financial crisis (which emerged with the fall of the Lehmann Bank in 2008). However, government, politicians or public services are still held responsible for almost any failure, be it a financial crisis or a governmental failure.

This contrasts with the reality. Nowadays public policies are administered through increasingly complex networks, decentralised governance structures,

255 Report of the United Nations Expert Group Meeting, Improving Public Sector Effectiveness, Dublin, Ireland 16-19 June 2003.

public-private partnerships and cooperative ventures between NGOs, consultants and government. The traditional concept of the public service as a single, unified employer is disappearing. Thus, the "old paradigm" of a clearly separated hierarchical, career public service no longer exists. Consequently, a public-private discussion on performance issues is the wrong starting point, since it is less clear as to who is responsible for poor quality services – government, the public service, NGOs, public-private partnerships, private providers of public services or public employees.

Also, too little analysis is done of why most countries have many efficient and inefficient, effective and ineffective, public organisations at the same time and in different sectors. For example, whereas in some countries the tax administration works very well, this may not be true as regards the implementation of a programme in the field of environmental protection by the Ministry of the Environment. Likewise, some may have a very effective anti-discrimination policy, but at the same time a high level of inequality between men and women. Or performance levels can be very different from school to school, police force to police force, hospital to hospital, juvenile delinquency programme to environmental protection programme etc. Too many experts link a big public sector, a high degree of regulation, high expenditure on public employment and high taxes too easily to bad public performance.

2.1 Are the public services functioning so badly? Why is performance management so popular?

Today, public performance is a tremendously popular issue. Without doubt, in the field of public management the issue of public performance is the most important of all. "Despite mounting critiques, managing performance continues to increase and is arguably now the dominant idea for governments"[256]. Why has this issue become so important within the last decade? Experts have so far offered a number of explanations which can be divided into five main categories.

1. Performance management can serve any political master, since everybody will agree that there is always a need and possibility to improve the performance of public organisations. The first and most important reason for this call for better performance is the underlying conviction that governments, public services and their personnel are not performing well enough. The reasons for this are identified in too much bureaucracy and red tape, too many rules, too little delegation and decentralisation, structures which are too centralised, procedures

256 Bouckaert/Halligan, op. cit., p. 13.

which are too slow. In this scenario, the public sector suffers from too many poor performers.

2. The second reason for the popularity of the performance management concept is political and ideological. “Bashing bureaucrats” is an evergreen on the political agenda no matter whether political affiliations are more left or right. Almost every political party or politician can be sure of the massive support of the electorate if measures are announced which aim at better public performance. Many citizens believe that the performance of the private sector is better than the public sector. Therefore, the public sector should try to enhance and to improve performance and take the private sector as a role model. For example, the introduction of performance-related pay is popular since it conveys a different and widely popular understanding of “justice” and “fairness”. Bureaucrats should only be paid for good performance and not automatically receive increments through “seniority”. The latter would be unfair.

3. A third reason is that improving public performance is an important objective in the discussions about the so-called Lisbon process and the role of Europe in global economic competition. In this discussion, public services are considered as a policy maker, regulator, service provider, investor, purchaser and employer. In all of these fields, the public sector plays an important role in economic and competition issues. Consequently, the Member States should seek to explore all possibilities in every sector for making better and more efficient contributions to sustainable growth and competitiveness.

4. Differently to the above-mentioned poor performance discussion, the issue of performance management also has a tremendous intuitive appeal to the public services “for it conveys that bureaucrats and public agencies are working hard and being held accountable” (Brewer). In fact, the national public services are increasingly eager to present their success stories in quality management: more customer friendly services, new standards for hospitals, electronic parking ticketing, improved waste collection, better public order policing, improved local public services through online and one-stop services, options for paying taxes online, enhanced public information and data management, more transparency etc.

5. Today, nobody doubts that the concept of improving public sector performance is to be welcomed. Why should somebody be against improving the quality and performance of governments, organisations and public employees, especially in times of growing awareness of cases of unacceptable and poor quality services in hospitals, schools, social and health care, risk management and in the daily lives of citizens? Thus, especially from a historical point of view, the call

for performance management and the introduction of new quality management systems like the CAF or Balanced Scorecards and new performance management systems are a great step forward. There is no doubt that the benefits of being clearer about the purposes and results of quality management, both inside and outside government, are undeniable. Despite the different concepts and interpretations of quality and performance in the public sector, performance management and measurement fulfils a number of important common criteria in all Member States, such as transparency in measuring and evaluating outputs; learning through experiencing what went well and what went wrong; judgement concerning the efficiency and effectiveness of an authority or an individual; and rewarding or punishing those who perform well or do not perform well.

Other arguments for the introduction of performance management schemes can be summarised as the following:

- They provide a statement of what an organisation is trying to achieve. They set out the aims and priorities for improving public services and the specific results government is aiming to deliver. Targets can also be used to set standards to achieve greater equity.
- They provide a focus on delivering results. "By starting from the outcome Government is trying to achieve, the targets encourage departments to think creatively about how their activities and policies contribute to delivering those results. They also encourage departments to look across boundaries to build partnerships with those they need to work with to be successful"[257].
- They "provide a basis for monitoring what is and isn't working. Being clear what you are aiming to achieve, and tracking progress, allows you to see if what you are doing is working. If it is, you can reward that success; if it isn't, you can do something about it"[258].
- They provide better public accountability. "Government is committed to regular public reporting of progress against targets. Targets are meant to be stretching. So not all targets can be hit. But everyone can see what progress is being made"[259].
- They can improve performance of public employees by a) increasing employee skills and abilities, b) promoting positive attitudes and increasing

---

257 See United Kingdom, House of Commons, Public Administration Select Committee, On Target? Government by Measurement, Fifth Report, 2002-2003, London, 22 July 2003, Vol. 1.

258 Ibid.

259 Ibid.

motivation, and c) providing employees with expanded responsibilities so that they can make full use of their abilities.

2.2. Comparative work in the field of performance management

It is very tempting to compare public performance in several countries, especially in those cases where Member States realise that other Member States perform differently (better/worse) in fields like education, health or social services. Logically, the more expensive or less efficient countries could learn from the "more efficient" and "cheaper" Member States. However, as the comparative "public sector performance" study makes clear: "We should note, though, that - at the present stage - it seems difficult to perform in-depth analyses, given the limited quality of and lack of detail in the data available"[260].

Only a "few studies exist that compare bureaucratic quality and/or administrative performance internationally"[261]. The existing comparative best practices base public sector performance mainly on quantifiable variables, e.g., the comparison of costs for the health sector, unemployment rates, economic growth, payments for social security systems etc. So far, there is no study that compares the performance of ministries, judiciaries or parliaments. The reason for this is obvious: it is still very difficult to compare the performance of qualitative services and services that have an impact on human rights.
Another important obstacle is to agree upon the choice of the right performance indicators such as the level of corruption, red tape, quality of the judiciary, the degree of accountability, political stability, rule of law, ability to implement programmes, tax compliance, etc. Although government indicators are expanding as rapidly as organisational performance indicators and individual performance indicators, there is still considerable confusion, (sometimes) contradiction and overlap as regards the right indicators and targets.

At the same time, there are also many obstacles in comparing public sector performance because of uncertain or problematic data: for example, how to get evidence and comparable data on the level of corruption in different countries (or how to measure the relationship between the level of corruption and public performance).

---

260 Steven Van de Walle, Measuring Bureaucratic Quality in Governance Indicators, Paper presented at the 8th Public Management Research Conference in Los Angeles, 29 September to 1 October 2005, p. 25.

261 Ibid., p. 3.

A study by the Instituut van de Overheid (2004) noted that researchers are "fortunately quite hesitant when it comes to comparing countries directly"[262]. There is growing awareness that the quality of bureaucracies is hard to measure and experts have different concepts when they discuss the quality of public organisations. In addition, "most (…) rely to some extent or completely on subjective indicators"[263].

According to OECD in "Management in Government: Feasibility Report on the Development of Comparative Data" (2005) the fact is that "public management reforms have been hampered by the lack of good quality comparative information, resulting in a situation where assessing progress made and learning from other countries' experiences remain limited. As a consequence, public management reforms have been driven significantly by assumptions concerning "best practices" rarely specified with any precision. Although there is significant growth in broad measures of "governance", most of these data are based on subjective assessments, and have little relevance for public management"[264].

As tempting as public sector comparisons seem to be for many, the comparability problems are still numerous. For example, it is difficult to say that countries which are supposed to have fewer bureaucratic structures, e.g., Sweden, the Netherlands, the United Kingdom, Finland or Estonia are quicker, more attractive, more effective and more efficient and that public officials are more motivated and perform better than in career systems. In fact, existing comparisons in public performance generally show that countries with traditional bureaucratic systems are not performing less well than other countries. Some traditional career countries (e.g., Luxemburg, France and Germany) are still rated as the best or – at least – as high performing countries[265]. Today, it is accepted that both career and post-bureaucratic systems have advantages and disadvantages at the same time. For example, countries with career systems may be flexible in many respects but also offer specific strengths, e.g., predictability, stability, rationality, predictable treatment, equitable treatment[266]. On the other hand, employees in the so-called post-bureaucratic system countries may be able to enter earlier into the organisational hierarchy. Thus, they have the possibility of making quicker

262 Ibid., p. 16.

263 Ibid., p. 27.

264 OECD, Management in Government: Feasibility Report on the Development of Comparative Data, Paris, October 2005.

265 Steven van de Walle/Mierkatrien Sterck/Wouter van Dooren/Geert Bouckaert, What You See Is Not Necessarily What You Get, Instituut voor de Overheid, Leuven, July 2004.

266 Bozeman, Bureaucracy and Red Tape, op. cit., p. 29.

career advances. At the same time, they also face more uncertainty about future career prospects.

However, the difficulties in making comparisons do not mean that it is not possible to compare public performance at all. For example, it is interesting that in almost all existing comparative public performance studies Denmark, Finland and Luxemburg are found among the top three countries according to several indicators, while some southern European countries do badly according to most indicators[267]. This illustrates that comparative studies may suffer from many deficiencies. This does not mean that they are totally irrelevant and misleading and that things cannot get better in the future. Even to the contrary. Since it is almost certain that performance will remain a focus of management and policy[268], improved Benchmarking Studies may in the long term even lead to a convergence (at least in part) of civil service structures. Thus, the performance movement is here to stay!

3. Alignment – reducing differences in working conditions and employment patterns

Studying the differences in status and working conditions between civil servants, other public employees and private sector employees take us to the heart of the reform process within the national civil services. In the past, civil servants had a different status (public law vs. private law status) and enjoyed very specific and different working conditions. They could only be dismissed for disciplinary reasons, (often) enjoyed generous specific pension entitlements, received a fixed salary which was based on age and qualification, worked fulltime, had specific qualifications (many were qualified in law), entered the civil service after having succeeded in specific recruitment procedures, moved slowly up the career ladder from an entry grade etc.

Today, these differences are fading. In almost all Member States the differences between civil servants and other public employees and civil servants and private sector employees have become fewer. Still, few Member States stick to the traditional patterns and maintain at least some traditional features. Other Member States have almost entirely aligned the working conditions within the public service and between the public- and private sector.

---

267 Van de Walle, Measuring, op. cit., p. 24.
268 Bouckaert/Halligan, op. cit., p. 196.

However, civil servants and other public employees still differ from each other, as can be discerned from Table 13 (see page 99). For example, in almost all countries civil servants enjoy a higher degree of job security. Moreover, in most countries civil servants are still recruited in specific recruitment procedures. Also ethical rules and rules on conflicts of interest are different. Overall, in most EU Member States, different rules still apply to civil servants regarding their legal status, recruitment procedures, job security, career and salary systems.

In Germany and Lithuania civil servants and other public employees are two clear-cut groups that have their own exclusive rules and standards. In these countries civil servants have, for example, different recruitment procedures, separate career and salary systems as well as very restricted strike right. In practice, however, German public employees have employment conditions which come close to those of the civil servants. For example, German public employees have lifetime job security after 15 years of service. The greatest difference still exists in the field of pensions and the right to strike. In both fields, civil servants are still treated (very) differently than public employees.

In most countries, in terms of disciplinary rules, social dialogue, pension systems and right to strike, civil servants and other public employees share the same or similar rules. According to the data, in the UK and the Czech Republic there are no significant differences at all between the civil servants and the other public employees. Next, the Scandinavian countries (Denmark, Sweden and Finland) have almost no differences between civil servants and public employees. From the group of continental countries only the Netherlands and Slovenia have relatively aligned employment conditions. Interestingly, Anglo-Saxon countries (Malta, Ireland and the United Kingdom) also differ sharply amongst themselves. From the group of the Mediterranean countries, Portugal (after the last reform) has also introduced a number of measures which led to an alignment of employment conditions for a great number of civil servants.

In our study we correlated a number of specific working condition features with each other. For example, we wanted to know if a positive correlation exists between the existence of a bureaucratic career system and other specific civil service features. The results are astonishing. For example, a positive correlation can be seen regarding the existence of a career system and other specific features. Thus, if a Member State still has a career system, it is very likely that this Member state also has a number of specific civil service features. Thus, bureaucratic career systems have in general sharper differences between civil servants and other public employees than post-bureaucratic countries. Comparisons between career structure countries and non-career structure countries indicate that the type of civil service system has a significant impact upon the differences between civil servants and other public employees.

Table 17: Main differences between civil servants and other public employees by type of civil service system

(Frequencies in parenthesis)

		Very different	Mixed	Very similar	Total
Type of civil service structure	Career structure	61 (11)	39 (7)	0 (0)	100 (18)
	Non-career structure	11 (1)	44 (4)	44 (4)	100 (9)
	Total	44 (12)	41 (11)	15 (4)	100 (27)

In the future, the alignment process may have further important implications on the reform of civil service laws (in a number of countries) in the future. If more Member States align the working conditions between civil servants and other public employees, the question arises as to why different categories of public employees are still needed. This again may enhance debates about the need for a uniform civil service or public employee law. So far, only very few Member States have a uniform civil service/public employee law for the whole public service. However, it may very well be the case that discussions will commence about the need for a more coherent legal approach as to the status of public employees. On the other hand (as we will see later on in this study), more Member States are also engaged in introducing measures, which facilitates the employment of flexible employees "at will". Therefore, the alignment of working conditions between civil servants and public employees may also bring the (paradoxical) emergence of a new class of public employees with different (weaker) working conditions. However, this trend is also connected with the decentralisation of HR responsibilities. If legal competences in the field of civil service law and HR policies will be further delegated and decentralised, this may also facilitate the creation of different forms of employment statuses and employment conditions.

4. Decentralisation

Practical experiences and empirical evidence so far suggest that decentralisation undoubtedly has positive effects, but also poses severe challenges in the field of HRM. The ultimate measure of any public service system is the results (for the country, common good, citizens etc.) that it delivers. Basically, the objectives can be achieved by either a more decentralised or a more centralised system, both of which have several benefits and risks; the advantages of one system often being the shortcomings of the other. Thus, finding a right balance between too much centralisation and too much decentralisation is a major challenge for all governments.

Centralisation in the field of HRM generally refers to the extent that decision-making powers are vested in bodies at a hierarchical level. These central powers or rules are often applicable to the entire public service and civil service. Centralised HR systems were put in place to guarantee politically neutral decision-making and protect employees against political coercion and patronage. Moreover, it has often been argued that the standardisation of HR practices secures coherence of policies and fairness.

Proponents of decentralising responsibilities to managers assert that this increases the efficiency and effectiveness of HRM and public administration in general. Decisions can be taken faster, recruitment can be tailored to the exact needs of the organisation, less complex procedures are needed etc. In addition, motivation and performance are increased, because decentralisation increases the manager's discretion and job control, thus enabling him to recruit, evaluate, offer incentives, promote, suggest training needs and communicate directly. The philosophy behind decentralisation and deregulation is a well-known argument: centralised HRM is rigid, unresponsive, slow and ineffective. Finally, there is very little evidence so far as to whether decentralised HR systems are really more vulnerable to cases of political pressure and politicisation.

On the other hand, highly decentralised systems may entail a decline in the professionalism of the core civil service, a certain loss of a civil service ethos, the fragmentation of policies from a strategic point of view, less stability and more cases of unfair HRM as long as the system lacks effective coordination and control mechanisms. In addition, according to the United Nations (2005), the problem with such a decentralised approach is the increased possibility of conflicts among the different actors and institutions – ministries, agencies or HRM authorities – if central coordination mechanisms are ineffective or non-existent. The success of decentralisation also seems to depend on the skills of managers and HR professionals to carry out their tasks and responsibilities. Thus, greater autonomy and decentralisation of responsibilities require considerable investment in management qualifications at all levels. It is important to combine decentralisation efforts with additional management training to provide the professional skills that are crucial for managing in a decentralised environment. As already mentioned, fairness, equity and the lack of a common ethos are other important issues to be discussed. What happens when centralised procedures are removed with regard to issues such as pay, promotion, diversity and equal opportunities? What happens if managers, different units, organisations and agencies apply their discretion (flexibility) too widely and in very different ways? Finally, decentralised HR systems may have unintended centralising effects if the HR functions are bundled and/or outsourced to one centralised entity (Coggburn 2005).

It seems to be obvious, that decentralisation goes along with the need for additional coordination and new accountability procedures. Consequently, the effectiveness of decentralised systems depends on the existence of very good coordination and monitoring systems. Furthermore, specific forms of deregulation to 'let managers manage' can be accompanied by re-regulation that imposes new, and perhaps more burdensome constraints and additional bureaucracy. In the literature and in general discussions, decentralisation and centralisation are often said to entail a range of expected and unexpected outcomes (see Table 18 and Table 19).

Table 18: Advantages and disadvantages of decentralisation and centralisation of HRM

	Advantages	Disadvantages
Centralisation	• better coordination to address state-wide issues (e.g., anti-discrimination) • improved policy coherence • protection against patronage and politicisation • more equity and fairness • efficiency gains through economies of scale • better qualification of HR officials	• information deficits at top level • slower and time consuming decision-making • less able to adapt to local situations and needs • less responsive and flexible to changes • more rigid • de-motivating for executives and employees
Decentralisation	• managers and HR officials with more flexibility, freedom and autonomy • adaptation of recruitment, pay, rewards or sanctions to local needs • enhancing individual motivation and performance due to higher responsibility and autonomy • avoiding work-overload at central level • beneficial competition in	• need for more coordination, monitoring and control • negative impact on accountability and policy coherence • negative effects if managers lack HR knowledge (decision quality, unfairness, inefficiency) • danger of political abuse and patronage • loss of civil service ethos • differences in HR policies can cause mobility obstacles

	the HRM field • increasing customer orientation • reduction of red tape	• higher costs to loss of economies of scale / synergies • in case of outsourcing often re-centralisation

Source: Demmke, Hammerschmid and Meyer, 2006

Table 19: Benefits and side-effects of decentralisation

Benefits of decentralisation	Side-effects of decentralisation
• increased focus on tasks and performance accountability • performance/productivity improvements • increased citizen satisfaction due to increased service speed and quality; more value for citizens • more flexible HRM functions better suited to local needs • more compatible pay levels • increased motivation • empowerment of management • regional benefits	• need for increased coordination and accountability • duplication and resource/competence deficits • danger of increasing personnel costs and salaries • higher transaction costs • lack of transparency • increasing politicisation

Source: Demmke, Hammerschmid and Meyer, 2006

From a first point of view the issue of centralisation and decentralisation does not seem to depend on the type of civil service structure. Usually decentralised systems are in use in the larger Member States. All countries with a population less than 5 million have a centralised civil service system. In fact, the state structure and the size of the country are the best factors to explain the degree of decentralisation of civil service system.

Table 20: Whether a highly centralised or decentralised civil service system exists in a certain EU Member State, by type of civil service structure

(Frequencies in parenthesis)

		Centralised	In-between	Decentralised	Total
Type of civil service structure	Career structure	78 (14)	0 (0)	22 (4)	100 (18)
	Non-career structure	56 (5)	33 (3)	11 (1)	100 (9)
	Total	70 (19)	11 (3)	19 (5)	100 (27)

In addition, there is a direct correlation between state structure and civil service systems. For example it is much more likely that federal or quasi-federal states also have a decentralised civil service system.

Table 21: Whether a highly centralised or decentralised civil service system exists in a certain EU Member State, by state structure

(Frequencies in parenthesis)

		Centralised	In-between	Decentralised	Total
Type of state structure	Federal or quasi-federal state	20 (1)	0 (0)	80 (4)	100 (5)
	Decentralised unitary state	43 (3)	33 (3)	14 (1)	100 (7)
	Unitary state	100 (15)	0 (0)	0 (0)	100 (15)
	Total	70 (19)	11 (3)	19 (5)	100 (27)

However, countries with a more bureaucratic career structure seem to have more structures that are centrally regulated than non-career structure countries (see Table 22 on page 146). This is evident when we view issues such as career structure, requirement procedures, career development procedures and performance appraisals. Career structure countries regulate the career structure by law and apply it to the whole civil service. Their recruitment procedures are regulated centrally more often than in non-career structure countries, and they have centralised rules about how and when to carry out performance appraisals.

Table 22: Level of central regulation by policy and by EU Member State
1=Centrally regulated, 2=Not centrally regulated

	A	B	C	D	E	F	G	H	*Mean*
Cyprus	1	1	1	1	1	1	1	1	*1.00*
Greece	1	1	1	1	1		1	1	*1.00*
Ireland	1	1	1	1	1	1	1	1	*1.00*
Luxembourg	1	1	1	1	1		1	1	*1.00*
Malta		1	1		1	1	1	1	*1.00*
Portugal	1	1	1	1	1	1	1	1	*1.00*
Romania	1	1		1	1	1	1	1	*1.00*
Hungary	1	1	1	1	1	2	1	1	*1.13*
Lithuania	1	1	1	1	1	1		2	*1.14*
Poland	1	1		1	1	1	1	2	*1.14*
France	1	1	1	1	1	2	1	2	*1.25*
Slovakia	1	1	1	1	1	1	2	2	*1.25*
Spain	1	1	1	1	1	2	1	2	*1.25*
Estonia	1	1	1	1	2	1		2	*1.29*
Bulgaria	1	1	1	2	2	1	1	2	*1.38*
Italy	1	1	1	2	1	1	2	2	*1.38*
Latvia	1	1	2	1	1	1	2	2	*1.38*
Slovenia	1	1	1	1	2	1	2	2	*1.38*
Denmark	1	1	1	2	2	2	2	2	*1.63*
Finland	1	1	1	2	2	2	2	2	*1.63*
Sweden	1	2	1	2	2	1	2	2	*1.63*
Netherlands	1	1		2	2	2	2	2	*1.71*
Germany	1	1	2	2	2	2	2	2	*1.75*
United Kingdom	1	2	1	2	2	2	2	2	*1.75*
Austria	1	2	2	2	2	2		2	*1.86*
Czech Republic	2	2	2	1	2	2	2	2	*1.88*
Belgium	2	2	2	2	2	2	2	2	*2.00*
Mean	*1.08*	*1.19*	*1.21*	*1.38*	*1.44*	*1.44*	*1.50*	*1.70*	

A = Equality and diversity policy

B = Legal status

C = Pension system

D = Basic salary

E = Recruitment procedure

F = Performance appraisals

G = Career structure

H = Career development policy

In a study carried out for the Austrian EU Presidency, Demmke and Hammerschmid and Meyer[269] analysed the degree of centralisation and decentralisation in the individual public administration and the involvement (main involvement, minor involvement, no involvement) of different actors in several typical HR decision-making situations *within* both, core administration and agencies. The authors distinguished between vertical decentralisation (which refers to the decision-making autonomy of management, e.g., to line managers) and horizontal decentralisation (which refers to the regulation and management of HR competencies at the level of central government within a central body, e.g., the Ministry of Finance, the State Chancellery or a Ministry for Public Administration).

Apart from the centralisation/decentralisation dimension, Demmke, Hammerschmid and Meyer also analysed the question of to what extent decisions are made by a single actor – indicating a strong individualisation of the system – or whether multiple actors and/or levels are involved[270]. "Increasing multi-actor involvement may be indicative of a higher decision-making complexity (with all advantages and disadvantages), and – depending on the type of actors to be involved – of increasing participation"[271].

4.1. Is there a 'new' decentralised model superseding the 'old' hierarchical bureaucracy?

The study by Demmke, Hammerschmid and Meyer confirms a general trend towards HR decentralisation but also other forms of decentralisation. However, despite the many initiatives to decentralise HR services, there is not a convergence trend in the direction of HR decentralisation. Thus, the multiple initiatives towards decentralisation do not seem to give rise to a shared new model taking shape or to a European-wide convergence of organisational models. It also seems unlikely that the bureaucratic model will be fully replaced by such a new model in the near future. Instead, the development of organisational structures in the European public administrations reflects the general tendency towards more differentiation in society. To what extent this diversity in the European public administrations will continue in the future remains open.

---

269 Christoph Demmke/Gerhard Hammerschmid/Renate Meyer, Decentralisation and Accountability as a Focus of Public Administration Modernisation, EIPA, Maastricht, 2006.

270 The multi-actor involvement index varies between 0 (single-actor involvement) and 1 (high degree of multi-actor involvement).

271 Demmke/ Hammerschmid/Meyer, op. cit.

Today, none of the 27 Member States have either completely centralised or completely decentralised HR systems. The pathways taken to organise HR services are multiple and vary greatly. Based on the typical HR decision-making situations we used in this study, we find a preference for hierarchically centralised organisation of HR issues e.g., in Cyprus, Greece, Luxembourg, or Romania. The organisation of HR in Sweden, on the other end of the spectrum, is the result of a step by step decentralisation over decades. We can find small countries both with high vertical centralisation (Cyprus, Luxembourg) and others that report a high degree of management autonomy (Estonia, Malta).

Overall, the results show that – at least with regard to the HR decision-making issues – central actors still tend to have greater responsibilities and involvement than the actual management level. This implies that, although the devolution of decision-making responsibilities towards the point of service delivery has been an important element in previous and current reform initiatives, the current picture is still rather centralised with only limited autonomy given to management.

As regards the involvement of multiple actors in HR decision-making, decision-making by individual actors is an exception and many HR issues are a shared responsibility of many different parts of the administration. Generally, decision-making in the field of HR is complex and – to different degrees – participative. In most cases, central units, ministers, and Directors-General are more or less strongly involved (depending on the issue at stake). In Greece or Luxembourg, low multi-actor involvement goes hand in hand with centralised decision-making. In Sweden, operational day to day HR issues are handled locally at agency level by line management or by staff experts with low multi-actor involvement; in more strategic issues, such as local pay policies, recruitment strategies etc. more actors, including the unions, are involved. Overall policy decisions, such as a new overall framework agreement, change of general working conditions, demand greater involvement from multiple actors.

Figure 3: Vertical decentralisation and multi-actor involvement in EU public administrations

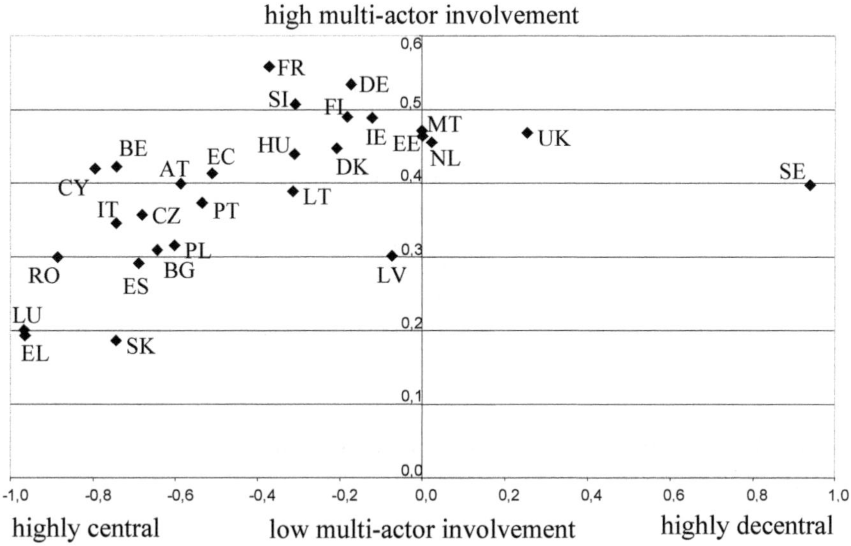

Source: Demmke, Hammerschmid and Meyer, op. cit., 2006, p. 51

The authors found a considerable relationship between decentralisation and multi-actor involvement, indicating that the responsibilities are rarely fully delegated to line management and/or lower hierarchical levels, but that they are rather involved in the decision-making processes. Central actors still have a major influence. It is unclear at this point in time whether this might be interpreted either as a particular form of organising in a transition period or as the emergence of a new, more stable form of arranging HRM.

In addition, authors found interesting interrelations between the degree of vertical decentralisation and priorities of public administration modernisation. For example, public administrations with a higher degree of HR decentralisation assess the relevance of administrative decentralisation and budgetary decentralisation higher than more centralised administrations indicating self-reinforcing dynamics. Furthermore, the more de-central HR functions are organised, the more relevance the public administrations assign to the use of market-type mechanisms, the alignment of public and private employment, private sector involvement, performance management, and accountability as priorities of public administration modernisation.

4.2. The importance of context: administrative traditions and HR systems

Moreover, administrative traditions and HR systems proved to be quite influential in explaining the organisation of HRM. Especially the Scandinavian and Anglo-Saxon countries have relatively decentralised HR structures with a high degree of multi-actor involvement. The Baltic countries and – to a lesser extent – Continental European countries take a middle position. In contrast, at the other end of the spectrum, the transition and Mediterranean countries have relatively centralised and (more or less) complex structures with little management autonomy regarding HR decisions. Small countries such as Estonia, Malta and Luxembourg have adopted quite different models for their public administrations, which are closely connected with their own history, tradition, administrative culture and (to some extent) geography. Estonia seems to be strongly influenced by the Nordic models (esp. Finland), Malta by the UK and Luxembourg by France and Germany. Our study also shows that, in terms of HR organisation, the Baltic countries are closer to the Scandinavian countries than to the other transition countries.

Table 23: Regulation of recruitment procedures by type of civil service structure

(Frequencies in parenthesis)

		Centrally regulated	Not centrally regulated	Total
Type of civil service structure	Career structure	72 (13)	28 (5)	100 (18)
	Non-career structure	22 (2)	78 (7)	100 (9)
	Total	56 (15)	44 (12)	100 (27)

According to the data, it is evident that career structure countries prefer centrally regulated recruitment procedures while non-career structure countries do not[272]. The more the systems deviate from the classical bureaucratic career system, the more they are characterised by a decentralised and more complex (in terms of multi-actor involvement) organisation of HR issues. Especially differences between countries within the same administrative tradition (e.g., between the UK and Ireland, or between the Netherlands, Luxembourg and Austria) can be related to the countries' adherence to different HR systems.

---

272 Five career countries, Austria, Belgium, Bulgaria, Germany and Slovenia do not use centrally regulated recruitment procedures, whereas two non-career countries, Latvia and Slovakia, use centrally regulated recruitment procedures.

Figure 4: Vertical decentralisation and multi-actor involvement according to size, administrative tradition and HR system

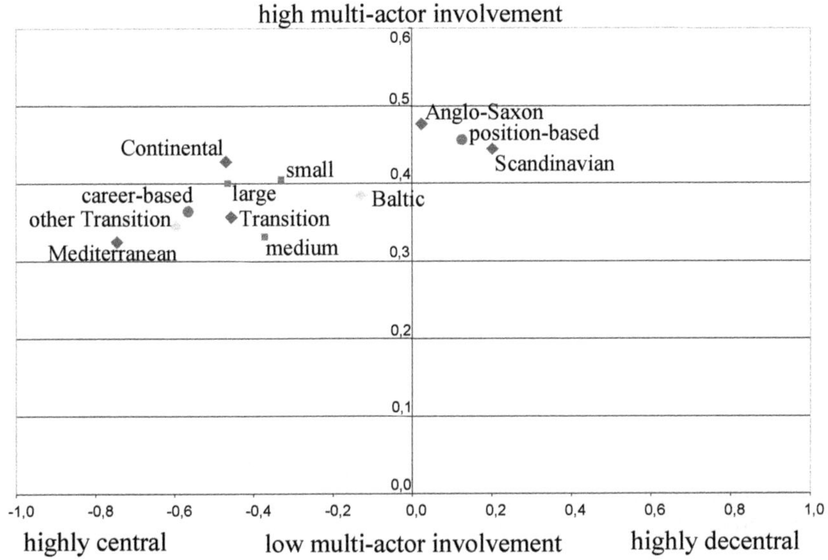

Source: Demmke, Hammerschmid and Meyer, op. cit., 2006, p. 54

Moreover, the size of a country (measured in terms of its population) is not a highly influential factor for the organisation of HR competencies. In addition, small countries also differ considerably with regard to the horizontal dimension of decentralisation. In Cyprus, most HR competences lie with a central body; in Luxembourg, most HR issues are decided by a central body (Ministry of Public Service and Personnel) or the line minister, whereas Malta and Estonia have central HR units within the individual ministries that are strongly involved in many decisions.

5. Increasing responsibility

An increasing number of public administrations are pursuing strategies to further give senior and line managers greater responsibility and discretion (especially as regards budgetary questions and performance management and recruitment issues). Overall, it seems, (senior) managers have indeed received more (strategic, financial and budgetary) responsibility and discretionary powers within the last years. As Table 24 shows, in almost all Member States top- and middle managers have been given more responsibilities in the field of HRM within recent years.

Table 24: Developments in top managers' and middle managers' responsibilities in recent years by type of civil service structure

(Frequencies in parenthesis)

		More	Same	Less	Total
Type of civil service structure	Career structure	78 (14)	22 (4)	0 (0)	100 (18)
	Non-career structure	78 (7)	22 (2)	0 (0)	100 (9)
	Total	78 (21)	22 (6)	0 (0)	100 (27)

As can be seen from Table 25 on page 153, this is mostly the case in the field of career development and training (but also in other fields such as recruitment and allocating performance-related pay). On the other hand, individual managers have little decision-making discretion in fields such as disciplinary issues, dismissals and code of conducts, as these are issues where several hierarchies and persons interact and take decisions. Although Bulgaria and Ireland seem to be cases where managers have been allocated more responsibilities than in other countries, this is not necessarily the case. For example, other countries may have already introduced more responsibilities to managers beforehand.

In fact, most important is the general trend towards more responsibilities. No Member States have actually decided to re-centralise responsibilities. Consequently, issues like good leadership will become even more important in the future. However, negative consequences of decentralisation on equity and fairness issues may also become more relevant in such cases where managers have been given important discretionary powers to take important HR decisions on their own (especially decisions on pay, recruitment, training, promotion and/or evaluation and appraisal of staff). It is only in these cases that we can talk about a real *individualisation* process. Our analysis of the situation reveals that managers are indeed given more responsibilities but this does not mean that this process can be described as an individualisation process. In most cases, managers do not have full discretion and decision-making powers and have to consult or coordinate their decisions with other, mostly hierarchically superior levels.

Table 25: Developments in top managers' and middle managers' responsibilities in recent years by HRM policy (1=lot more, 2=some more, 3=same, 4=some less, 5=lot less)

	A	B	C	D	E	F	G	H	I	J	K	L	M	N
Bulgaria	1	1	1	1	1	1	2	1	1	1	2	1	2	*1.23*
Ireland	1	1	1	1	2	1	1	2	1	1	2	1	1	*1.23*
Czech Republic	1	2	1	1	1	1	1	2	2	2	1	1	2	*1.38*
Portugal	1	1	1	2	1	2	1	2	1	1	2	1	2	*1.38*
Belgium	1	1	2	2	2	2	1	1	1	1	1	2	2	*1.46*
Latvia	2	2	1	1	1	1	2	1	2	2	1	2	1	*1.46*
Denmark	1	1	1	2	1	2	2	1	1	2	1	2	2	*1.46*
Greece	1	1	1	1	2	1	2	2	2	1	2	2	2	*1.54*
Slovenia	1	1	2	2	1	1	1	2	2	1	2	2	2	*1.54*
France	1	2	2	1	1	1	1	2	2	1	2	2	2	*1.54*
Finland	1	2	1	2	1	2	1	1	1	2	2	2	2	*1.54*
Sweden	1	1	2	1	1	1	2	1	2	2	2	2	2	*1.54*
Italy	2	1	2	2	1	2	1	1	2	2	2	2	1	*1.62*
Malta	1	1	2	2	2	2	1	1	2	2	2	2	1	*1.62*
Spain	1	2	1	2	2	1	2	1	2	2	1	2	2	*1.62*
Luxembourg		1		1		2	2				2	2	2	*1.71*
Estonia	2	2	1	1	2	2	1	2	2	2	2	2	2	*1.77*
Austria	1	1	2	2	2	2	2	2	1	2	2	2	2	*1.77*
Netherlands	1	1	1	1	2	1	3	2	1	2	3	2	3	*1.77*
Slovakia	2	2	2	1	2	2	1	2	2	2	2	2	2	*1.85*
Romania	1	2	1	2	2	2	2	2	2	2	2	2	2	*1.85*
Hungary	2	1	2	2	2	2	2	2	2	2	2	2	2	*1.92*
Poland	2	2	2	1	2	2	2	2	2	2	2	2	2	*1.92*
Germany	2	2	2	2	2	2	2	2	2	2	2	2	2	2.00
United Kingdom	2	2	2	2	2	2	2	2	2	2	2	2	2	*2.00*
Lithuania	2	2	2	2	2	2	2	2	2	2	2	2	2	*2.00*
Cyprus	2	2	2	2	2	2	2	2	2	2	2	2	2	2.00
Mean	*1.38*	*1.48*	*1.54*	*1.56*	*1.62*	*1.63*	*1.63*	*1.65*	*1.69*	*1.73*	*1.85*	*1.85*	*1.89*	

A = Career development, B = Training, C = Relocating, D = Recruitment, E = Performance pay, F = Promotions, G = Working time, H = Diversity policy, I =Performance plans, J = Poor performance, K = Code of conduct, L = Dismissal, M = Discipline, N = Mean

With regard to the HR issues covered in the Demmke, Hammerschmid and Meyer study, line managers are given important responsibilities in all three Anglo-Saxon countries but also in the Scandinavian and Baltic States (especially Estonia) and in the Netherlands. On the other hand, in the Mediterranean (especially Greece, Italy, Cyprus), or in Luxembourg, Belgium, Slovakia and Romania, line management is endowed with only few decision-making rights. Also interesting is the fact that countries that are supposed to have rather hierarchical organisational and decision-making structures seem to involve line management to a quite considerable extent (e.g., Germany). Only in the UK and Ireland, do lower hierarchical levels play a relevant role. Overall, line managers and lower hierarchical levels are given more responsibilities in post-bureaucratic systems. Mostly, line managers have responsibilities in the field of performance management (apart from the Anglo-Saxon and Scandinavian countries; also in Slovenia, the Netherlands, Portugal or the Accession States; least so in Greece for example), performance-related pay, career development and training issues, as well as disciplinary and dismissal issues.

The ongoing trend towards responsibilisation and delegation of HR responsibilities reveals a surprising deficit in management research. In the course of this Europe-wide development towards decentralisation of personnel management responsibilities, the medium management level is primarily entrusted with additional staff assignments, without always ensuring that this level is able to cope with and "manage" these tasks. Until today, no one has appeared to seriously address the question of how managers handle these new challenges and are capable of adapting to these developments. Questions on further training, competency development and on motivation and incentives are becoming more and more important; but far too little is being done in administration reality for managers to accept and cope with the new challenges.

Thus the question arises as to whether not too much is being expected of superiors? Are expectations at all realistic? Don't the employees expect too much? A simple and general answer to these challenges seems difficult at the very least: there is indeed a dilemma in all European public services if superiors are more and more frequently of the opinion that the effort involved in the delegation of HR responsibilities has currently already reached a very high level and could increase even more in the future.

Where the concepts of "competency management", "lifelong learning", "employee interview", "target agreement", "feedback" and "performance management and appraisal" are concerned, it becomes clear that in recent times cooperative styles of management are increasingly gaining ground in performance management (or should do so). Although this is to be welcomed in principle, as yet the issue remains mainly unsolved as to whether cooperative styles of management actually do have the desired control effect constantly attributed to them. If this is supposed to be the case, employee interviews and target agreements should have been introduced into administration reality a long time ago[273].

In reality, however, it frequently seems to be a case of false labelling – despite the (Europe-wide) positive significance and surge of popularity of the employee interview. At times, the impression is created that cooperative forms of management style are asserting themselves more and more and are – in any case – relatively unproblematic. In reality the workload and the increased responsibility of managers seem to be the very things that cause them simply not to have enough time for employee interviews. In addition, the discourse surrounding employee interviews, performance agreements and performance contracts frequently omits to consider that work processes in most European administrations (still) function according to hierarchic structures, and cooperative, supportive and even friendly structures do not represent the customary picture. Thus it can be seen that in many EU Member States the civil servant relationship still follows the classic model of superordinate and subordinate. The compulsory habit of following instructions corresponds to the specification of targets by the superiors. Hence a target agreement questions this classic relationship.

Indeed, several Member States are of the opinion that hierarchic administration structures still represent a challenge. A look at the actual situation shows that popular ideas of a consensual and supportive staff relationship between superiors and employees have to be freed first of all from all too naive expectations. Another problem is even more obvious: particularly in times of financial straits and performance cut-backs, many employees find consensual working styles and motivation management to be rather cynical. On the other hand, trendy management advisers often spin an unrealistic yarn about administration by giving the impression that hierarchic and bureaucratic administrative structures have long since ceased to exist. In reality, nearly all European administrative models continue to be based on the principle of "hierarchy" and bureaucracy. Hence trendy ideas such as participation, information, agreement, feedback and communication frequently contradict administrative reality. The superior-employee relationship is still shaped in practice by a (sometimes exceedingly) hierarchic work style, and forms of cooperation that show mutual trust cannot be taken for granted.

---

273 Jürgen Lorse, Personalmanagement im öffentlichen Dienst, Luchterhand, Neuwied und Kriftel, 2001, p. 223

Often the relationship between superior and employee looks completely different in reality. Wehrle describes this reality in *Der Feind in meinem Büro* (The Enemy in my Office) as follows: If the boss is the first to go home, he's lazy in the eyes of his colleagues and employees. If he is the last at his desk, he is a workaholic. If he leaves everything as it always was, he is missing the boat. If he pushes changes through, he is seen as a reckless gambler who hazards the future (...). A boss does everything wrong because he is the boss. And his employees are the know-alls because they are the employees[274].

The greatest problem in the relationship between bosses and employees consists of the following: that information between bosses and employees does not flow; that hierarchy levels are sometimes as impenetrable as concrete ceilings; that everyone has an idea what the other person wants, but does not know exactly. Most employees know the menu in the canteen far better than the expectations their boss has of them[275]. Vice versa, employees are more capable of estimating their boss's performance than the bosses themselves[276]. A remarkably high number of superiors often have a distorted view of their own performance and overestimate their competencies and skills.

6. Increasing flexibility

For decades, conventional wisdom simply assumed that organisational and personnel stability contribute to public administrative performance und impartiality. Originally, rigid careers and the seniority principle were invented in order to avoid patronage and in order to prevent political influence in the field of career development policies[277]. Therefore most organisations were heavily influenced by hierarchical command and control methods.

This has drastically changed. In particular, the literature on public administration reform in recent years has heavily emphasised connected flexibility with the themes of mobility, organisational change, adaptability and – in the case of same countries – the abolition of the lifetime tenure, career structure and seniority principles. Today, issues such as flexibilisation and decentralisation have become quasi sacrosanct principles. Almost everybody is in favour of them. Prin-

---

274 Martin Wehrle, Der Feind in meinem Büro, Berlin 2005, p. 25.

275 Ibid., p. 219.

276 Ibid., p. 33.

277 Matthias Pechstein, Das Laufbahnrecht in der Gesetzgebungskompetenz des Bundes, in: Siegfried Magiera/Karl-Peter Sommermann/Jacques Ziller (Hrsg.), Verwaltungswissenschaft und Verwaltungspraxis in nationaler und transnationaler Perspektive, Dunker und Humblot, Berlin, 2008, p. 673.

ciples and values like stability and centralisation are "out". Furthermore, careers are seen as old-fashioned and rigid structures. In the modern literature, almost few experts still defend their usefulness[278]. By contrast, nothing seems more attractive than novelty, flexibility and innovation.

This general trend is a pity since it is obvious that organisational stability as such can be helpful to organisations. Expertise, a strong public service ethos, centralised structures and a professional knowledge management system are also helpful[279]. Next, job stability and clear job perspectives have a strong and positive impact on organisational performance and individual motivation. Moreover, it may well be that enhancing the mobility of top officials may also have negative effects in building competence, mutual trust, and long-term commitment. While new flows of human resources may bring innovation into an organisation, they may also have the negative side effects mentioned above. An empirical study by O'Toole and Meier on Personnel Stability and Organisational Performance reveals that general personnel stability and stability at the top often seem to matter[280]. Moreover, the authors claim that personnel stability can be an important determinant of public organisational performance. The findings of the authors "fly in the face of those who would celebrate impermanence, mobility…"[281].

As can be seen, flexibility can be defined in many ways: in the book "The Corrosion of Character" Richard Sennett described (mostly) the negative sides of the flexibilisation of our working life. On the other hand, Anneke Goudswaard differentiates in the study on "Flexible labour – sustainable labour?" between different types of flexibility (qualitative flexibility, quantitative flexibility, flexible work and ad-hoc flexibility etc.). She comes to the conclusion that positive effects of flexibility depend "on the type of labour flexibility and, more importantly, on the conditions at work"[282]

278 Ibid.

279 Niklas Luhmann/Renate Mayntz, Personal im öffentlichen Dienst, Baden Baden, Nomos-Verlagsgesellschaft, 1973, p. 75.

280 Laurence J. O'Toole Jr./Kenneth Meier, Plus ca Change. Public Management, Personnel Stability, and Organizational Change, in: Journal of Public Administration Research and Theory, Vol. 13, No.1, p. 56.

281 Ibid., p. 62.

282 Anneke Goudswaard, Flexible Labour – Sustainable Labour?, The Situation in the Netherlands After Twenty Years of Increasing Flexibility, Dissertation, Catholic University of Nijmegen, 7 October 2003.

Expressed in general terms flexibilisation embraces the different tools and processes with which the supply and demand of employees can be managed. The most important regulating tools and approaches for flexibilisation are:

- The regulations and protection standards under law with regard to health, income, pension security and job security;
- The provisions in law on working time, contractual status, work contents and tasks;
- The work organisation, in particular the organisation of work and tasks and the management with regard to the reconciliation of work and private requirements;
- Flexibilisation of recruitment and selection procedures for external candidates, recruitment at mid-career, recruitment for a limited amount of time etc.

Flexibilisation strategies are often differentiated in organisational practices by whether they have a quantitative or qualitative character and whether they are organised internally or externally. Quantitative or numerical flexibility uses working time flexibilisation, part-time employment and temporary work to permit the volume of workers to be adapted to fluctuations in demand. Qualitative or functional flexibility uses procedures of work organisation and qualifications to permit workers to be deployed for different tasks; job enrichment and job rotation being included here. External flexibilisation comprises temporary and seasonal work, outsourcing and subcontracting.

As the results of our study show, most Member States are engaged in enhancing different forms of flexibility. The measures and instruments are wide and include reforms in order to make it easier to dismiss civil servants, to facilitate and speed up recruitment procedures, to ease administrative burdens and to facilitate occupational mobility of civil servants, to make it easier to change jobs between the public- and private sector, and to move between different careers etc. Mostly, flexibilisation and decentralisation are, by nature, ambivalent constructions.

One good example for many other national reforms is the new law on mobility and career paths which was adopted in France in July 2009. The law aims to promote the mobility of civil servants, whose departments are being reorganised, and also to make staff management easier. The law is part of the process of the general revision of public policies (*Révision générale des politiques publiques*, RGPP). The main measure of the new law aims to promote geographical and occupational mobility of civil servants, especially those whose position is abolished or changed by the RGPP. The workers concerned are placed in a 'situation of occupational reorientation'. After drawing up an occupational plan with their line managers, these staff members have to engage in 'occupational guidance, training and validation of work-derived experience'. Their department must propose redeployment solutions in line with their pay grade and personal career plans. These proposals must take into account where the worker lives, as well as their family situation. If three proposals are refused, the civil servant concerned can be placed in non-active status (*disponibilité*) and thus lose their pay, or can be forced to retire. The law also provides for increasing possibilities for civil servants to combine part-time jobs and to make it easier to recruit staff on private law employment contracts – that is, without civil service status. Moreover, the law extends the recruitment of temporary agency staff to the national civil service and local authorities – this option was previously only possible in public service hospitals. Examples like these are frequent mostly in bureaucratic career system countries. They illustrate that career system countries are engaged in various efforts to flexibilise their (formerly) overly rigid, hierarchical and formalised systems.

This study also gives an impressive illustration of how much the former rigid, closed and hierarchical civil services have changed. Most Member States reformed or even abolished their careers, enhanced mobility, streamlined and opened up recruitment procedures, enabled recruitments from the private sector (and at mid-career level) and replaced or even abolished the seniority principle. Today, many public employees work part-time or use other new flexible working patterns. Moreover, more public services allow for the recruitment of top-managers (also from the private sector) for a limited period of time (and based on performance contracts).

Our research in this study does not reveal enough evidence on the impact of more mobility and flexibility on individual and organisational performance. Therefore, one suggestion would be to analyse in more detail why organisational change, innovation, reform, and flexibilisation as such seem to attract such a great deal of attention (although change can also destroy tradition, values, knowledge and institutions). Equally, it would also be important to invest more research time into the concept of "administrative conservatorship" (Terry)[283] and on whether administrative stability is automatically in conflict with change[284].

283 Larry D. Terry, Leadership of Public Bureaucracies: The Administrator as Conservator. Thousand Oaks, Sage, 1995.

284 Ibid., p. 35.

7. From closed to open systems: reforming organisational structures

7.1. The reform of recruitment systems

Traditionally, all European civil services were closed systems. Civil servants were recruited for a clearly specified career path. Normally, entry into these systems took place in an entry grade which was normally at the lowest end of the career. From here, civil servants would slowly move up in the hierarchy. The bureaucratic career system and the seniority principle allowed civil servants to move up steadily, but only from one grade to the next. Mid-career access to civil service functions was impossible, as was the recruitment of outsiders from the private sector into the civil service. This was to protect the administration from patronage and political influence. Classical civil services were built on the belief that civil servants remained in their positions for their whole life. They would neither move to other organisations nor leave the public sector to the private sector. Consequently, mobility policies did not exist as this could lead to a too strong politicisation of the civil services. Also, communication was highly formalised and followed hierarchical rules. Direct contact to citizens and NGOs was highly unusual.

Although much of this looks old-fashioned in the eyes of the (post-) modern observer, there were good reasons for this. Public services should follow fair recruitment procedures. Posts should only be allocated according to objective criteria (e.g., merit, qualification, competence) and should not be subject to the influence of money, power, family ties or tradition. Thus, for a long time, the market was not seen as an alternative to public recruitment procedures. In "Spheres of Justice. A Defense of Plurality and Equality" Walzer explains the underlying reasons for this[285]: We do not like to expose people to public officials who are given jobs only because of personal reasons (and not because of merit and qualification). And we do not like to expose people to public officials who lack the necessary competence and qualification of the post in question. It would be unfair to allocate jobs to applicants as a result of non-transparent and corrupt practices. Thus, posts must be allocated to those who have succeeded in fair and neutral recruitment procedures and who are qualified enough to carry out these posts. Consequently, impartial and neutral recruitment procedures should not be privatised.

---

285 We have used the German version. Michael Walzer, Sphären der Gerechtigkeit, Ein Plädoyer fuer Pluralität und Gleichheit, Frankfurt/New York, 2006, p. 198.

For a long time recruitment procedures were also different from those in the private sector. Because of the specific duties and obligations of civil servants they had to undergo a specific recruitment procedure. Traditionally, all Member States required candidates to pass specific concours, state exams and/or training if they wanted to be recruited as civil servants. Until today, this principle has not changed very much. Specific recruitment procedures still form an essential part of the bureaucratic career systems. As the results of our study show, almost all Member States still have specific formalised recruitment requirements.

Table 26: Specific formalised recruitment requirements in civil service by type of civil service structure

(Frequencies in parenthesis)

		Formalised requirements	No formalised requirements	Total
Type of civil service structure	Career structure	100 (18)	0 (0)	100 (18)
	Non- career structure	44 (4)	56 (5)	100 (9)
	Total	81 (22)	19 (5)	100 (27)

Traditionally, all Member States required candidates to pass specific concours, state exams and/or trainings if they wanted to be recruited as civil servants. Even today, this principle has not changed very much. Specific recruitment procedures still form an essential part of the bureaucratic career systems.

Most career countries use open competitions (*concours*) or state exams to recruit permanent staff. In Spain there are many public exams which are different for the State, the Autonomous Regions and the Local Governments. In Austria recruitment is decentralised to the level of each ministry. Initial recruitment is based on examinations or application followed by an interview. Recruitment is often followed by training at the Federal Administration Academy and completed by an exam.

Open competitions are also popular among non-career structure countries. For example, Estonia, Latvia and the United Kingdom also use recruitment concours. In Finland an academic degree is required for most civil service positions. However, the recruitment process itself is open to all applicants.

Despite the fact that almost all Member States still have specific recruitment procedures, all other traditional features in the field of recruitment are about to change. The reasons for this cannot only be found in the change of values and the alignment of the public- and private sectors in general. In fact, many Member States are forced to open up their civil services because of demographic changes, more competition between the public and private sector and trends in the field of mobility.

Within the next few decades, demographic changes will lead to the population of the European Union consisting of an increasing number of elderly people. In addition, the ageing of society will result in a growing number of employees leaving the public sector. On the other hand, the present developments may also lead to increasing demands in different fields (such as in the field of data protection, fight against terrorism, sustainable administration, IT and in the field of social services (in particular). This *demographic problem* affects all Member States of the EU, but to differing extents. The different age structure of the Member States suggests that the demographic situation of a country is only one (although important) parameter when evaluating the impact of national recruitment policies and the attractiveness of the public sector in general. As such, it is even possible that countries with a high birth rate and an ageing population will anticipate more recruitment problems in the future (e.g., in Sweden). However, today, almost all Member States do or will face recruitment problems in specific sectors.

One of the greatest challenges seems to be in anticipating the exact number of recruitment shortages there will be per sector and the amount of possible recruitment. At the same time, a number of Member States aim to reduce the number of personnel mainly because of budgetary constraints. On the other hand, the Member States have (politically) committed themselves to pursue policies which aim at a high level of employment (as agreed upon during the Lisbon Summit).

At first sight the situation appears obvious: new staff are needed at a time when demographic trends suggest that the supply of employees will not keep up with the pace of demand and large numbers of public employees who are retiring (often still too early). The ratio of leavers to entrants over total public employment in many countries has been increasing in the past ten years, influenced by changes such as the restructuring of government functions, privatisation, and cuts in personnel spending. A number of Member States face the additional problem that the number of candidates for public posts is decreasing.

Generally, the measures taken in the Member States to enhance the attractiveness of the public sector, to recruit a sufficient number of qualified employees and to face the demographic challenge involve a series of (often combined) measures:

- reducing the demand for personnel (e.g., by "doing more with less", or doing more with the same number of personnel, reducing tasks, etc.),
- increasing the number of potential applicants, internally and externally, (extending working life, reducing early retirement, offering incentives to those interested in working for the public sector),
- Introducing measures to retain personnel (improving working conditions, offering incentives, opportunities and career development possibilities).

Table 27: Main strategies and measures to enhance the attractiveness of the public sector

Main Strategies	Possible Measures
Reducing the demand for personnel	Increase efficiency in work processes Reduce duplication of work Reduce rules and procedures Extend working life Reduce public tasks Reduce early retirement Reduce sickness absenteeism
Increasing the number of potential candidates	Improve image Organise marketing campaigns More and better information Stress advantage of working conditions Offer (material and immaterial) incentives
Introducing measures to retain personnel	Interesting jobs Challenges and career development Responsibility Combination of private life and work Flexibility in working time (flexitime) Mobility International dimension Attractive salaries Leadership and training Good working atmosphere

As regards recruitment, we can differentiate between:

- Investing in image campaigns, the setting up of websites for public sector vacancies, improved access to information about public sector jobs,
- Reform, flexibilisation and diversification of recruitment methods,

- Speeding up of recruitment procedures,
- Measures to further decentralise recruitment procedures and responsibilities.

Especially in the field of recruitment policies the current reform trends contradict long established routines. In the past, the public sector was not very active in attracting possible candidates through career fairs, marketing campaigns, etc. Overall, there was too little information about vacant positions, career development possibilities and working conditions in the public sector. As a result, it was "mostly up to talented employees to find government, not vice versa" (Light, 1999). This lack of information and knowledge about work in the public sector contributed to an image of work in the public sector that does not always match the reality. The longer the recruitment procedure, the more likely it is that the candidates will find another job in the private sector during the process.

Recruitment and career development policies may aim at making entry positions more attractive (through higher initial pay), and may shorten and facilitate the recruitment procedure and introduce measures to increase mobility between the public and private sectors at middle and senior level, etc. Other possibilities include raising awareness about existing vacancies, marketing public sector employment, initiating image campaigns, distributing information or improving cooperation with universities in order to attract more young graduates.

Where recruitment policies are concerned, many Member States have altered selection methods with a view to achieving faster and more efficient throughput in competitions (for example the introduction of a "fast-track" recruitment system). The fact that recruitment needs will be very different in the future has also convinced a number of Member States to decentralise their recruitment procedures. Today, only half of all Member States still have central rules in place that regulate the recruitment procedures. Also career countries like Austria, Belgium, Bulgaria, Slovenia and Germany do not have central rules in place (anymore).

Table 28: Regulation of recruitment procedures by type of civil service structure

(Frequencies in parenthesis)

		Centrally regulated	Not centrally regulated	Total
Type of civil service structure	Career structure	72 (13)	28 (5)	100 (18)
	Non-career structure	22 (2)	78 (7)	100 (9)
	Total	56 (15)	44 (12)	100 (27)

Overall, all ministries face different recruitment needs at different times. This is why recruitment procedures and processes are being made more flexible, speeded up and decentralised. Nowadays, more and more authorities, ministries and agencies are recruiting their own staff, and are thereby able to act flexibly to achieve, keep and develop the competences they need. This process is very likely to continue in the future.

In addition, a number of Member States are introducing measures to facilitate greater mobility, as well as to reform and "flatten" the various career tracks in order to make it easier to reach the top of the career scale. In this context of introducing greater flexibility between and within careers, one additional objective is to increase mobility between the public and private sectors and with international organisations.

These measures also aim to alter traditional recruitment and career development policies. One reason for this is that the traditional career civil service is seen as increasingly unattractive to younger applicants who wish to change careers, positions and sectors more frequently. In addition, managers are increasingly prepared to switch jobs or are more reluctant to stay in one job for lengthy periods.

However, mobility between the public and private sectors is in many respects still difficult: the path into government service at mid-career is often difficult, and middle and senior level positions are rarely broadly advertised. Moreover, senior positions are often not attractive for candidates from the private sector since salaries in the public sector are generally lower. Enhancing HR mobility between the private and public sectors as well as within the government helps to motivate employees by offering interesting career prospects, and it can also increase organisational competences. In some countries there is a need to transfer staff from diminishing sectors to expanding ones. In other countries, the challenge for mobility lies in movement from the private sector to the public sector.

Overall, it seems that despite all the efforts being made in a number of Member States, it is very difficult to attract senior managers from the private sector to positions in the public service. Other Member States face legal and political burdens in opening up the different career paths in the civil services.

7.2. The change in recruitment policies

Today, only 9 out of 27 Member States still follow the principle that recruitment generally takes place at the lowest level/rank/position in the relevant career. All of these countries belong to the group of bureaucratic career systems. However, this principle only applies to half of the countries that have a career structure. In non-career structure countries any applicant with sufficient qualifications can be appointed to any position. Therefore, recruitment does not necessarily go through the lowest level, rank or position.

Table 29: Recruitment in civil service generally takes place at the lowest level/rank/position in the relevant career/corps/hierarchical level by type of civil service structure

(Frequencies in parenthesis)

		Mainly yes	No	Total
Type of civil service structure	Career structure	50 (9)	50 (9)	100 (18)
	Non-career structure	0 (0)	100 (9)	100 (9)
	Total	33 (9)	67 (18)	100 (27)

Another changing feature concerns the traditional principle of promotion to the next rank or grade (see Table 30). In some countries (e.g., France, Spain, Estonia) it is necessary to pass an internal concours before a promotion can take place. Although this instrument is more frequently used in career structure countries than in non-career countries, all career countries do not use it[286]. In general promotions can be done in a rather flexible manner in both types of the civil service structures.

---

286 Five career system countries reported that this instrument is not in use: Austria, Germany, Poland, Portugal and Slovenia.

Table 30: Necessity to pass a specific internal concours/exam before a promotion can take place, by type of civil service structure

(Frequencies in parenthesis)

		Yes	In some cases	No	Total
Type of civil service structure	Career structure	28 (5)	44 (8)	28 (5)	100 (18)
	Non-career structure	11 (1)	33 (3)	56 (5)	100 (9)
	Total	22 (6)	41 (11)	37 (10)	100 (27)

Whereas in some countries the regulatory framework related to promotion is still quite rigid, in others there is more flexibility. In Denmark and Sweden, for instance, promotion is first and foremost based on the candidate's competence and merit. Another example for the many different approaches that exist is the Irish civil service: promotion in the Irish civil service is based on merit. Officials having served two years in their current grade, and graded 3 or better in their most recent Performance Management and Development System (PMDS) review are eligible to compete for promotion to the next grade. The official must also be certified by the Personnel Officer as being satisfactory in respect of performance in the current post, sick-leave and general conduct. Promotion may take place as a result of a competition confined to eligible civil servants within their current Department or by way of an interdepartmental competition, open to all eligible officials, across the civil service. Fifty per cent of vacancies to be filled by promotion are filled following departmental competitions. The remaining fifty per cent are filled by a combination of interdepartmental competition and open recruitment.

As regards promotion in **Portuga**l, the former rules apply to appointed staff until the entering into force of a new regulation of such careers. Therefore, in order to be promoted it is compulsory to be approved in a specific internal open competition and the promotion takes place to the next grade of the corresponding career. With regard to contracted staff a new terminology is applicable to this matter. Thus, rather than promotion it is more accurate to apply career advancement or, concerning the general uni-grade career, change of the remuneration pay step.

In Germany, Article 23 of the *Bundeslaufbahnverordnung* (BLV) allows for the recruitment of "outsiders" in certain cases as well as the recruitment of civil servants at mid-career level (Art. 25 BLV). Also in Belgium, "the federal employment system is relatively open. It remains in essence a career-based system, but where entries in the past were only possible at junior level and advancement slow, heavily regulated and following fixed quotas, entries can now be at more senior levels and advancement is subject to personnel planning and financial means, and of course the presence of required competencies. The Flemish government set up its own employment system at an early stage, but stayed within the boundaries set by the Royal Degree. The Flemish employment system remains a career-based system. The movement away from the traditional career-based system has been similar to that at the federal level, with a mandate system coupled with some opening up of posts for lateral entry at senior grades. The same goes for the Brussels Capital Region and the Walloon Region. In principle, statutory recruitment is the main way to enter the administration – and entry into the administration is only possible at the level of recruiting grades. Some exceptions do exist through recruitment on a contract basis"[287].

Table 31: Is it also possible to promote candidates to other positions at mid-career or top-level by type of civil service structure

(Frequencies in parenthesis)

		Yes	No	Total
Type of civil service structure	Career structure	89 (16)	11 (2)	100 (18)
	Non-career structure	100 (9)	0 (0)	100 (9)
	Total	93 (25)	7 (2)	100 (27)

The trend in Germany, Portugal, Ireland and Belgium is symptomatic for many bureaucratic career system countries and illustrates the general development towards post-bureaucratic structures.

Many things have also changed in the field of recruitment of private sector managers. Today, at least theoretically, the possibility to recruit managers from the private sector is increasingly becoming a possibility in the civil services. As can be seen from Table 32, non-career structure countries are more flexible than career countries as regards recruiting a senior manager from the private sector. However, the difference is not significant since most career structure countries (78%) also allow for the recruitment of managers from the private sector. However, some countries still apply for exceptions. For example, in Cyprus senior managers have to be hired from the public sector; while Greece, Poland and

287 OECD, Challenges of Human Resources Management for Multi-level Government, Paris, December 2008.

Romania face constitutional restraints in relation to the recruitment of private sector managers.

Table 32: Is it possible to recruit senior managers from private sector for a limited period of time by type of civil service structure

(Frequencies in parenthesis)

		Fully or partially	No	Total
Type of civil service structure	Career structure	78 (14)	22 (4)	100 (18)
	Non-career structure	100 (9)	0 (0)	100 (9)
	Total	85 (23)	15 (4)	100 (27)

The trend towards the opening up of civil services can also be observed in the recognition of professional experience outside the public sector. A majority of Member States take into account professional experience outside the public service (even though there may be restrictions) in the recruitment process and the classification into the salary structure. However, also here, post-bureaucratic systems are more flexible than career systems countries (and the newer Member States are more flexible than the older Member States of EU-15). As can be seen from Table 33, all post-bureaucratic system countries take into account private sector professional experience in the recruitment process and in the classification in the (salary) hierarchy. As regards the career systems, a majority recognises the private sector experience.

Table 33: Is professional experience in private sector taken into account in recruitment processes and in the classification in the (salary) hierarchy by type of civil service structure

(Frequencies in parenthesis)

		Fully or partially	No	Total
Type of civil service structure	Career structure	67 (12)	33 (6)	100 (18)
	Non-career structure	100 (9)	0 (0)	100 (9)
	Total	74 (20)	26 (7)	100 (27)

A different observation must be made for the recognition of experience in the private sector for the calculation of pension rights. Here, differences between post-bureaucratic and career systems are less significant. In the meantime most Member States – either partially or fully – take into consideration professional experience in the private sector as regards the calculation of public pension rights. However, eight Member States still do not recognise professional experience in the private sector in the calculation of (public) pension rights.

Table 34: Is professional experience in private sector recognised in calculation of pension rights by type of civil service structure

(Frequencies in parenthesis)

		Fully or partially	No	Total
Type of civil service structure	Career structure	76 (13)	24 (4)	100 (17)
	Non-career structure	56 (5)	44 (4)	100 (9)
	Total	69 (18)	31 (8)	100 (26)

Missing: Ireland

7.3. Conclusions

The field of recruitment and mobility policies illustrate the enormous changes that have taken place and the general move towards new post-bureaucratic features. Today, the national civil services are no longer closed-off entities. Instead, they have become much more open towards society. Still, post-bureaucratic countries like Sweden, Finland or the Netherlands have opened up their civil services to a higher degree than the bureaucratic career system countries. The OECD composite index (see Figure 5) "indicates the level of openness of the recruitment process in central government, and particularly its openness to applicants coming from outside the public service at all levels of the organisation, above entry level"[288].

288 OECD, The State of the Public Service, op. cit., p. 27.

Figure 5: Composite index of openness of the HRM system in central government

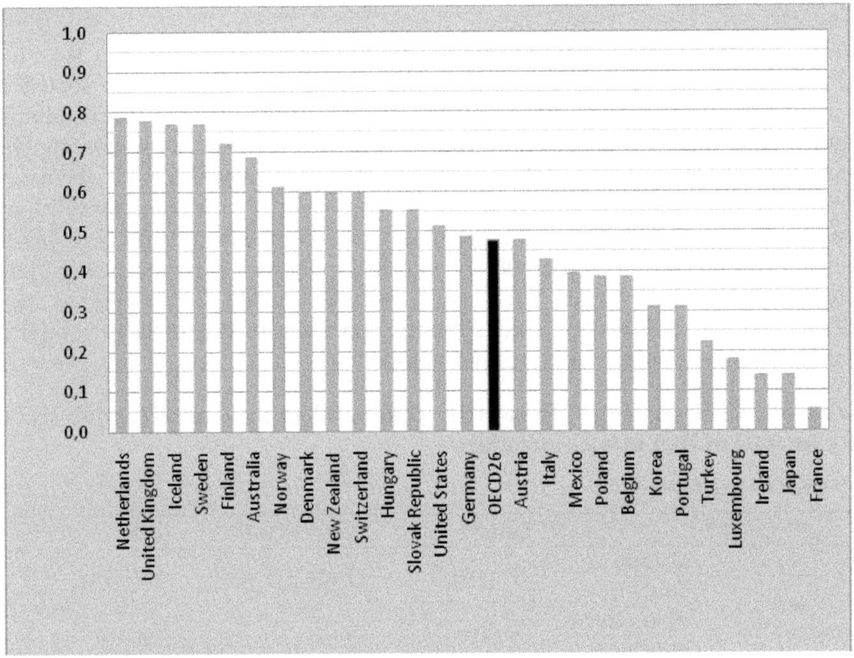

Source: OECD, The State of the Public Service, op. cit., p. 27

The overview illustrates the existing differences amongst the OECD countries. In the meantime, countries such as France and Portugal have introduced laws that will also open up their civil services to the level of most of the other countries.

Thus, the trend towards more flexibilisation in recruitment and career development policies is a continuous process in all countries. Most Member States open up their civil service, introduce flexible recruitment procedures, allow for the recruitment of outsiders from the private sector, permit mid-career access, allow for the promotion to higher grades, enhance mobility policies, introduce possibilities for the recruitment of candidates who have not passed a specific recruitment procedure (and therefore do not fulfil the necessary criteria to be recruited as a civil servant) etc.

8. Other reform policies

8.1 Reforming job security

Writers on public administration have long suggested that without a specific status, legal protection, lifetime tenure and special ethical rules, our societies would be open to terrible corruption (*furchtbarer Korruption* – Weber) and this would undermine the capacity of the state to rule society. Consequently, in 2003, the French *Conseil d'Etat* came to the following conclusion: "....the main objectives of the successive statutes of 1946, 1959 and 1983, were to establish in France an ethical, competent and non-politicised civil service, that is to say a civil service loyal towards the public authority, and which is protected from political and partisan pressures. This result is without doubt to be regarded as successful..."[289]. Consequently, civil servants' job security is still largely higher than in the private sector (see Table 35 below)[290].

Table 35: Civil servants' job security compared to private sector job security by type of civil service structure

(Frequencies in parenthesis)

		Differs	Does not differ	Total
Type of civil service structure	Career structure	89 (16)	11 (2)	100 (18)
	Non-career structure	56 (5)	44 (4)	100 (9)
	Total	78 (21)	22 (6)	100 (27)

From the point of view of the civil servants (and the Trade Unions), the criterion security is especially important in times of economic crisis. Another aspect of public service employment is the function of job security as a motivational instrument. In most Member States, job security in the public sector is an important motivational element for the recruitment and the retention of staff. At present, therefore, most Member States still agree with this argument that job security is important, but also argue that more job security can only be justified for specific positions and functions. Consequently, job security seems to be widely accepted as an important motivational factor. This is also in line with many stud-

289 Council of State, Public Report of the Council of State, Studies and Documents, Reflections on the Civil Service, Paris, 2003.

290 According to data, only in Hungary, Poland, the Czech Republic, Denmark, Slovakia and Sweden civil servants' job security does not differ significantly from the private sector job security.

ies that show the detrimental effects of job insecurity[291]. In this way, it is striking that almost one third of all Member States allow for the dismissal of civil servants in times of economic difficulties.

The attractiveness of the public sector as an employer is also closely linked to the security of the workplace. In recent times, however, the "relative" decline of the economy has led to an increasing interest in government jobs. In recent years many EU Member States have faced increasing recruitment problems, though the current slowdown in the economy is leading to an improvement in the situation. This, however, supports a false image of the public sector, since the number of jobs in it will be cut over the next few years. In the past, new recruitment only took place in a very limited way and because of this, the public sector has felt little incentive to present itself as an attractive employer. In the future almost all European countries are expected to face recruitment problems in the fields of social services, IT and education.

Yet, lifetime employment seems to be less important than it was some decades ago. As we can see many Member States are moving away from the classical lifetime tenure principle. In more countries it is now possible to dismiss civil servants for various reasons (and mostly in cases of poor performance). In our study we have correlated the existence of a career structure with the existence of job security (see Table 36and Table 37 on page 175). The results show that countries with a career system also have a higher degree of job security. Thus, if a country decides to reform its traditional career structure it is also likely that it will reform traditional job security patterns.

Furthermore, it is also true that – in some countries – the degree of security between jobs in the public and the private sectors does not differ very much; in other countries like Germany and Austria, job security does not differ (very much anymore) between civil servants and other public employees. In both cases job security can be very high.

---

291 Bert Klandermans/Tinka van Vuuren, Job Insecurity: Introduction, in: European Journal of Work and Organizational Psychology, Vol. 8, 1999, pp. 145-153; Hans de Witte, Job Insecurity and Psychological Well-being: Review of the Literature and Exploration of Some Unresolved Issues, in: European Journal of Work and Organizational Psychology, Vol. 8, 1999, pp. 155-177; Johnny Hellgren/Markus Sverke/Kerstin Isaksson, A Two-dimensional Approach to Job Insecurity: Consequences for Employees Attitudes and Well-being, in: European Journal of Work and Organizational Psychology, Vol. 8, 1999, pp. 179-195; see also the case studies about Finland and the Netherlands.

Furthermore, in some Member States governments pursue policies of reducing public employment. In the meantime 17 EU countries allow for downsizing policies in the civil services. These developments show that it would be misleading to speak in a general way about the "stability of public service employment". In fact, it is also true that people often have a false image of employment in the public sector since they believe that public employment is more stable than employment in the private sector. In fact, the issue of job security is still surrounded by many myths. For example, whereas people believe that all public employees enjoy lifetime tenure and greater job security, this is not always the case. In most Member States, public employees can be dismissed for many (mostly theoretical) reasons.

Today, almost all Member States have maintained a system in which civil servants are enjoying a very high or a high degree of job security. In countries such as Germany or Ireland, lifetime tenure is seen as protecting the independence of civil servants, particularly given the requirement that they are able to give unbiased advice to the Government of the day. Civil servants are also expected to exercise high ethical standards of fairness in the discharge of their duties without bias i.e. in relation to enforcement of regulations. Thus the instrument of job security is seen as important instrument as it protects the civil servant against political pressure. Therefore, job security is mostly higher for civil servants than for other public- and private employees. For example, in Denmark, civil servants are entitled to three years pay if they are dismissed due to abolition of positions.

Here, one may distinguish between countries with lifetime tenure (where dismissal is only possible as a result of disciplinary procedures) and systems with a high degree of job security (where it is possible to dismiss civil servants under specific conditions). In both cases dismissal of civil servants exists more in theory than in practice. Overall, 14 Member States still offer a lifetime tenure. According to data, career structure countries provide stronger job security than non-career countries (see Table 36). The only country that has indicated having weaker job security is Latvia. Latvia is currently struggling with serious economic problems, forcing layoffs in the public sector. Also other Eastern European countries (e.g., Slovakia) have relative weak job protections for civil servants.

Table 36: Generally, do civil servants with public law status have lifetime tenure or a limited, fixed-term contract by type of civil service structure

(Frequencies in parenthesis)

		++	+	0	-	- -	Total
Type of civil service system	Career structure	67 (12)	22 (4)	11 (2)	0 (0)	0 (0)	100 (18)
	Non-career structure	22 (2)	22 (2)	44 (4)	11 (1)	0 (0)	100 (9)
	Total	52 (14)	22 (6)	22 (6)	4 (1)	0 (0)	100 (27)

Overall, countries with a bureaucratic career structure allow dismissals mainly for disciplinary reasons. In non-career countries civil servants' employment can be terminated for various different reasons, for example for poor performance or economic difficulties.

Table 37: Termination of civil servant employment by type of civil service structure

(Frequencies in parenthesis)

		Few reasons (1-2)	Some reasons (3-5)	Many reasons (6-7)	Total
Type of civil service system	Career structure	50 (9)	28 (5)	22 (4)	100 (18)
	Non-career structure	0 (0)	44 (4)	56 (5)	100 (9)
	Total	33 (9)	33 (9)	33 (9)	100 (27)

In a study "Are civil servants different because they are civil servants?"[292] most Member States agreed that job security can be justified in order to protect employees from external pressure or political pressure[293]. On the other hand, the privileged treatment of public employees regarding job security and specific social security schemes seems to have caused frustrations in some Member States. Many people believe that public employees should not be treated differently to

292 Demmke, Are Civil Servants Different Because They Are Civil Servants? EIPA, Maastricht, 2006.

293 The participating Member States agreed with the following statement: "The main argument in favour of lifetime tenure is that it compensates for the generally higher private sector salaries and, even more, enhances job protection for those employees with a regulatory or enforcement function and with jobs needing protection against individual and political pressure".

private employees. In addition, many believe that job security (or job tenure) will not enhance performance since public employees do not fear dismissal or sanctions in the event of poor performance. In the above-mentioned survey, Member States were also asked whether *"The possibility of firing staff for poor performance may lead to higher performance levels, since staff would believe they are subject to sharper discipline"*. Most Member States did not agree with this hypothesis; only Denmark, the Netherlands, Lithuania, Cyprus and Italy were inclined to agree.

Most Member States stated that "*dismissing people for poor performance is not a way to ensure higher performance*", and dismissal is a last resort. The **French** contribution to the survey stated that it is difficult to improve employees' performance on the basis of fear of dismissal *("la crainte du licenciement")*. The highest possible effectiveness should be sought via positive incentives, e.g., organisation of the work, individual performance management, training, promotion, etc. With regard to this point, job guarantee is an important motivational factor which should be exploited dynamically.

Table 38: Civil servants' job security trend by type of civil service structure

(Frequencies in parenthesis)

		Increasing	Status quo	Decreasing	Total
Type of civil service structure	Career structure	0 (0)	83 (15)	17 (3)	100 (18)
	Non-career structure	0 (0)	44 (4)	56 (5)	100 (9)
	Total	0 (0)	70 (19)	30 (8)	100 (27)

In each of the EU-27 countries, civil servants' employment can be terminated due to disciplinary reasons. As the country analysis **(table below)** shows, countries such as Germany, Greece and Lithuania only allow for the dismissal of civil servants due to disciplinary reasons. In many countries poor performance also seems to be an adequate reason for termination. Restructuring, downsizing and re-organisation are reasons to terminate the relationship in more than half of the countries. However, despite the fact that these operations can analytically be distinguished from each other, it seems that in practice they measure the same thing and respondents find it difficult to differentiate between restructuring and downsizing. However, the general trend is towards a (slight) weakening of job protection for civil servants.

In the meantime, more countries also allow for other reasons (such as poor performance and bad performance assessment) to dismiss civil servants. However, in all of these countries it is still rare that civil servants are dismissed because of poor performance. The same is true for the Netherlands, Finland and Denmark. Although it is possible to dismiss civil servants in these countries for various reasons, in reality civil servants have a relatively strong (judicial) job protection. For example, in Sweden, job protection is managed relatively well although life-time tenure does not exist. For Swedish civil servants, there is a special job protection agreement that increases the already beneficial general conditions on the Swedish labour market. The aim for assistance in case of redundancy is to find a new job in the labour market as a whole, not only in the civil service. Even firing staff for bad performance is certainly not easy. Employers have to prove an employee's misconduct or deliberate misuse of power or resources. From the Swedish point of view the possibility of firing staff for bad performance would have a disadvantageous side effect: the risk of losing trust between management and staff. Investments in enjoying work, encouraging confidence and promoting the common interest seem to be better ways of raising performance rather than strengthening discipline and stressing the internal formal execution of power.

However, the situation is different in many of the central- and Eastern European Member States who offer a relatively weak job protection. For example, in Bulgaria civil servants can also be dismissed when conflicts of interests arise. In Slovakia dismissals are possible in the case of loss of the civil servants' capability to carry out legal acts.

8.2 Remuneration systems: from seniority-based to performance-related pay

Traditional remuneration systems were established decades ago and for a long time they changed very little. The traditional focus on careers, stability, seniority and positions made sense when the vast majority in the public service had similar qualifications and jobs. The classical pay system was adapted to the dominant values at the time: bureaucratisation, standardisation and equality.

Table 39: Termination of civil servant employment by EU Member State

0 = No, 1 = Yes

	A	B	C	D	E	F	G	H
Germany	1	0	0	0	0	0	0	*1*
Greece	1	0	0	0	0	0	0	*1*
Luxembourg	1	0	0	0	0	0	0	*1*
Belgium	1	1	0	0	0	0	0	*2*
Cyprus	1	0	0	0	0	0	1	*2*
Ireland	1	1	0	0	0	0	0	*2*
Italy	1	1	0	0	0	0	0	*2*
Portugal	1	1	0	0	0	0	0	*2*
Spain	1	1	0	0	0	0	0	*2*
Austria	1	1	0	0	0	0	1	*3*
Malta	1	0	1	1	0	0	0	*3*
Sweden	1	0	1	1	0	0	0	*3*
Czech Republic	1	0	1	1	1	0	0	*4*
Estonia	1	1	1	1	1	0	0	*5*
France	1	1	1	1	1	0	0	*5*
Hungary	1	0	1	1	1	1	0	*5*
Lithuania	1	1	1	1	1	0	0	*5*
United Kingdom	1	1	1	1	1	0	0	*5*
Bulgaria	1	1	1	1	1	0	1	*6*
Denmark	1	1	1	1	1	1	0	*6*
Finland	1	1	1	1	1	1	0	*6*
Latvia	1	1	1	1	1	1	0	*6*
Netherlands	1	1	1	1	1	1	0	*6*
Poland	1	1	1	1	1	1	0	*6*
Slovakia	1	1	1	1	1	0	1	*6*
Slovenia	1	1	1	1	1	1	0	*6*
Romania	1	1	1	1	1	1	1	*7*
Mean	*1.00*	*0.71*	*0.61*	*0.61*	*0.54*	*0.29*	*0.18*	*3.93*

A = Disciplinary reasons
B = Poor performance
C = Restructuring
D = Downsizing
E = Re-organisation
F = Economic difficulties
G = Other
H = Sum

During the past decades, the workforce and the work itself have changed greatly. In particular, qualifications have become much more diverse and work has become highly skilled and increasingly specialised knowledge work. In addition, important changes in values have taken place. Today, civil servants want to be seen as "individuals" and to be treated individually. It seems traditional pay systems with their career ladders, time-based pay increases and specific allowances are increasingly reflecting a slowly disappearing concept of employment. "That model is designed to reward loyalty by providing stable and secure employment, reflecting and meeting those needs"[294]. Today, employees themselves expect immediate rewards and recognition for their individual accomplishments.

Thus, the above-mentioned European-wide process of responsbilisation, flexibilisation and decentralisation can also be seen in the field of pay. However, the national pay systems differ enormously. Whereas Sweden has a relatively individualised pay system (every agency negotiates individually with its employees), pay is decentralised between the federal and the regional level in Germany. In other countries pay is rather centralised.

Basic salary is still regulated by law in most Member States (22). Majority of the countries have centralised salary systems that are applicable to the whole civil service (13) or to the federal/central level (4). The remaining countries have either a hybrid system consisting of centralised elements and decentralised discretion by departments or agencies (8), or they have fully decentralised their remuneration system, including elements that are determined on the basis of individual negotiations (2). As Table 40 illustrates, career structure countries have more often traditional salary systems that are based to a much larger extent on seniority, age and experience. However, not all post-bureaucratic Member States have completely abandoned the principle of seniority (e.g., the Netherlands).

Table 40: Seniority-based wage system by type of civil service structure

(Frequencies in parenthesis)

		Yes	To some extent	No	Total
Type of civil service structure	Career structure	56 (10)	39 (7)	6 (1)	100 (18)
	Non-career structure	11 (1)	33 (3)	56 (5)	100 (9)
	Total	41 (11)	37 (10)	22 (6)	100 (27)

294 US Office of Personnel Management, Performance Related Pay, Washington D.C, April 2002, p. 4.

Non-career countries are also strongly represented among the civil service systems foreseeing wage schemes, calculated on the basis of performance and target agreements. This is true for most of the Scandinavian and Anglo-Saxon tradition countries. Continental tradition countries were less prone to incorporate criteria of performance and objectives are systems. Performance-related pay is widely applied in the United Kingdom, the Czech Republic, Hungary, and in Denmark (and partly in Finland). It is just being introduced in Germany, Spain and France. In other countries it is only used for top officials (e.g., Ireland). The amount of the reward also differs considerably amongst the European countries.

Figure 6: Composite index on the intensity of the use of performance-related pay in OECD member countries reporting to have PRP systems in place

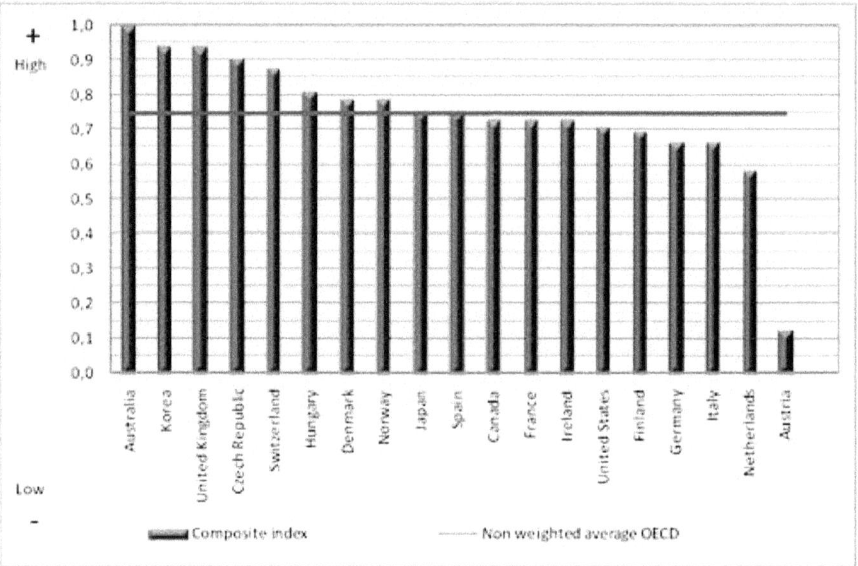

Source: OECD, The State of the Public Service, op. cit., p. 43[295]

The main purpose of integrating performance-oriented pay into HRM is to increase the individual performance of employees and to reward those who perform well. Mostly, PRP is allocated to individuals after the completion of annual appraisals and evaluation, which show whether someone has achieved or ex-

295 Greece, Iceland, Luxemburg, Mexico, Poland, Portugal, Slovakia and Sweden reported not having a PRP system (OECD: The State of the Public Service, op. cit.).

ceeded performance targets (mostly set by their superiors or by the organisation).

When evaluating the effectiveness of PRP, it is necessary to place it in the context of other performance management instruments. Generally, performance-orientation of the workforce can be realised by appropriate HRM concepts and tools[296]:

- Improving communication
- Enhancing training systems and career development opportunities
- Reforming recruitment and selection procedures
- Introducing personnel and management leadership and development plans
- Offering training courses in negotiation, decision-making skills and leadership
- Defining the competences needed and putting the right people in the right jobs
- Defining incentive systems which motivate performance
- Offering the right mix between stability and mobility of personnel
- Modernising and improving personnel appraisal systems
- Rewarding good performance with material and non-material rewards (including performance-related pay).

Stimulating *incentive systems* play a major role in motivating employees towards performance orientation. There is clear empirical evidence that public employees – at least in industrialised countries – want a pluralist incentive system ("cafeteria system") which offers a broad choice of extrinsic and intrinsic incentives and rewards[297]. In the past, several civil service systems were still predominantly based on immaterial incentives and (more or less) automatic promotion as a motivator.

Although more Member States of the European Union have implemented performance-related pay systems in recent years, comparative and empirical studies on successes and failures in implementing these reforms are scarce[298]. The main reason for introducing PRP cited in most cases is to enhance the motivation of employees and thus to improve performance and efficiency. In addition, the re-

296 See also Christoph Reichard, Assessing Performance-oriented HRM Activities in Selected OECD Countries, A Review of Ten Years of Modernisation, The HRM Perspective, PUMA/HRM (2002) 9, 24 September 2002.

297 Ibid.

298 To our knowledge the only one so far has been the one from the OECD.

form of pay systems is followed by a strong tendency to decentralise the remuneration system to regional and local authorities, or to agencies and even to line management. Performance-related pay is used to improve the pay of those employees that the organisation wishes to retain. However, it is not clear if this is the actual outcome, and PRP schemes may, in fact, be detrimental to the motivation of individuals if not handled very carefully. Another problem is that it is not yet clear whether rewards should follow, rather than precede, performance. This is in contrast to behaviourist theory, which maintains that rewards induce performance[299].

The complexity surrounding reward management is just one of the difficulties faced by human resource management. The main argument put forward in favour of PRP is that it acts as a motivator, by providing extrinsic rewards in the form of pay and intrinsic rewards through the recognition of effort and achievement. PRP is also seen as helping employees to identify closely with the goals of the organisation, leading to increased productivity, quality, flexibility and teamwork. In addition, PRP is seen to be useful in the recruitment and retention of staff.

For the past 50 years, many researchers, however, have questioned whether PRP actually acts as a motivator, or, indeed, if money can motivate. Most managers are aware of Herzberg's view that the job itself is the source of true motivation, not the pay or even the conditions of work. Herbert Simon (1961) already emphasised that "material incentives – salaries, wages, or bonuses – are probably not the most important influences that induce an employee to give his active and enthusiastic support to an organisation"[300]. In Germany, Siedentopf (1978) raised similar concerns in the 1970s[301]. So far, most of the recent literature in the field remains very sceptical as to the expected positive effects of PRP[302].

---

299 Sally Coleman Selden/Gene A. Brewer, Work Motivation in the Senior Executive Service: Testing the High Performance Cycle Theory, in Journal of Public Administration Research and Theory, 2000, Vol 10. No 3, p. 545.

300 Herbert Simon/Victor A. Thompson, Donald W. Smithburg, Public Administration, New York 1961, p. 63.

301 Heinrich Siedentopf (ed.), Bewertungssysteme für den öffentlichen Dienst, Nomos, Baden-Baden 1978.

302 Due to time and space restraints we will refrain from quoting the mass of publications in the field. One of the last examples are Virginie Forest, Performance-related Pay and Work Motivation: Theoretical and Empirical Perspectives for the French Civil Service, in: International Review of Administrative Sciences, Vol. 74, No. 2, 2008, pp. 325-329, and James S. Bowman, The Success of Failure: The Paradox of Performance Pay, in: Review of Public Personnel Administration, Vol. 30, No. 1, March 2010, pp. 70-89.

Despite these limitations of pay as a motivator the main question is what to learn from this. Should PRP be abandoned? Should the national civil services move back to the old standardised systems? The latter option may already pose a problem since many public employees themselves consider the traditional pay systems in the civil services (pay according to seniority) to be unfair. Although traditional pay systems may correspond to the principle of equality, they do not match with new expectations and value changes. Today, more public employees want to combine the principle of equality with the principle of autonomy and performance. In short: they want to be treated more as individuals.

People constantly compare their performance with the performance of their colleagues (Note: and mostly believe that they are better than others). In the case of standardised pay, many employees believe that their pay is not fair since they perform better than their colleagues. In Dubet's research 72.9% of all people interviewed find performance-related pay fairer than seniority pay[303]. However, the problems are not solved once PRP is introduced and civil servants are paid according to performance.

From now on, new feelings of being treated unfairly emerge and, in many instances, people are even more demotivated and frustrated after the introduction of PRP. Since people constantly compare themselves with other colleagues, they also tend to believe that colleagues who receive bonuses and PRP do not deserve them. Often, employees who do not receive PRP are becoming demotivated since they expected to get bonuses etc. Another dilemma concerns the fact that many employees do not trust their superiors to take fair decisions on the allocation of PRP. Consequently, many people feel that they are treated unfairly because of unprofessional or unfair pay decisions of their superiors. In all of these cases, the expectation to be treated individually conflicts with the expectation to be treated equally.

Thus, as long as traditional pay systems exist they will always be seen as unfair and not corresponding to new value developments. However, any alternative may not be better. In the future one main challenge will be to better balance the three principles of equality, autonomy and performance in the field of performance-related pay.

---

303 Dubet, Ungerechtigkeiten, op. cit.

Demmke[304] suggests that modern Performance-Related Pay Schemes are not necessarily fairer than traditional seniority pay. Rather questions of unfair and fair pay are simply different in centralised, standardised and decentralised systems. Whereas in the former system, the principle of seniority (everybody receives salary increases independently of his or her performance) may be at the centre of the "unfairness" debate in systems with PRP and individual pay setting, the problem is the pay discretion of managers (and the subjective allocation of PRP to those people who are supposed to perform better) and the perception of employees' (different) pay to that of their colleagues.

However, returning to the traditional centralised and seniority pay schemes is not an option. Rather, it is important to design fairer pay systems under decentralised conditions. For this, one major challenge will also be to avoid discrimination in allocating bonuses and PRP. In 2008, a study by the European Foundation for the Improvement of Living and Working Conditions revealed that "men are not only paid bonuses more often but the sums they are paid are also larger. Some 13% of male wage and salary earners had received at least €1,000 as a bonus for the previous year, whereas only 5% of women received such a bonus. A significant gender pay gap is also evident with respect to medium-sized bonuses of between €500 and €1,000"[305]. So far, only few empirical studies have analysed the pay gap between full-time employees and part-time employees, older versus younger employees, top-civil servants versus line managers and other employees etc. In the future, the legitimacy of performance-related pay systems will very much depend on the question whether bonuses are paid as a result of a non-discriminatory process. One may doubt whether this is the case today.

Major challenges also exist between the views of managers and employees on employee motivation. Managers thought money would top the list of possible incentives, while employees listed job satisfaction as the top motivator. Sufficient evidence is still missing, but it seems that, where motivation is concerned, (dis-) *satisfaction with management* and (lack of) *career opportunities* rank higher than pay and are especially important factors for workers leaving an organisation and becoming de-motivated.

The incentives created by different forms of pay and reward, and their impact on performance, can indeed be complex. As job security is considered by civil ser-

---

304 Christoph Demmke, Leistungsbezahlung in den Oeffentlichen Diensten der EU-Staaten, in: Der moderne Staat, No. 1/2009, pp. 53-73.

305 European Foundation for the Improvement of Living and Working Conditions, Effect of Performance-related Bonuses on Gender Pay Gap, Dublin 2008.

vants to be an important element of their reward package, Member States wishing to introduce new public-management style contractual arrangements (to reward performance) may have to offer a higher rate of basic pay to compensate for lost job security. In reality, however, the funding crisis in the public sector has not increased pay, but has often led instead to lower salaries, which have been frozen due to financial constraints. For example, in Germany a number of public services have cut the Christmas allowances for their civil servants.

Apart from fairness, other problems associated with PRP include a tendency towards a short-term focus on quantifiable goals, to the neglect of more long-term issues. Organisational problems also play a role. For example, in the United Kingdom pay is a competence delegated to individual authorities. But what will happen if different departments, agencies or units pay differently? How will this affect mobility policies?

As regards measurement problems, studies by Demmke and by Demmke, Hammerschmid and Meyer on individual and organisational performance management systems reveal numerous problems in appraising employees' performance, including difficulties in measuring the work of public servants and subjectivity. Another study by the Danish Ministry of Finance[306] on motivation reveals a further paradox: while employees strongly welcome the introduction of individual rewards and the introduction of PRP, once it is implemented it creates frustration and the feeling of being treated unfairly. It is therefore clear that communication and agreement on objectives and standards of performance are central to the success of the scheme. Finally, an empirical study on the reform of the remuneration system in the US state of Georgia[307] revealed that only about 50% of employees said that performance ratings were done fairly[308]; 70% disagreed that PRP was a good way to motivate state employees and 75% of supervisors questioned the motivational effects of PRP[309]. Furthermore, 90% were of the opinion that no additional money was made available and 82% believed that the main purpose of the new PRP system was to control the state payroll[310]. Finally, over 90% of state employees did not believe good performers were being rewarded

---

306 Danish Ministry of Finance, op. cit.

307 Edward Kellough/Lloyd G. Nigro, Pay for Performance in Georgia State Government: Employee Perspectives on Georgia Gain after Five Years, University of Georgia, Manuscript, July 16, 2001.

308 Ibid., p. 8.

309 Ibid., p. 9.

310 Ibid., p. 12.

with meaningful pay rises[311]. The authors come to the conclusion that there is regrettably little evidence that PRP has yielded any desirable outcomes.

Thus, the results of most studies seem to suggest that PRP should not be overrated. It may be only one instrument in certain situations and when:

- Managers are sufficiently trained and have time to measure performance;
- Managers are motivated to carry out performance assessment and sanctioned if they do not carry out assessments properly;
- Managers better learn how to set and evaluate the achievement of annual targets;
- Both parties have an interest, are able to communicate with each other and are motivated to do the appraisals;
- The evaluated tasks are specific, measurable and linked to a single individual;
- The performance due to effort can be distinguished from that due to pure luck;
- Performance can be attributed to one person or one group;
- Financial rewards seem to be important for employees and sufficiently high;
- Performance management systems are transparent and fair.

On the other hand, difficulties arise when:

- Bonuses are too low;
- Financial rewards are not seen as incentives by employees;
- People already earn enough;
- PRP is paid to a small number of employees and the rest feel punished;
- Focus is on rewards to high performance and less care is taken of poor-performers;
- The position and task is as such that performance cannot be measured and is qualitative;
- The incentive function might be lost when paid over a long period.

Our analysis has shown that – despite all challenges – the trend is clearly towards more flexible, decentralised and individualised pay in the future. Post-bureaucratic systems offer more flexible pay arrangements for their civil servants. However, this is an ambivalent development. More employees will feel

311 Ibid., p. 15.

that they are treated unfairly. In fact, we believe that the main future challenge is not performance-related pay. Instead, it is the impact of the financial crisis on the (future) salary systems. In the future it may be likely that more bureaucratic and post-bureaucratic Member States will no longer be willing (or able) to offer more competitive salary systems. Some Member States will even be forced to reduce salaries. It is clear that this development will come with a price attached: declining attractiveness of the public sector. Performance-related pay will also become a problem because budgets for PRP will be reduced. But how should this enhance motivation?

9. Reform overview: from traditional bureaucracy to post-bureaucracy?

In the previous chapters we have discussed various organisational and HRM reforms. The aim of this chapter is to summarise the main developments and to present an overview of where the EU-27 countries stand. For this purpose we have created a model which measures how well the civil service system follows the basic elements of a traditional bureaucracy as described by Max Weber. The components of the model were introduced in Chapter II on methodology (see pages). Thus, we tried to empirically measure which countries are more bureaucratic and which are less bureaucratic.

The results can be seen from Table 41, where we have ranked the EU Member States according to their score. All career structure countries were closer to traditional bureaucratic model than any non-career structure country. The career structure countries' scores vary from 7.2% (Cyprus) to 29.5% (Slovania). The average score is 19.1%[312]. The non-career countries' score range from 38.8% (Estonia) to 81.4% (Sweden). The average is 57.5%.

As can be seen the national civil services of the EU Member States are a rather heterogeneous group of countries with different structural characteristics. Two interlinked structural features help us to understand how and why the Member States have adopted different civil service models. The first structural feature is the population. In general, the more inhabitants there are, the bigger the bureaucratic system that is required. The second structural feature is the state structure (see pages 46-51). Small countries are typically unitary states, medium-sized countries are decentralised unitary states and big countries are typically federal or quasi-federal states. When these two structural factors are taken into account, it is possible to detect a visible pattern of how the countries are grouped. Firstly,

312 European Commission's score is 12.1% which indicates that it is a rather traditional bureaucracy.

it is easy to see that decentralised unitary states as a group can be considered post-bureaucratic countries (with the exception of France). Secondly, federal or quasi-federal states have adopted a rather traditional bureaucratic model. Thirdly, unitary states are somewhere in-between the other two groups. This finding is interesting and it helps us to understand the underlying logic of different reform paths.

Table 41: Traditional bureaucracy: post-bureaucracy continuum score by EU Member State

0% = traditional bureaucracy, 100% = post-bureaucracy

Member State	Score
Greece	7.2
Luxembourg	7.2
Cyprus	9.8
Ireland	13.6
Portugal	16.3
France	16.3
Germany	16.6
Belgium	18.6
Spain	19.1
Romania	19.8
Italy	20.4
Hungary	22.9
Austria	23.7
Lithuania	24.3
Poland	27.7
Bulgaria	28.9
Malta	29.3
Slovenia	29.5
Estonia (*)	38.8
Latvia (*)	40.2
Netherlands (*)	47.1
Slovakia (*)	51.0
Finland (*)	53.4
United Kingdom (*)	64.1
Denmark (*)	68.2
Czech Republic (*)	73.0
Sweden (*)	81.4
Mean	32.2

(*) Non-career system country

Of course, another interesting question is to anticipate the future developments of the national civil services. Since we do not want to enter the field of speculation we will refrain from discussing potential future trends. Clearly, the trends within the last two decades went clearly into the direction of post-bureaucratic models. However, this does not allow for the conclusion that the times of bureaucratic civil services are over. Instead, what seems to be more important is to discuss the quality of the ongoing reform trends and reform outcomes. What do we know about the reform outcomes? What are successes, what could be the failures? And what can (should) we learn from this?

Figure 7: Bureaucracy – post-bureaucracy continuum model by population and by state structure

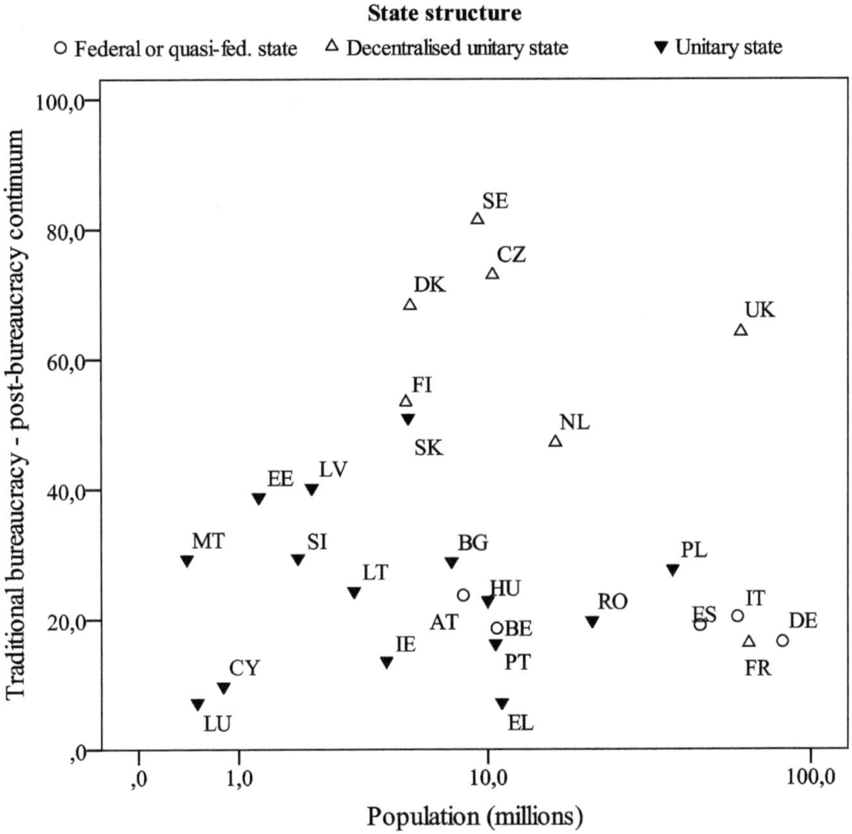

VI. EVALUATING REFORM OUTCOMES

1. The employment of public employees: growing inconsistencies

The traditional question of which tasks and which functions should be performed solely by civil servants has never been answered definitively[313]. In addition, the question as to the differences between public employees and civil servants is handled differently not only throughout the European Union, but also worldwide. At the national level, in some Member States, e.g., Denmark, Germany, Spain and Greece, either the constitution and/or constitutional courts' jurisprudence or the civil service act (or a combination) require the establishment of a statutory system of official employment. These requirements do not exclude the possibility of concluding normal employment contracts in the national civil services. However, public employment should normally consist of civil servants subject to public law and the employment of employees subject to labour law should be an exception. However, our analysis shows that in many countries, the possibility of employing staff in terms of employment contracts is NOT treated as an exception[314]. On the other hand, many civil servants are employed in fields, e.g., in relation to technical tasks (maintenance, automation, technical assistance, etc.) which do not necessarily require the employment of public law civil servants.

Another problem concerns the national inconsistencies as regards the employment of public employees in civil service employment positions (although many national civil service laws do not allow for the employment of public employees in civil service tasks). Several Member States apply different employment relationships in the same sectors and – sometimes – for the same professions. Furthermore, as mobility has increased and careers are in the process of being reformed (or even abolished), there is less reason to treat different groups of public employees differently. Therefore, some countries provide for derogation and exception clauses in their national civil service laws. For example, France allows in Art. 20 of the Law n. 2009-972 of 3 August 2009 (*relative à la mobilité et aux parcours professionnels dans la fonction publique*) that non-tenured personnel may be recruited in tenured positions in special cases. Also Art. 21 of the Portuguese law 12 a/2008 allows for the recruitment of employment contracts to

313 Christoph Demmke/Uta Linke, Who's a National and Who's an European? Exercising Public Power and the Legitimacy of Art. 39 4 EC in the 21st Century, in: EIPASCOPE 2003/2.

314 Ministerio de Administraciones Públicas, Civil Service in Spain, op. cit., p. 40.

meet “urgent public and temporary needs” (Art. 22)[315]. In both cases, the derogations may be interpreted widely. Also in Belgium the civil service law allows for the recruitment of public employees in civil service positions in certain cases.

When considering the situation in all Member States, the following conclusion can be drawn: although most Member States apply a distinction between civil servants and other public employees and between public employees and private sector employees, this distinction as such is no longer decisive for deciding which tasks are carried out by whom. At the same time, differences in working conditions amongst the different categories of public employees are decreasing. The conviction is growing that public employees can exercise important state tasks just as well or badly as civil servants under public law. Moreover, more Member States are of the opinion that specific legal and ethical requirements in the national civil services can also be adopted under labour law: the need to act impartially, specific ethical requirements, fairness, rule of law and standardised treatment, etc. Here, pressures for alignment come from EU obligations. One such example is European labour- and anti-discrimination law. Here, many directives apply in the same way as to the public and private sector. The case law of the European Court of Justice is also relevant. In cases like Adeneler (C-212/04) and Del Cerro Alonso (C-307/05) the ECJ ruled that employees with flexible contracts should not be discriminated against in comparison with permanent employees as regards aspects such as pay and the length-of-service allowance. In the future the case law on the interpretation of Directive 1999/70/EC may further blur the distinction between civil servants and other public employees.

As regards the latter, the Directive 1999/70/EC requires that employees in the public and private sectors should not be offered an unlimited number of limited contracts (provided that the objective reasons cannot be proved to be necessary). In fact, employees should be offered an unlimited contract after a certain period of employment. It is clear that the transposition of this Directive has led to a dif-

---

315 In France Art. 20 of the Law on Mobility states that « Toutefois, des agents non titulaires peuvent être recrutés pour assurer le remplacement momentané de fonctionnaires autorisés à exercer leurs fonctions à temps partiel ou indisponibles en raison d’un congé de maladie, d’un congé de maternité, d’un congé parental, d’un congé de présence parentale, de l’accomplissement du service civil ou national, du rappel ou du maintien sous les drapeaux ou de leur participation à des activités dans le cadre de l’une des réserves mentionnées à l’article 53, ou pour faire face temporairement et pour une durée maximale d’un an à la vacance d’un emploi qui ne peut être immédiatement pourvu dans les conditions prévues par le présent titre».

ficult alignment process in some Member States. The reason for this is rather simple: the Member States are to some extent forced to align of working conditions between civil servants and other public employees. For example, in **France** the law n° 2005-843 from 26 July 2005 as regards the measures taken in order to transpose the Community law into national law has modified "*le statut de la fonction publique*" in relation to a number of points. For example, the law has implemented the Directive 1999/70/CEE from 28 July 1999 and introduced measures on how to better protect the situation of employees with fixed-term contracts. The law has limited the possibility to recruit public employees with fixed contracts (for a maximum of six years after they need to be offered an unlimited contract if the administration wishes to continue the work relation)[316]. The situation in **France** is representative of the situation in other countries because community law forces all Member States to align the contractual situation of the different categories of public employees.

Despite the growing importance of EU law, each Member State still follows a specific, not always rational, national logic. As regards public employment and the employment of civil servants and other public employees, different national models have developed and brought their own paradoxes and complexities. For example, in the **Netherlands** and in **Austria**, approximately half of all teachers either have a public law status or are employed as employees subject to labour law. In Germany, too, teachers are civil servants in some *Länder*, whereas they are public employees subject to labour law (or *Bundesangestellten Tarif* – BAT) in others.

Germany has *Beamte* (civil servants) and *Angestellte* (contractual staff) working in the public service. However, both groups may perform tasks which are related to the exercise of official powers (although the German Constitution (*Grundgesetz*) and the case law of the Federal Constitutional Court stipulate differently). In the various job categories, tasks are carried out which are also performed in the private sector. It is precisely because of this inconsistency in the allocation of tasks, that the question of why the differences between *Beamte* and *Angestellte* actually exist is being raised continually. If *Angestellte* can perform functions which are supposed to be just as well (or badly) reserved for civil servants, the meaning of the concept of "function connected with the exercise of official powers" is being questioned. Until now, no evidence has been presented that *Angestellte* carry out their tasks differently to civil servants.

---

316 Rapport annuel sur l'état de la fonction publique, 2009, op. cit.

Similar inconsistencies can be found in other countries (e.g., in **Belgium** and **Spain**).

In **Denmark,** there has been a change in the state area from employment as civil servants and civil servant-like employment, to employment under collective agreements. In theory, Denmark employs civil servants, civil servant-like employees and other public employees although the differences amongst these three groups have become less.

Figure 8: Trends in the proportion of appointments of civil servants in Denmark (1996 -2005)

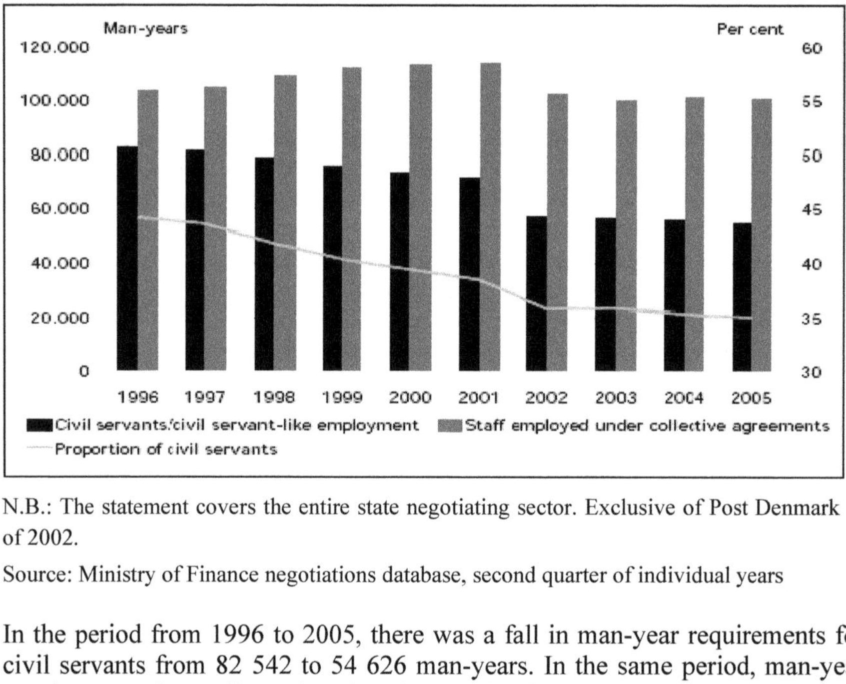

N.B.: The statement covers the entire state negotiating sector. Exclusive of Post Denmark as of 2002.

Source: Ministry of Finance negotiations database, second quarter of individual years

In the period from 1996 to 2005, there was a fall in man-year requirements for civil servants from 82 542 to 54 626 man-years. In the same period, man-year requirements for staff employed under a collective agreement dropped merely from 104 157 to 101 093. Thus, the proportion of civil servants fell from 44% in 1996 to 35% in 2005. Further considerable reductions are to be expected in the number of civil servants as a result of new rules limiting civil servant appointments. At the same time, there is an imbalance in the age composition among civil servants in that there are relatively many elderly employees"[317]. The percentages of civil servants vary sharply from ministry to ministry. As a 2002 report shows, whereas 84% of those employed by the Ministry of Ecclesiastical Affairs are employed as civil servants, the 2% are employed in that capacity by the Ministry of Refugee, Immigration and Integration Affairs. On the other hand, 68% of all employees at Danish State Railways (DSB) are civil servants; this figure is 56% at Ministry of Taxation, but only 18% at the Ministry of Finance. Because of these differences in employment relationships, one may wonder why the Ministry of Finance employed so few civil servants and the Ministry of Taxation so many[318].

France is one of the few countries with a relatively homogenous and uniform public service. However, in the meantime the three *fonctions publiques* also employ almost 200 000 non-tenured personnel (mostly employed by the ministries). "The recourse to non-tenured personnel is linked to the absence of employment limits because of certain recruitment needs (IT personnel for example) and the fact that in certain occupational sectors recruitment essentially involves non-permanent jobs, in response to occasional or seasonal requirements,"[319]. In the technical sector, one employee in five is non-tenured[320]. Another development concerns the fact that some persons exercise several jobs in the civil service. It even happens that an employee is working in the public and private sectors at the same time or in different *fonctions publiques*[321]. This tendency towards a fragmentation of employment and employment relationships contrasts with the original French concept regarding a uniform Civil Service. In the future the Law *no 2009-972 of 3 August 2009* (which seeks to further enhance the mobility and flexibility in recruitment matters within the French Public Service) will – despite its positive intentions – further obscure the difference between "*des agents non titulaires*" and "*agents titulaires*".

In **Belgium,** the Law from 22 July 1993 (*M.B. du 14.8.1993 portant certaines mesures en matière de fonction publique*) stipulates in Art. 3 that civil servants

---

317 Danish Ministry of Finance, State Sector Personnel, 2005, Copenhagen 2006. http://www.perst.dk/Publications/2006/State%20Sector%20Personnel%20in%20Denmark%202005.aspx

318 Figures are taken from the Report of the Danish Ministry of Finance, State Sector Personnel in Denmark, Copenhagen, November 2002, p. 40.

319 France, The Public Employment Observatory, Annual Report 2003, Speech by Mr Jean-Paul Delevoye at the Meeting of the Steering Committee of the Public Employment Observatory, 9 December 2003, Paris 2003, pp. 28-29.

320 Ibid., p. 29.

321 Rapport Annuel, 2007-2008, op. cit.

with a public law status should be recruited as the rule in clearly defined areas and organisations. However, Art. 4 of the Law allows public employers to employ contractual employment as an exception and if the conditions are met which are enumerated in the Art 4.1 to 4.4. Art. 4 paragraph 10 also allows for more flexibility for the employment of non statutory personnel[322]. Today, one may indeed wonder whether the "theory of the status as a rule" and the "contract as an exception" is still applied in practice[323]. In the meantime many public employees are employed in jobs which should principally be reserved for civil servants in accordance with Art. 3 of the Law.

According to the OECD[324] Belgium is indeed "specific in that contractual staff are employed under rules that are clearly considered different from what should be general government employment rules, and their increasing number appears to have been unplanned, bypassing basic employment regulations too often, and resulting in a very large proportion of long-term employees not being properly managed. (…). The situation is very unsatisfactory both from a governance and an equity perspective, although it is to be noted that governments are making specific efforts to improve the management of contractual employees (…). It seems that the most important reason for hiring contractual staff lies in the cumbersome recruitment process for statutory staff, due partially to *ex ante* internal controls in each government and, although much less clearly, to the SELOR procedure. In addition, with a low level of outsourcing compared to other OECD member countries, governments have instead used a large proportion of contractual employment to fill in some of the lower skilled positions such as drivers, cleaning personnel and canteen personnel"[325].

In the **Netherlands,** the majority of people working in the public service have employment relationships governed by public law. However, employment rela-

---

322 « A partir d'une date qui doit être fixée par arrêté royal (article 450, § 1er, de la loi programme (I) du 24 décembre 2002), l'article 4 devra se lire comme suit: Par dérogation à l'article 3 et sans préjudice des dispositions de la loi du 3 juillet 1978 relative aux contrats de travail, sur proposition du ministre qui a la Fonction publique dans ses attributions, le Roi détermine par arrêté délibéré en Conseil des Ministres, les circonstances dans lesquelles il peut être procédé à l'engagement de personnes sous contrat de travail, les conditions et les modalités de leur engagement et leurs conditions de travail ».

323 Steunpunt Bestuurlijke Organisatie Vlaanderen, Jaarboek 2002, Tussen Bestuurkunde en Bestuurpratijk, Spoor HRM, De mythe van het statut voorbij?, Katleen Janssens, Ria Janvier, p. 124, 2003.

324 OECD Reviews of Human Resource Management in Government, Belgium, Executive Summary, OECD 2007.

325 Ibid.

tionships in the public sector have mostly been aligned with those in the private sector, though the public service performs functions which traditionally involve the exercise of official powers. For example, labour laws relating to working hours, works councils, equal opportunities, etc. are also applicable to the public service. However, a unified civil service no longer exists, following a decision in 1999 to divide the public sector into 12 sectors. On 16 December 1998, an Advice Relating to Civil Service Status report (*Advies van de Raad voor het Overheidspersonnelsbeleid inzake de Ambtelijke Status*) was published in the Netherlands. The report discussed whether the Dutch policy of aligning the public sector employment relationships with the private sector should be continued, and examined the consequences of a possible abolition of civil service status in the case of:

- recruitment procedures for civil servants;
- the possibility of dismissing civil servants and terminating their contracts;
- the procedural rules for civil servants;
- the budget;
- fundamental rights;
- social security;
- the image of the public service;
- the integrity of the public service;
- social dialogue;
- incompatibilities between public and private law status;
- the oath.

The report concluded very pragmatically that the normalisation process in the Netherlands should be continued. However, total abolition of public law status was not recommended – not so much on the grounds of substantive reasons, but because such a step would take at least four years and would be a complex and time consuming process. In addition, the report concluded that "the right time" for the total abolition of civil service status had not yet arrived. Furthermore, the question of whether the costs for the process would outweigh the benefits[326] would also have to be considered. In the Netherlands, this very pragmatic approach still raises the question of the legitimacy of the public-law employment relationship. Why not abolish it too ?

---

326 Advies van de Raad voor het Overheidspersonnelsbeleid inzake de Ambtelijke Status, Adviesnummer 17, The Hague, 16 December 1998 (official document without author), pp. 3-4.

In **Slovenia,** many civil servants have a public-law status and their employment relationship is still somewhat different to that in the private sector. In this respect, the question could be raised as to why so many employment relationships are governed by public law (approximately 80% in the ministries), while many tasks are of an ancillary or technical nature and are not related to the exercise of official powers, and could just as well be regulated by employment contracts modelled on the private sector. Some of the officials in Slovenia perform official tasks, e.g., some institutes employ meteorologists, statisticians or veterinary surgeons. Although these people do not execute official tasks, they are offered a special status as these are better paid.

In **Italy,** the central public service was "privatised" in 1993. Since then, a distinction must be made between civil servants subject to public-law status (who were excluded from all privatisation, e.g., judges, state advocates, military personnel, police officials, diplomats, prefects and to some extent professors and researchers[327]), public servants under a special private status, (e.g., prison officers, most employees in ministries and agencies, etc.), and private employees, (e.g., teachers and employees in hospitals such as doctors). In this respect, one may wonder why, for example, most professors are still civil servants, whereas many civil servants in ministries, many top-officials and teachers are mostly private status civil servants.

In Poland, the Civil Service Corps consists of positions in clearly defined public organisations and sectors. This exact and precise enumeration of civil service corps positions and functions reveals the question of why these and not also other positions that also exercise important public powers were included in the definition of the civil service corps. For example, regional and local administration does not belong to the civil service.

In **Spain** according to article 2, the Basic Statute of the Public Employee is applicable to all public employees (civil servants and contracted personnel) employed by the following public administrations:

- general state administration;
- governments of the autonomous communities and the cities of Ceuta y Melilla;
- governments of local government bodies;

327 Roberto Caranta, Point de vue sur les réformes récentes en matières de fonction publique en Italie, in Council of State (Conseil d'Etat), Public report of the Council of State, Studies and Documents, Reflections on the Civil Service, Paris, 2003, p. 405.

- public organisations, agencies and other bodies under public law with their own legal personality, linked or reporting to any of the public administrations;
- public universities. In Spain, positions in Spanish public service may be given to employees subject to labour law only under certain conditions[328].

The positions that can be held by employees with employment contracts are as follows:

- non-permanent positions;
- positions that involve everyday tasks, such as security, caretaking, transport and other similar;
- instrumental positions that relate to matters such as the maintenance of buildings, equipment and facilities, graphic arts, surveys, public safety and social communication;
- positions that require specialised technical knowledge, provided that no one is available from the ranks of the public officials to fulfil these tasks;
- positions that involve performing auxiliary functions of an instrumental nature or the provision of administrative support; and
- positions in foreign offices that entail administrative tasks which are procedural or auxiliary in nature and that involve the operation of machinery, filing or similar tasks.

However, figures show that the percentage of employees subject to conditions other than public-law contracts is relatively high (and increasing from central to local level). Similarly, the term "subject to certain conditions" may be interpreted in a relatively flexible way.

In **Sweden,** the competence to recruit and to define working conditions is highly decentralised. From a comparative perspective, almost all Swedish public employees could be termed as civil servants or private employees at the same time. Public employees enjoy almost the same legal situation in the public sector as in other sectors in the labour market. Only a very small minority of employees enjoy a type of specific status, i.e. judges. As a result, less than 1% of all public employees have a working relationship that is clearly distinct from those working in the private sector. The following question can therefore be asked: what is the point of having specific civil service rules for judges and military personnel if not for other central government personnel who are also exercising important

328 Ministerio de Administraciones Públicas, Civil Service in Spain, op. cit., p. 39.

public powers. Or, are these tasks less important and do they not need specific job protection? One could also argue: what is the purpose of having a distinct public sector as an alternative to the private sector?

In **Portugal** drastic public service reforms have introduced new rules, rights and duties to public employees which have been influenced by private labour law. Interestingly, despite all innovations and the wave of "privatisation into the Portuguese Public Sector" all three categories of public employees are still subject to public law. However, only the group of appointed staff (which according to the law n° 12-A/2008 of 27 February 2008 compromises staff in some well defined services: the Military, the Foreign Office, State Security Information; Criminal Investigation; Public Security; Inspection Activities) has maintained the former rules and rights. From an outsider point of view this reveals many questions. One should be able to question the importance of a "public law status" as such. Why introduce radical civil service reforms but keep the public law status?[329]

The **United Kingdom** is a very specific case since crown civil servants have never enjoyed a public law status. The basis of the civil service as we know it today dates back to the Northcote-Trevelyan Report of 1854. The Report set out the enduring core values and key principles that underpin the role and governance of the civil service – integrity, honesty, impartiality and objectivity. The Report also recommended that these values and principles should be enshrined in legislation. However, no Government ever took forward this recommendation. Instead, over the last 150 years or so, Ministers have exercised powers in relation to the civil service under the royal prerogative. In recent years, the merits of civil service legislation have been the subject of considerable debate, and there have been growing calls to implement the Northcote-Trevelyan recommendation and bring forward legislation for the civil service. In 2003, the House of Commons Public Administration Select Committee published a draft Civil Service Bill and, building on this, the Government launched a consultation *A draft Civil Service Bill – A Consultation Document* (CM 6373, November 2004). These consultation processes and other public debates have revealed a considerable body of opinion in favour of civil service legislation. Therefore, the Government announced in July 2007, in its Green Paper, *The Governance of Britain* (CM 7170), that it intended to bring forward legislation which would *"include*

329 This highly interesting (but also highly theoretical) topic has been discussed for years in Germany. See Pechstein/Summer, Beiträge zum Beamtenrecht, op. cit.

measures which will enshrine the core principles and values of the Civil Service in law"[330].

From the approx. 500,000 employees in the British civil service, 10 820 were employed as casual staff[331]. In the past, special advisors could be appointed in the United Kingdom "solely for the purpose of providing advice". However, this has caused some uncertainty over the years and special advisors did work which extended beyond giving advice. In the future, it is planned to redefine the special advisor's general functions as "assisting" the minister. The planned civil service bill will also clarify the tasks that special advisors are not permitted to do, e.g., authorising expenditure, exercising line management supervision over the civil service or discharging any statutory powers[332].

2. HR reforms and outcomes: successes and failures

Studying cases of good administration, good governance and *successes* in public services take us to the heart of current debates about the modern public service capacities to govern and to manage public services. To affix the label "successes" to public services is risky business. The risk is doubled when "successes" is attributed to new ideas, innovation and improvements in the field of public services whereas – at the same time – ideas are widespread that public services are not innovative and the poor performance of public services is a major reason for public distrust. Not surprisingly, many researchers are more interested in cases that are likely attract a lot of attention, such as cases of corruption, public scandals, waste of public money, poor performance and quality management etc.

Even though this focus is understandable, it clearly hinders the development of evidence, knowledge and awareness of positive developments and cases of "good administration". What is clearly missing is literature and studies about improvements in the field of HRM and the attitude of public employees about the nature and effects of recent developments in this area. There is also very little evidence about the impact of recent HR reforms on motivation, satisfaction etc., progress in working conditions, developments as regards the attractiveness of public service employment, as well as recruitment and HR policies in com-

330 Ministry of Justice, the Governance of Britain, Draft Constitutional Renewal Bill, London, March 2008, p. 66.

331 United Kingdom, Cabinet Office, Personnel Statistics, Media Brief, 1 April 2004.

332 United Kingdom, Cabinet Office, A Draft Civil Service Bill, A Consultation Document, p. 13.

parison to the private sector. Moreover, little is known on whether certain categories of staff (managers, older employees, women, minorities etc.) have witnessed improvements over the last few years whilst other categories of staff have not.

The discussion of what has been achieved (or not) in civil service reforms throughout the last few decades is most controversial. Given the limited attention and knowledge of the dimension of positive developments, it is not surprising that there is no specific theory on "good administration" and "successes". Discussing successes may also be seen as naïve if the emphasis is put purely on positive aspects while excluding other more critical issues. In the literature, many experts feel strongly on what to conclude about public services failures even though it turns out to be very difficult to find clear answers. Yet, in the future it is important to find empirically based and more accurate responses to the positive and critical effects of (HR-) reforms within recent decades. Still, there is also evidence about the impact of recent HR reforms on performance, motivation, satisfaction, (un-)ethical behaviour, working conditions etc.

Accusations that civil services are not innovative, not ready to reform and suffering from reform inertia are clearly wrong. Contrary to this, HR reforms seem to produce as many positive as negative reform outcomes. Despite these many changes, the public perception is still that civil servants work in an environment, which is clearly separated from the private sector. In some countries the civil servant is seen as a protected person, set apart from the outside world. In reality, customer and citizen orientation, as well as transparency, have increased and many working conditions have been aligned to those in the private sector. Nowadays the differences between public and private employees in status, working time, pay, pensions, holidays, recruitment and competency requirements are less significant than they were previously.

However, despite these many reforms, surprisingly little is known about the effects of organisational and human resource management reforms. One reason for this is obvious and relatively banal. There are many methodological problems involved in measuring the impact of HRM reforms on performance, motivation and work satisfaction.

One reason for the lack of evidence as to the effects of public service and HR evaluations can be found in the specific historical development of public service organisations. In the early 20th century only few public organisations conducted public service- and HR evaluations. Organisational performance assessments were even more the exception.

Because of the prevalence of national economical, institutional, social and political differences identifying common successes, role models and best practices in the field of "successful HR management" remains a huge theoretical and practical challenge. Thus, analysing positive and negative reform outcomes in the public services of the EU Member States involves some of the greatest challenges and difficulties in legal, political and administrative science.

However, at present, the discussion about what has been achieved during the last few decades is the most controversial issue of all. Whereas it seems to be relatively easy to conclude on public services failures (and to identify cases of corruption, public scandals, waste of public money, organisational and individual poor performance, organisational inefficiency, administrative burdens and red tape etc.), it is much more complicated (and less popular) to identify positive reform outcomes. One explanation for this may be that positive results of administrative reforms are more difficult to define because performance standards are not limited to economic as well as quality and customer satisfaction criteria. Instead they also include constitutional, regulatory and political standards, as well as the duty to serve the common interest.

Stereotypes and images about public services are common all over the globe and have existed for long. Many still exist today and are the same in all Member States despite differences in culture, tradition and structure. In his dissertation, Steven van de Walle[333] illustrates an important paradox. When citizens consider public services as individual services which are no different to private services (e.g., banks, insurance, companies, shopping), their evaluations will probably be focused more on the service quality actually experienced[334] and not on whether they are services provided by the state administration. However, even if most people are satisfied with specific public services, they tend to be negative towards the public sector in general. Similarly, it seems that specific objects are always perceived more favourably than general ones. For example, it is very possible that citizens combine a positive attitude towards a specific train, with a negative attitude towards the public railways company[335]. The same perception is true as regards the term 'public service' or 'public administration'. People may have positive attitudes towards and perceptions of specific public services (police, water supply, fire brigade, etc.), but negative attitudes towards public services in general. For example, even if people are satisfied with the motorway network, the police, the telephone service, water supply, the courts, justice, col-

333 Steven van de Walle, Perceptions of Administrative Performance: The Key to Trust in Government? Dissertation at the Catholic University of Leuven, 2004.

334 Ibid.

335 Ibid., p. 189.

lection of household rubbish, this does not mean that they are satisfied with the public services in general. Katz et al. found that even though users were satisfied with the way service agencies handled their problem and with fair treatment, this opinion was not necessarily generalised to all agencies or government offices. However, when citizens felt they were treated badly, they generalised their experience to the public sector as a whole.[336]

Today, concepts such as participation, communication, transparency, change management, performance management, decentralisation of HR responsibilities, knowledge management, lifelong learning, total quality management (TQM), value management, competence management, accountability, and performance-related pay (PRP) have been introduced in almost all national public administrations. In addition, in many public services, decentralisation trends were introduced, organisational structures and recruitment procedures have changed, budgets reduced, working time patterns were modified, performance management systems adopted, (top) officials were nominated on time, pay- and pension systems reformed and – more generally – alignment trends between the public- and private sector continued. Also within the public services, the civil servants have become more demanding and are asking for more responsibility, job control, job autonomy, transparency, pluralism, flexibility, diversity, decentralisation of responsibilities and involvement in decisions.

Despite all reforms, a gap between citizen's expectations and reform measures can be noticed. Whereas many citizens do not believe that the public services have really changed, the public administrations have been very eager to strengthen citizen rights, facilitating access to information, increasing efforts in satisfying citizen- and customer needs and informing citizens about their rights in their fight against any form of maladministration (and against too many "administrative burdens"). Throughout the last few years almost all Member States (and the European institutions) have been very active in fighting against different forms of maladministration[337]. In the meantime, core principles of good administration have been transformed into legally binding rules in almost all Member States of the European Union such as the right:

- to have ones affairs handled impartially and fairly and within a reasonable time;
- to be heard before any individual measure is taken that would affect the citizen adversely;

---

336 Quoted from Steven van de Walle, op. cit., p. 12.
337 Statskontoret, Principles of Good Administration, Stockholm 2005.

- to have access to his or her file, regarding any individual measure that would affect him or her;
- the obligation to state reasons in writing for all decisions;
- the right of access to documents.

The European institutions have also adopted a European Code of Good Administrative Behaviour, which includes substantive principles for establishing a good administration (lawfulness, non-discrimination and proportionality) as well as a number of obligations for the different EU administrations. At the national level, also the Member States have increased their efforts in order to help and support citizens in their fight against any form of maladministration (which includes issues such as unreasonable delay in responding to citizen requests, impoliteness, failure to apply the law or rules properly, failure to provide information etc). Moreover, the Member States and the European Commission have launched an ambitious Action Programme to reduce the administrative burden of existing regulation in the EU. As part of this, a reduction target of 25% was agreed by the EU and Member States to be achieved by 2012.

Thus, whereas many citizens do not believe that the public services have really changed[338], the public administrations have been very eager to strengthen citizen rights, facilitate access to information, increase efforts to satisfy citizen- and customer needs and inform citizens about their rights in their fight against any form of maladministration (and against too many "administrative burdens"). Overall, the present trend towards the introduction of new reforms and growing expectations as well as the call for new values are highly ambivalent developments in all European public services. The requirements for more "transparency" in public policies is one of the best examples: Although transparency is very often linked with "Good Governance", simply introducing more transparency policy outcomes can be very ambivalent and may have as many positive as negative side-effects[339].

Thus, accusations that public services are not innovative, not ready to reform and are suffering from reform inertia are clearly wrong. Nowadays the differences between public and private employees are less significant than they were previously. However, many changes do not seem to have reached the public. Still, most people have perceptions about public services, public servants and working conditions in the public services that reflect the situation from a long

---

338 See for exp. Social Research Institute, Survey of Public Attitudes Towards Conduct in Public Life, London 2006.

339 Christopher Hood/David Heald, Transparency: The Key to better Government, Oxford University Press, 2006.

time ago. At the same time, public expectations as to the tasks, responsibilities and the quality of the public services are rising and are becoming increasingly contradictory.

In order to shed more light on the negative as well as the positive effects of public service and HR reforms a comparative study was carried out under the Slovenian EU Presidency (2008) which should evaluate the effects of a number of HRM reforms in the Member States of the EU[340]. The survey was carried out thanks to the official support of 363 higher public employees and HR experts from all of the EU Member States[341] (from the central governmental level) who contributed to the study. Furthermore, the empirical findings were discussed and cross-checked in two additional workshops with HRM experts (mostly personnel managers) from all Member States of the EU. The workshops were held in January 2008 (in Brussels) and in April 2008 (in Slovenia).

Since all respondents to the study worked for the central governmental level this put some restrictions on the scope of this study. Only in rare cases were respondents able to answer for the whole civil service and also not for the regional and local level. The participation rate to the survey and to the questionnaire (363 replies from higher ranking public employees from the central public services) allowed for the identification of general trends on the central level. However, the participation rate also shows that the data was still too low and probably rather elitist in the sense that the percentage of (top) managers was relatively high and all respondents had to answer in the English language (which is not a custom in many countries). The following discussions present the main findings of that study.

3. Changing public services and the perception of change

As we have seen in this study, at the beginning of the 21st century there is no longer a civil service model that could be described as a 'classical bureaucratic career model'. Moreover, pure bureaucratic career systems or pure non-bureaucratic systems simply do not exist (anymore). Instead of clear-cut categories, there seems to be a trend towards a middle way where Member States "throw" away a number of classical bureaucratic features. At the same time they keep some elements which used to be specific to the civil service (e.g., higher job security, public law status, specific recruitment procedures). Despite this, an

---

340 Demmke/Henökl/Moilanen, Slovenian Study, op. cit.

341 From these were 198 higher employees, 122 line managers and 43 top managers. See Demmke/Henökl/Moilanen, Slovenian Study, op. cit.

analysis of the different national HR systems shows that there are considerable differences between the HR systems in the various countries but no trend towards a European model of civil service.

Most respondents to the above-mentioned Slovenian study from all Member States, administrative traditions, public service systems, staff categories, ages and sexes evaluated these public service and HR reform developments as overall positive. However, there are some important clarifications to be made. For example, top managers see the developments as more positive than other categories of staff. Whereas more than 80% of all top managers made a positive assessment, approximately 60% of the employees had a positive opinion[342]. Despite these differences the positive ratings from the employees are still considerably higher than the negative ratings. Moreover, the overall positive evaluation of the reform developments differs amongst the different administrative traditions. Figures range between 85% (from Mediterranean countries) and 47% (from Eastern European career tradition)[343]. In more detail, respondents from Hungary, Lithuania, Poland and Slovakia were less optimistic than their colleagues from the other countries. Surprisingly, the respondents from the Eastern European position countries (Czech Republic and Latvia) were much more positive than their colleagues from the other Eastern European career-system countries.

Although a vast majority of respondents to the Slovenian study considered that HR policies have improved during the last years, this does not mean that they are considered as competitive with HR policies in the private sector. Concerning almost all HR policies, the respondents replied that they consider the working conditions in the private sector to be better than those in the public sector. Overall these replies were disastrous for the public services.

As can be discerned from Figure 9, competitive advantages of the public sector are only seen in the field of working time, involvement of staff in management decisions and pension policies (and partly health policies). However, as regards the pension policies, the situation in the national public services differs enormously. Whereas most pension systems in Cyprus, Greece, Spain and Portugal are seen as competitive with the private sector, this cannot be said for the public pension systems in Eastern Europe which are seen as partly much worse than those existing in the private sector. Here, 25% of all respondents of this study replied that the pension systems would not be competitive with those in the pri-

---

342 Demmke/Henökl/Moilanen, Slovenian Study, op. cit., p. 52.
343 Ibid., p. 53.

vate sector[344]. Compared to these figures, only 8% of all respondents from the above-mentioned Mediterranean countries were of the opinion that the pension systems are not competitive. As regards the latter group, 81% of all respondents are of the opinion that the pension systems are competitive (compared to 32% in the Eastern European countries and 33% in the Scandinavian countries)[345].

Figure 9: HR policy performance – private services vs. public administration

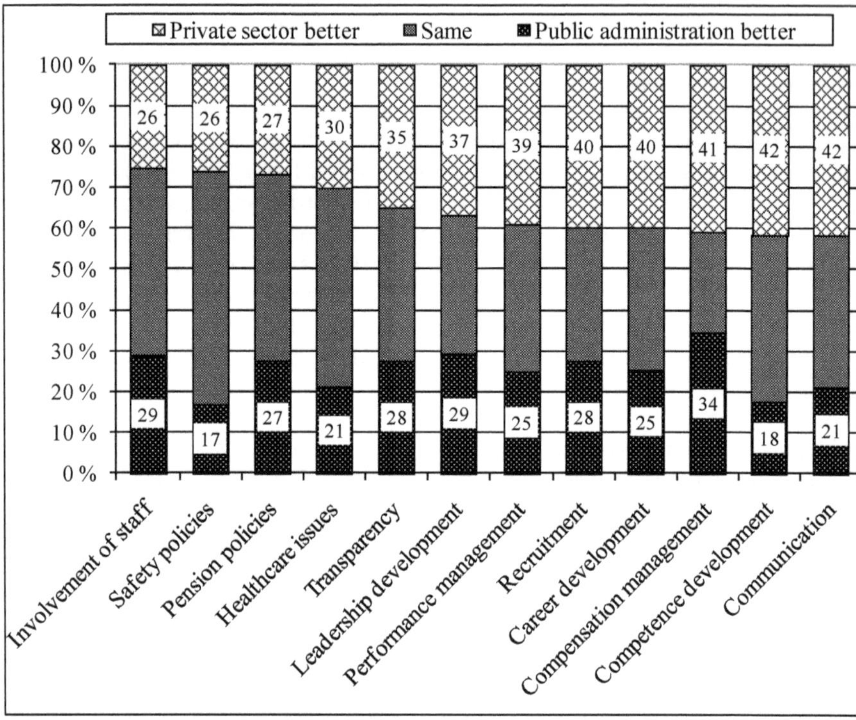

Source: Demmke, Henökl and Moilanen, Slovenian Study, op. cit., p. 79

From an individual point of view the statistics also suggest that public pensions for top- and middle-level managers are more competitive with private sector pensions than those for employees. The same remarks can be made as to the quality of healthcare and safety policies. Whereas in some country clusters these

344 Demmke/Henökl/Moilanen, Slovenian Study, op. cit., p. 79.
345 Ibid.

policies are seen as superior to those existing in the private sector, in other countries these are seen as worse and not competitive.

4. Public pay versus private pay

As regards pay issues, the Slovenian study reveals no surprising news. As can be seen, the great majority of respondents replied that salaries in the public services are not competitive in relation to the private sector.

Figure 10: Public services' competitiveness in relation to private sector

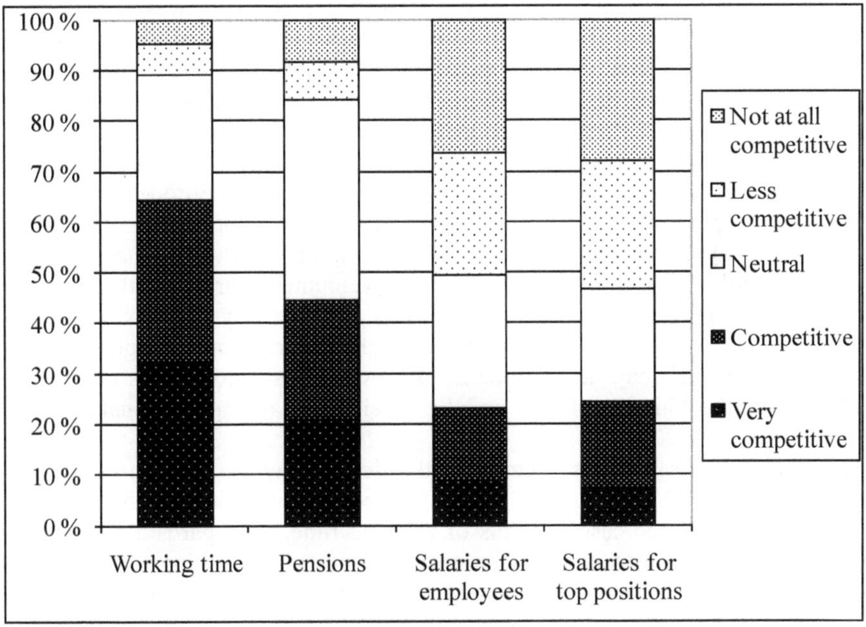

Source: Demmke, Henökl and Moilanen, Slovenian Study, op. cit., p. 84

However, it is interesting to make some geographical distinctions. For example 38% of all respondents from some Eastern European countries were of the opinion that salaries for employees are not competitive at all. This is in striking contrast with the situation in Austria, France, Germany, Belgium and Luxemburg, where only few respondents were of the opinion that the salaries of employees are not competitive[346]. In addition, different categories of staff differed with regard to the perception of whether the salaries of public employees are competi-

346 Demmke/Henökl/Moilanen, Slovenian Study, op. cit., p. 84.

tive with those in the private sector. Mostly, the top management had a much more positive attitude than the public employees. Whereas only 7% of all top managers who replied to the study believe that the salaries of employees are not competitive at all, this figure was almost 30% among employees[347]. Thus, top managers and employees differ a lot in their opinions regarding the competitive situation of public employees' salaries.

The situation was slightly different as regards the salaries of top managers. Overall, only 24% were of the opinion that the salaries of top managers are competitive with the salaries in the private sector. Most respondents replied that the salaries are less competitive or not competitive at all. However, also here, important geographical distinctions must be made. Only 8% of all respondents from the Mediterranean countries are of the opinion that the salaries of top managers are competitive; the figure is much higher for the Eastern European countries (36%). In total 73% of all respondents from the continental European countries were of the opinion that the salaries for top managers are not competitive compared to only 38% of the respondents from the Eastern European countries. A more European-wide comparison as regards the developments in the field of pay (better pay, fairer pay, and motivational pay), job security, working time and flexible working time reveals that pay developments are slightly positive. Mostly Scandinavian employees at all levels are relatively happy with the development of pay. In the continental European countries top managers are less satisfied with their pay developments. However, satisfaction levels drop when asked about the "fairness of pay" and the development of "motivational pay"[348].

The greatest contrast to the situation in the field of pay can be seen in the field of working time. Whereas pay is mostly not seen as competitive with the private sector, this is not the case in terms of working time. As regards the latter, the public services seem to be very competitive concerning working time developments and working time flexibility. Most respondents to the study were of the opinion that the working time arrangements in the public services are even very competitive or competitive. The highest degree of competitiveness could be found in the Mediterranean countries with a career system (Spain, Portugal, Cyprus and Greece).

347 Ibid., p. 86.
348 Ibid., p. 88.

Figure 11: Developments of working conditions

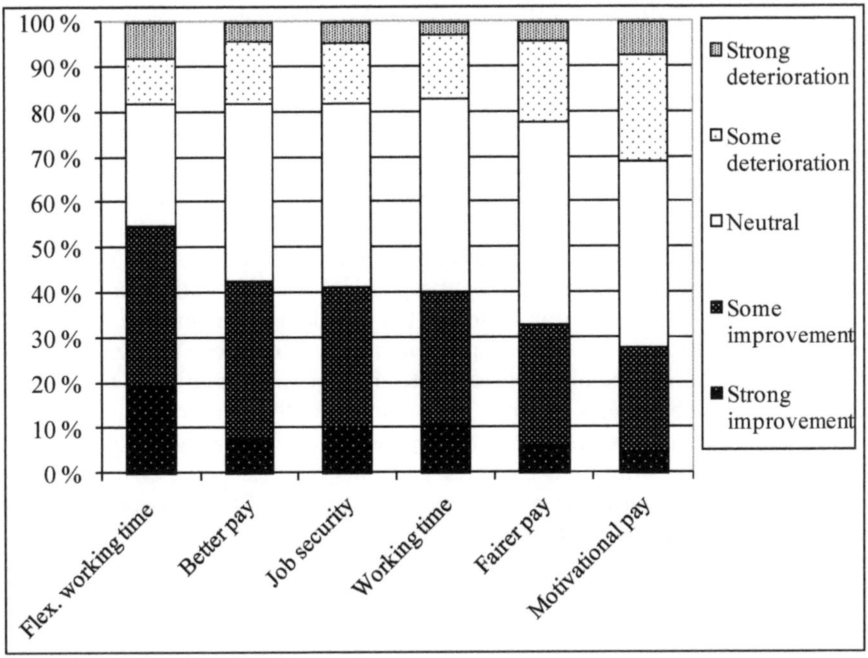

Source: Demmke, Henökl and Moilanen, Slovenian Study, op. cit., p. 89

5. Positive trends in public service reforms

Since evidence on the effects of personnel management is rare, one important interest in the Slovenian study was to get more evidence regarding general developments in the field of HRM policies. We asked the respondents to reply to whether the public services had become more transparent, more customer- and citizen friendly, whether citizens' complaints are managed quicker and whether civil servants have become friendlier. More specifically we also wanted to know whether HR reforms have improved within the last 15 years, administrative costs could be reduced, the public services have become less rule-oriented, anti-discrimination and ethics policies could be modernised etc.

The most positive outcome was the fact that more than 65% of all respondents were of the opinion that the public services have become more customer and citizen friendly. About 11% believed that this is not the case. Another very positive result concerns the fact that citizens' complaints and requests are managed quicker than before[349]. On the other side, the perception of positive and/or negative developments differ (at least sometimes) very much according to the different public service systems, administrative traditions, the different categories of staff and amongst men and women. Thus the perception of the results and effects in the field of reducing administrative costs and bureaucracy are also very much linked to institutional and cultural issues.

Overall, about 45% of all respondents replied that the public services were successful in reducing administrative costs. In many Member States this is seen a very positive development since reducing administrative costs and easing administrative burdens figures high on the political agenda of all countries (and also of the agenda of European Union in the Lisbon agenda context). However, it is important to note the existing great national differences. Whereas 54% of the respondents from the old Member States have a positive opinion, the figures for the new Member States are only 30%. A total of 59% of all respondents from the Continental career-system countries agree that administrative costs were reduced, but only 24% from all Eastern European countries. Some 28% of the respondents from Eastern European countries are even of the opinion that their countries are not successful in reducing costs[350].

It is important to note that almost all categories of employees (top-employees, middle-management and other employees) also reported positively about the developments in these areas. One should note, however, that top managers (62%) are much more positive than employees (36%). Next to the overall positive evaluation of the cost developments in the public services 44% of the respondents from the old Member States and 25% of the new Member States were also of the opinion that rules and bureaucracy could be reduced. A cluster analysis shows that percentages range from almost 52% (in the Scandinavian countries) to 22% (in the Eastern European countries). In the latter countries, 31% of all respondents were of the opinion that rules and bureaucracy had even increased. Especially the respondents from the career-system countries Austria, Belgium, Germany, France, Luxemburg, Hungary, Lithuania, Poland and Slovakia were less positive, whereas the position countries Denmark, Estonia, Finland and Sweden were of the opinion that rules and bureaucracy could be reduced. Thus mostly respondents from the Scandinavian tradition countries believe that bureaucracy could be reduced[351].

---

349 Demmke/Henökl/Moilanen, Slovenian Study, op. cit., p. 54.

350 Ibid., p. 56.

351 Ibid., p. 57.

As regards the question of whether rule and bureaucracy could be reduced significantly differences could be found between employees and top managers. Overall employees are more sceptical of whether these objectives could be achieved (26% are positive) than top managers who are much more optimistic (60%).

Thus, the answers to the question as to whether rules and bureaucracy could be reduced are – although still promising – less positive than those concerning the overall cost developments and cost reduction. These mixed results can be explained by the – almost paradoxical – developments in the continental career system countries, which seem to be very successful in reducing administrative (personnel?) costs. On the other hand, these countries are much less successful in reducing rules and "bureaucracy". The situation is even more problematic in some Eastern European States who have also not succeeded in reducing costs. The most positive developments have taken place in the Scandinavian countries where costs and rules/bureaucracy could be reduced[352].

Another important question concerned the development of customer and citizen satisfaction. In the survey we asked the question of whether the public services have become more citizen- and customer friendly. The answers to this question were also (mostly) positive. Overall 60% of all respondents to this study were of the opinion that the public services have succeeded in becoming more customer/citizen friendly. When analysing the figures in more detail, the positive percentages are slightly higher for the older Member States. Again, top managers were more positive than other public employees and women were more positive than men. Since these differences are considerable they require another in-depth analysis[353]. Unfortunately, there is no space here to discuss these interesting (gender) differences.

The different results regarding the developments in this field indicate again that different public service systems and administrative traditions produce different reform outcomes. Moreover, different categories of staff have sometimes very different perceptions of the impact and effects of HR reforms. As such, perception levels are very much linked to gender and hierarchical (or power) issues. As such top managers are almost always more positive than other public employees. At least as regards some issues, women are either more positive or more critical than men. Although these findings are not altogether surprising it would be nev-

352 Demmke/Henökl/Moilanen, Slovenian Study, op. cit., p. 56-59.
353 Ibid., p. 59.

ertheless important (and interesting) to further invest more research in identifying the reasons for these differences.

6. Successes and failures in selected HR policies

Another objective in the Slovenian study was to analyse whether progress could be achieved in certain HR policy areas. To achieve this, respondents were asked questions regarding the development of remuneration policies (better pay, fairer pay, motivational pay), job security, working time and working time flexibility, job responsibility, job autonomy, training, vacations, work-life balance, leadership, the distribution of top positions amongst men and women, diversity and anti-discrimination policies, stress etc.

6.1. Positive features

6.1.1. General positive development: which policies are improving?

From a general point of view, the respondents from all Member States were of the opinion that improvements could be noted in the following HR policies:

- Job security (only in the new Member States),
- Development of qualification of civil servants,
- Flexible working time,
- (some aspects of) Pay policies,
- Recruitment policies are faster and more transparent (old Member States),
- Knowledge management,
- Job responsibility,
- Job autonomy,
- Work life balance,
- Vacations,
- Top positions for women,
- Equality,
- Anti-discrimination,
- Diversity,
- Leadership,
- Training, and
- Ethics.

Amongst these policies the strongest improvements could be noted in the field of flexible working time. In total 19% of all respondents reported strong improvements in this field and 55% of all respondents noted general improvements. However, the situation seems to be more positive in the older 15 Member

States. In this country cluster 66% of all respondents observe strong or some improvements compared to 45% of all respondents from the new Member States. Many respondents (46%) also observed improvements in the field of work/life balance and vacations and leave (45%). Another success story seems to be recruitment policies ("Recruitment policies are faster and more transparent"). Especially the old Member States seem to have successfully introduced selection methods with a view to achieving faster and more efficient recruitments (for example through the introduction of a "fast-track" recruitment system). The same is true as to the ability of the public services to retain staff/leaders in the public services. Also here, the older Member States are more successful than the new Member States. However, one should also note once more that top managers see the developments in the field of recruitment and training staff/leaders more positively than all other categories of employees[354].

6.1.2. Decentralisation of responsibilities, job autonomy and job control

The replies to the Slovenian Study also confirm an ongoing trend towards the decentralisation and delegation of HR responsibilities to line managers and public employees. As a result, many employees observe strong or some improvements as regards the delegation of job responsibilities and the degree of job autonomy and job control. Overall 59% of all respondents are of the opinion that employees were allocated more job responsibilities[355]. Not surprisingly, employees from the Scandinavian countries are most positive about the degree of responsibilities at work. This result confirms the result of a study which was carried out under the Austrian EU Presidency[356] (which came to the conclusion that HR responsibilities are most decentralised in the Anglo-Saxon and Scandinavian countries). However, many employees also from Spain, Portugal, Greece and Cyprus (who formerly had relatively centralised HR responsibilities) observe strong improvements towards the delegation of more responsibilities.

Moreover, public employees are – generally – increasingly positive towards the degree of autonomy and the amount of job control. Overall, 71% of all respondents indicated that they are very positive or positive as to the degree of job responsibility, and 61% with the degree of autonomy and job control. In addition, many employees observe further improvements in these areas. Not surprisingly,

354 Demmke/Henökl/Moilanen, Slovenian Study, op. cit., p. 61.

355 Ibid., p. 63.

356 Demmke/Hammerschmid/Meyer, Decentralisation and Accountability as Focus of Public Modernisation Reforms, Office of Official Publications of the EU, Luxemburg, 2006.

top managers are even more positive than other employees. However, overall all categories of staff evaluate the present situation as positive. These overall positive findings contradict the widespread perception that work in the public services is hierarchical and employees have little responsibility and job control. In reality, many public employees are satisfied with the degree of decentralisation of responsibilities and the amount of job autonomy and job control[357].

6.1.3. Developments in the field of anti-discrimination and diversity

Other areas where improvements could be noted are the areas of anti-discrimination, diversity management and ethics. The vast majority of employees who responded to the Slovenian Study are of the opinion that the equality between the sexes had improved (63%)[358].

Overall, 73% of the respondents from the old Member States observe improvements, and 54% of the respondents from the new Member States are of the same opinion. A similar pattern can also be seen regarding the distribution of top positions between men and women. Whereas 55% of all respondents from the older Member States observed that improvements are occurring, this percentage was "only" 47% in the new Member States. Mostly the respondents from the Mediterranean countries (Cyprus, Spain, Portugal, and Greece) and – to a lesser extent – from Austria, France, Germany, Belgium and Luxemburg were of the opinion that more women were recruited in top positions. From these figures one may conclude that anti-discrimination and diversity policies are more advanced in the older than the newer Member States. However, the general trend is positive in all Member States[359].

Despite this country-wide comparison, another important difference has to be noted with regard to the differences in opinion between men and women (see Table 42 on page 217). In all Member States, women are more critical than men as regards the question of whether improvements (in relation to the distribution of top positions between men and women) have taken place and also whether improvements have taken place in the field of diversity policies. Almost twice as many women than men are of the opinion that the equality of sexes has not improved.

---

357 At this place we should highlight again that almost all respondents to this study were from the central level and assume relatively high positions. See Demmke/Henökl/Moilanen, Slovenian Study, op. cit., p. 61.

358 Demmke/Henökl/Moilanen, Slovenian Study, op. cit., p. 65.

359 Ibid.

Table 42: Development of gender equality by sex and by position

(Frequencies in parenthesis)

		Improved	Same	Deteriorated	Total
Employee	Male	62 (41)	29 (19)	9 (6)	100 (66)
	Female	57 (71)	23 (29)	19 (24)	100 (124)
Middle management	Male	66 (33)	22 (11)	12 (6)	100 (50)
	Female	46 (31)	33 (22)	21 (14)	100 (67)
Top management	Male	79 (15)	16 (3)	5 (1)	100 (19)
	Female	68 (15)	14 (3)	18 (4)	100 (22)
	Total	59 (206)	25 (87)	16 (55)	100 (348)

Source: Demmke, Henökl and Moilanen, Slovenian Study, op. cit., p. 67

These differences can also be observed in relation to the developments in the field of diversity policies. From a general point of view 60% of all respondents noted that improvements had taken place in the area of anti-discrimination. More particularly, mostly countries like Austria, France, Germany, Belgium, Luxemburg, Portugal, Spain, Greece and Cyprus noted progress in the area.

6.2. Negative developments

From a general point of view, the respondents from all administrative traditions were of the opinion that deteriorations could be noted in the following HR policies:

- Stress and time pressure,
- Pay policies (fairer pay, motivational pay),
- Performance assessment,
- Rewarding staff for good performance,
- Poor performers policies,
- Promotion policies,
- Recruiting potential talented candidates,
- Retention policies.

One of the most critical developments in all European public services seems to be the fact that stress levels are rising and time pressure is increasing. More than 42% of all respondents were of the opinion that stress-related developments and "time pressure" were negative and that the current developments led to deteriorations. The respondents were also highly critical as to the current developments in the field of performance management and promotion policies. Especially the developments in the field of poor performance policies and (to a lesser extent rewarding policies) are seen to be not successful. The picture related to recruitment policies is very mixed. A third of all respondents are of the opinion that recruitment policies are either successful or not successful.

Figure 12: Developments in performance management and recruitment policies

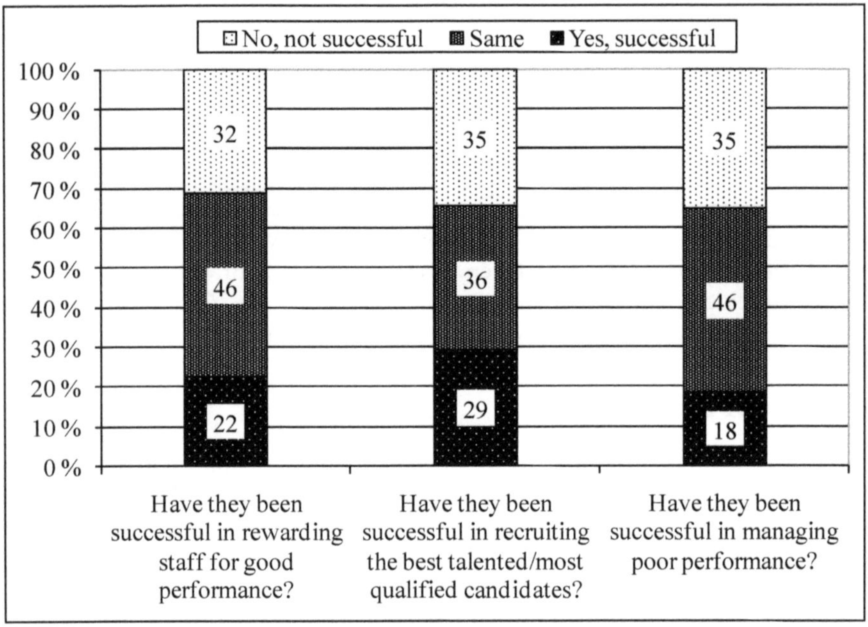

Source: Demmke, Henökl and Moilanen, Slovenian Study, op. cit., p. 69

Despite these challenges, the greatest problems can be found in the field of promotion and performance assessment (see Table 43 on page 219). As regards both policy fields, a relatively broad majority of respondents noted that promotion policies have not become fairer and performance assessment not less subjective. In relation to both issues less than 22% of all respondents were positive about the developments in these fields.

Table 43: Attitudes towards promotion and performance assessment procedures

(Frequencies in parenthesis)

	Promotion procedures are fairer	Performance assessment systems are less subjective
Fully agree	4,0 (13)	3,8 (12)
Agree	17,0 (55)	18,2 (57)
Neutral	45,5 (147)	41,9 (131)
Disagree	21,1 (68)	20,4 (64)
Fully disagree	12,4 (40)	15,7 (49)
Total	100,0 (323)	100,0 (313)

Source: Demmke, Henökl and Moilanen, Slovenian Study, op. cit., p. 70

The situation seems to be particularly worrying in countries like Austria, Germany, France, Belgium and Luxemburg as well as in a number of Mediterranean countries. Many respondents from these countries were not of the opinion that promotion procedures had become fairer. Only the respondents from the position-based systems, i.e. Scandinavian countries (DK, EE, FI, SE) and Eastern European Position System (CZ, LV) were slightly positive. In particular, the developments in the field of performance assessment are not perceived in a positive way. Only 19% of all respondents agreed that performance rewards are more transparent than before and are allocated quicker. Overall, most respondents do not agree that performance assessment systems have become less subjective. Only the respondents from the Scandinavian countries evaluate performance assessment systems (much) less critically than their colleagues from the Mediterranean countries and some continental career-system countries.

Other critical developments concerned the development of promotion procedures. In total, only 22% agreed that present performance assessment systems are less subjective. Again, top managers are much more optimistic than employees as regards the question of whether the public services are successful in rewarding good performance. Whereas 40% of all top managers responded that the developments have been successful, only 21% of the employees shared this opinion. Top managers are also much more optimistic than employees in view of the successes of poor performers' policies. However, positive figures are very low. Overall, only 18% of all respondents are of the opinion that managing poor performance has been successful. From these, 26% were top managers but only 14% were employees. Especially the replies from the Mediterranean countries showed a particularly high percentage of dissatisfaction with existing poor performers' policies[360].

7. Successes and failures in various administrative contexts

The results of the Slovenian study were very much in line with our civil service survey. Both surveys show that the nature and effects of public service reforms must be seen much more in the context of the different public administrative traditions, geographical and cultural differences as well as the importance of different organisational structures. In a way the findings of the studies give a fascinating insight into the differences and similarities of the public service systems in Europe. Whereas in some areas similar reform trends and reform outcomes can be observed, in other fields differences are prevailing or – even increasing. Still, continental- and Eastern European, Scandinavian, Anglo-Saxon, South-Eastern and Mediterranean countries "produce" their "own" successes and failures as a result of public service reforms. However, as the outcomes show, many Eastern European countries face (more) challenges that do not exist in the former "old" Member States. It is also difficult to judge whether bureaucratic career-system countries face more or fewer challenges than post-bureaucratic countries. What is clear is that both systems face different challenges. Another interesting result is that continental career-system countries seem to be successful in reducing administrative costs. On the other hand, career-system countries face more challenges with (a too high number of) rules in the field of HRM. Other findings in the Slovenian Study (which could not be presented here) reveal that "civil servants" are (mostly) satisfied with their work. In most cases, they are ready to take over new responsibilities and enjoy more job autonomy and job control. In this respect, the traditional image of the public executor who receives orders and executes them definitely belongs to the past.

However, the results also reveal an interesting paradox: whereas most respondents to the Slovenian Study considered that HR policies have improved over the last few years, they are not happy with career development policies, performance assessment, performance management issues, stress developments, pay policies and – to a lesser extent – their leaders. Thus, although the modern public service world is much less "dull and boring" than is commonly acknowledged, much more needs to be done in order to call public HR policies a "success. This also concerns the need to invest more in "perception management" as most public officials themselves believe that HR policies are not competitive with those in the private sector. A totally different question is whether this perception reflects the reality.

---

360 Demmke/Henökl/Moilanen, Slovenian Study, op. cit., p. 71.

VII. FUTURE OF THE CIVIL SERVICE – DO WE STILL NEED CIVIL SERVANTS?

1. Introduction

As we have seen in this study a tremendous reform trend is taking place. This shift is bringing a change in working conditions, values and organisational structures. Moreover, the differences in work, working conditions and contractual relationships between civil servants and other public employees are decreasing. All of these developments raise the question about the legitimacy of a specific civil service. This is one of the fundamental results of this study. Do we really need a specific civil service in the 21st century? Many current reform developments put into question the legitimacy of – at least – the traditional civil service. Consequently, in this chapter we will discuss the most important arguments in favour and against a specific civil service. We will also discuss the potential consequences of what would happen if a specific civil service were abolished. Here, our search for benchmarks has led us to the United States and, more specifically, the States of Florida and Georgia.

The purpose of this chapter is not to present European-wide conclusions and recommendations. As we have seen before in this study, all suggestions for reforms must take into consideration the existing traditions, legal philosophies, culture, experience and differences in political systems.

1.1. Arguments for differences between civil servants and other employees

Arguments *for* maintaining a specific civil service status that differs from an ordinary employment contract are often based on the following assertions.

Proponents for maintaining differences between public and private sector employees argue that work in the public service is specific and – by nature – different from work in the private sector. Consequently, civil servants should also be treated differently because they:

- are given considerable power and responsibilities;
- set legal and normative standards for citizens;
- have a responsibility to provide leadership;
- may intervene directly in the basic rights of citizens, e.g., police;

- are financed and paid from the public purse in order to carry out work for the public[361].

The specific tasks of civil servants also require a specific link to the state. In particular, those employees who are directly participating in the exercise of powers, who are intervening in the fundamental rights of the citizens, who spend public money and who are safeguarding the general interest of the state (or of other public authorities) should have a specific status which binds them to a public interest. Since civil servants spend public money, raise taxes, hunt down criminals, protect the society against enemies, diseases, pandemics etc., they must take decisions which have a tremendous impact on the fundamental rights of citizens. The level of power or responsibility awarded to public officials can be seen as requiring the imposition of some specific duties, rights and obligations for carrying out that role properly. For all these important tasks, it is important that the public servants exercise their role properly, and act lawfully, honestly and loyally without acquiring any personal advantage. In short, this means that they must have a specific ethos as the exercise of public tasks requires fairness and leadership as regards a number of principles (equity, equality, non-discrimination, impartiality, loyalty and neutrality). In particular, experiences in many former communist countries show that the public service can be used as an instrument for the political elite. But the need for a specific civil service is also seen on a less political scale. For example, it can be argued that teachers must be civil servants because they bear special responsibilities in educating school children, by deciding on the futures of millions of pupils. Thus, teachers exercise a real important public function for the state and the society and it is imperative that they do it in a professional, fair and impartial way.

Following this argument, it is important to define clearly those categories and posts which fall within these categories. Some Member States have done so for work in the ministries, agencies, courts, police, fire prevention, defence sector, etc. In particular, judges, the judicial authorities, police, defence bodies and the financial sector are in need of specific working conditions. Consequently, many Member States do not allow police officers the right to strike.

Another important argument for a specific status, specific working conditions, specific recruitment procedures, life-time tenure or unlimited contracts, etc., is

---

361 National Centre for Social Research/Centre for Research into Elections and Social Trends, Guiding Principles: Public Attitudes towards Conduct in Public Life, January 2003, p. 22.

to reduce as much as possible the risk of too much political influence[362] and instability of the government. According to the French philosophy, the principle argument in favour of the lifetime principle and a specific remuneration system is the protection of the civil servant. The employment guarantee is also an independence guarantee against all pressures, either private or political. But this protection is not sufficient in itself. It is also necessary that they benefit from a protection *"against all threats, violence (...) etc."* from which they could be victim when exercising their position"[363]. Seen from this logic it is precisely the current trend towards alignment which leads to a blurring of boundaries between the public and private sector, closer contacts between the private and public sector, more direct exchanges with citizens and companies, more mobility between the public and private sector etc., which in turn provokes discussion about the need for a specific status or ethical status.

Another argument for maintaining traditional civil service features is performance. Despite popular doubts, there is no denying that most Member States with relatively traditional civil service systems are performing well. Almost all existing benchmarking studies on public sector performance cannot prove that reformed public services perform better than traditional public services. In addition, countries with high public expenditures mostly have a good economic performance and are highly competitive countries. Indeed, as unfounded as some of these arguments look to most people, they are grounded on traditional and long-standing assertions that are supported by many. In addition, proponents of a specific civil service status sometimes argue that many of the new management reforms do not produce only positive results. In fact, many reforms have also produced new problems (see Table 44).

---

362 Politicisation as such can be interpreted in many ways: public servants working in a political environment; ministers or others intervening in the recruitment and appointment on merit; advice and expertise selected and judged on the basis of whether an individual is "one of us"; a system which is based on political appointees; and performance-related rewards and individual careers depending on the commitment to an ideology, whether it is that of a minister or non-minister. Alternatively, the individual perception that giving unwelcome advice may prejudice that individual's career.

363 Section 11 of the law of 13 July 1983 pertaining to the rights and obligations of civil servants.

Table 44: Shortcomings and problems in the field of HRM in many reformed public services

• problems in performance measurement and fair treatment of employees;
• new administrative burdens due to the introduction of new targets, performance contracts and performance measurement;
• growing importance of (poor) leadership as a consequence of the decentralisation of more responsibilities;
• more value conflicts and emergence of new ethical dilemmas;
• more fragmentation of the national civil services and coordination challenges;
• more stress and overwork of employees (also related to downsizing policies);
• frustration because of new budgetary constraints;
• too much focus on results instead of quality, administrative law;
• new rules (particularly due to new accountability requirements) despite trends to deregulate and attempts to introduce regulatory impact assessments;
• lack of career development, promotion opportunities and perspectives.

1.2. Civil servant as a dying species?

In those Member States where different categories of public employees are employed (often in the same positions), the legal status of public employees has little or no additional impact on the loyalty and impartiality of the civil servant. It cannot be observed that civil servants act differently than other public employees. Or, in Sweden it cannot be observed that the 99.5% of public employees who are employed under a labour law status carry out their work differently than their colleagues in other Member States.

These developments provoke the question of what would happen if a specific civil service were to be abolished and civil servants were no longer any different to other public employees and employees in the private sector? Would corruption and unethical behaviour increase, would politicisation be enhanced, and would fairness and the rule of law vanish? Are civil servants less politicised than other employees? Are they less corrupt? "Today it is impossible to study the politicisation of the civil service without taking into account the social evolution, political culture and the history of the various countries…"[364]. This means that the introduction of a career system or a specific legal status will not – as probably expected – reduce the politicisation of the national public service. For this, a number of other cultural, political and sociological elements will have to

364 Luc Rouban, Politicisation of the Civil Service, in: Peters/Pierre, op. cit., p. 310.

change too. In fact, having a specific civil service system will not have much impact on the degree of politicisation.

However, it has a different impact on individual and organisational performance. Many experts who are in favour of more alignment reforms so far have offered a number of explanations of why the behaviour and performance of civil servants differs from other employees, e.g., too many rules, too little delegation and decentralisation, too much political influence, too little motivation, not enough performance incentives, no individualised development strategies and tools, decision-making procedures that are too slow. Another widely believed explanation is that public employees have too much protection against being laid off, too few incentives to perform, too little external pressure (from clients and citizens) and too many privileges. With their structures, the story goes, public employees do not have to work hard and well since it will be very difficult to dismiss or discipline them for poor performance. In this scenario, the public sector suffers from too many poor performers.

Opponents of a specific civil service status argue that the tasks of civil servants are not more specific or more valuable than those carried out in the private sector. In addition, critics of traditional civil services point to the disadvantages of traditional career civil services. Their arguments can be summarised as follows.

First argument: even if public tasks are specific, this does not require a specific civil service status or specific legal contractual status. For example, any specific requirements can be easily arranged in an ordinary employment law contract (which is often based on collective agreements).

Second argument: the terms "essential functions of the state" and "safeguarding the general interest" are difficult to interpret. In addition, it is also not possible to argue that civil servants carry out more important tasks than private employees. Are doctors, workers in chemical companies, nuclear power station employees, farmers, bank and biotechnology staff not carrying out public interest tasks?

Third argument: many current reform trends reveal an enormous paradox in many Member States with a specific career system. In these countries, working processes, working conditions and organisation structures are different in private and public organisations. However, there is very little evidence that the actual behaviour of public employees differs from those working in the private sector. In addition, traditional career models suffer from many well-known shortcomings as described in Table 45. But what is then the point of having public employees who are treated differently than other employees?

Table 45: Shortcomings of traditional career civil services

- long decision-making procedures in traditional bureaucratic structures;
- too strong separation between the state and the society;
- too little transparency, openness and citizen orientation;
- too little focus on results;
- too little performance incentives for employees;
- too long and too complex recruitment procedures;
- focus on rigidity and centralisation and too little mobility;
- too much rigidity, e.g., in working time flexibility;
- too strong focus on seniority and political favouritism;
- too little career development possibilities for older staff;
- too little incentives for the young to assume leadership positions;
- too little training and possibilities for lifelong learning.

Fourth argument: the public service is often seen as an apolitical apparatus which is supposed to be neutral when implementing government policies. However, more and more civil service critics agree that this classical model of public service was shaped in a world that no longer exists. Today, the national public services have become much more complex and the separation between the state and the private sector is diminishing through the creation of agencies, public-private partnerships, quangos, outsourced and decentralised authorities, inspection authorities, etc. Consequently, the general development is that the public sector is becoming increasingly intermixed with the private sector. Government is developing into governance.

Fifth argument: in some Member States, the constitution provides for an obligation that public service tasks should generally be carried out by civil servants with a special status. In reality, however more and more contractual employees are also being employed in these countries. Evidence so far suggests that these employees do not perform differently to civil servants. At present, therefore, it is becoming more difficult to justify why civil servants should be treated differently at all. Are these employees really in need of specific ethical obligations? Would these groups perform worse or differently if they were just the same as anybody else?

Sixth argument: today, many Member States are also in a process of changing organisational structures, introducing more mobility, abolishing career structures and seniority principles, and aligning working conditions and working patterns to those existing in the private sector. As regards the civil service status, all of these developments are followed by a bottom-up process, which means that more public employees at local and regional level, rather than central level, are being offered a private law status. As a consequence, the number of public officials with a specific status is decreasing. So far, there is very little evidence that local services deteriorate due to the changing status.

Seventh argument: in a growing number of Member States, changes in the national civil service and also in HRM reforms also derive from the simple conviction that, as far as most of the civil service is concerned, there is no longer any cogent reason to consider the public function performed by the state to be of greater value than the functions designated to the private sector[365], so no greater value is attached to the public interest than to the private[366]. However, this popular conviction challenges not only career systems, but also the traditional justification for a specific civil servant status and specific ethics. When the state ceases to be above society and stands alongside it, a special relationship between public servants and the state seems superfluous. In addition, this makes civil servants with a specific legal status dispensable. While it is true that civil servants work with a view to protecting order, life and freedom, they have only taken on a job different to an employee working in a bank or a chemical plant who is fulfilling an equally valuable function in his or her job (which is essential to ensure the stability and preservation of the social system). A doctor working in a private hospital therefore performs just as important a function as a public servant such as a police officer or tax official. In addition, it would be difficult to argue why teachers should be civil servants with specific ethics in one country if they perform well in other countries without that civil service status.

Eighth argument: specific structural and organisational differences between public and private employment are not important for upholding specific ethical requirements and for carrying out public functions properly. What is more important for establishing an efficient and effective civil service are good working conditions, an appropriate administrative culture, openness, accountability, fairness and legal correctness, etc. For example, the fact that Sweden has a very low level of corruption seems to justify this opinion that working conditions and culture are more important than specific structures and questions of status.

Ninth argument: in many Member States, civil servants are more expensive than other public employees.

---

365 See Christoph Demmke, Civil Services between Tradition and Reform, EIPA, Maastricht 2004.

366 Ibid.

Table 46: Are differences between the public and private sector necessary? Considering the case of Sweden

Traditional Bureaucratic Principles	The case of Sweden
Specific ethical requirements (e.g., taking an oath, specific principles, codes of ethics, rules on conflicts of interest, values)	Generally, ethics are better managed by an integrity-based approach and less by a compliance-based approach (although generally applicable rules are also important instruments). A specific public ethos is important. However, it is difficult to generate in the Swedish public service
Specific public law status and enhanced job security, e.g., life-time tenure, more difficult to dismiss civil servants	No lifetime tenure needed but high job security
Specific and centralised pay and social security systems	Recognition that public service is competing in the market, no further differences necessary. Pay should be decentralised
Specific organisational structure and careers	No need to have a closed off bureaucratic organisation and careers which differ from other organisations. However, principles such as hierarchy and formalised treatment, good administration etc. are needed just as everywhere else
Specific recruitment, procedures	Recruitment should fit the purpose needed to get the competencies needed but there is no explicit reason for specific recruitment procedures
Rule-oriented HRM (need to centralise certain responsibilities in HRM), e.g., pay, right to strike, social security, working time	No need for centralisation. Equality and fairness can be attained through other means
Specific working conditions	Specific working conditions only needed in the military and for judges

In other words, depending on the nature of the various positions, there is no need for a specific public service (organisational) and specific public service requirements, e.g., ethical requirements could be laid down and arranged in individual employment contracts. Alternatively, differences are indispensable in order to guarantee a specific public service behaviour. Surprisingly, we still have very little knowledge, empirical evidence and hard facts which could validate or reject one of the two positions.

2. What if statutory civil servants were abolished?

In the future much of the administrative reform that will be conducted will no longer be done in the belief of the market as the better provider for public services. Instead, the focus of the debate is likely to become much more pragmatic and at the same time dominated by effectiveness, efficiency and sustainability considerations. Another future trend will be to make exchanges between the private sector, citizens and the public bureaucracy easier. Overall, there will be a much stronger "emphasis on proximity – if not physical, at least technological – between the public sector and clients"[367]. It may also be that the future holds a sizeable civil service because it remains a fairly labour-intensive sector. Thus, there will not be less "government", but different government. It is also likely that a civil service will continue to exist. However, as the results of our study show it is unclear whether and how the civil servants will differ from the public employees (but also from private sector employees) in the future.

In general, supporters and opponents of eliminating the differences between public and private employees make a number of predictions about the beneficial or negative effects for the performance and stability of public sector employment. Mostly, critics of alignment and privatisation policies argue that a total privatisation would lead to a decline in loyalty to the organisation, increase the danger of conflicts of interests and provoke political instability, etc. Instead, partisans of privatisation and alignment may argue that a too strong separation of the public and private sector would contradict new developments in almost all modern societies which require new models of governance. Furthermore, civil service reforms will also free civil servants and managers from ineffective and inefficient bureaucratic restraints, increase their authority and flexibility, improve performance by individuals and organisations and give employees more control and responsibility over work. In addition, the alignment of working conditions between the public and private sector, the possibility of dismissing employees (other than for disciplinary reasons), the introduction of performance contracts and the individualisation of pay would lead to higher performance levels, as employees would be more motivated due to the fear of losing their jobs as a result of poor performance (in extreme cases).

---

367 B. Guy Peters/Jon Pierre (eds.), Handbook of Public Administration, 2nd edition, SAGE, London, Thousand Oaks, New Delhi, 2003, p. 4.

In 1982, Niessen in his report to the Dutch government underlined the fact that many private individuals exercise tasks for the public good and no greater value should be attached to the public interest than to the private[368]. Niessen's report not only challenged the traditional career systems, but also the traditional justification for specific organisational structures and a specific legal status for civil servants. If the civil servant appears identical to a bank employer or a farmer, a special legal relationship would seem superfluous. Therefore the question arises whether a specific status and specific working conditions are needed in order to carry out public tasks properly.

Niessen argued that private employees fulfil an equally valuable role for the society, irrespective of whether they are working in a bank, a chemical plant or in the field of biotechnology (which is essential to ensure the stability and preservation of the social system). Consequently, a technician in a nuclear power station, a doctor or a teacher perform just as important a function as a police officer or a tax official in a ministry. In addition, it would be difficult to argue why teachers (if they are civil servants) should be civil servants with specific ethics in one country if they perform well in other countries without that civil service status. All these arguments support the position that "civil servants are not different because they are civil servants." In fact, differences in mentality, motivation or job attitude have more to do with individual characteristics and the sector in which they work, but not with the fact that people have a specific legal status and work in a specific organisational environment. Today, this opinion is widely shared in the Member States.

In Austria an interesting discussion unfolded in 2008 as to the future of the legal regime of public employees[369]. Austria employs civil servants under public law

---

368 C.R. Niessen, Preliminary report to the Dutch Government 1982, Bestaat er aanleiding de rechtspositionele verschillen tussen ambtenaren en civielrechtlijke werknemers te handhaven? [Is it necessary to maintain a distinction between civil servants and private sector employees regarding legal status?], p. 146.

369 It should be noted that – unlike the situation in Germany – the Austrian constitution does not require that certain public tasks must be carried out by civil servants. However, some constitutional principles require the employment of civil servants. ("Ein allgemeiner Funktionsvorbehalt in dem Sinn, dass Beamten zwingend die Ausübung aller hoheitlichen Befugnisse zu übertragen wäre, gilt nach österreichischem B-VG bekanntlich nicht (vgl Art 33 Abs 4 dt GG).4 Ein solcher ist – jedenfalls (…) – auch nicht etwa mittelbar aus Art 20 Abs 1 B-VG ableitbar.5 Das heißt, dass auch Vertragsbediensteten hoheitliche Befugnisse übertragen werden können. ….Da eine Reihe verfassungsrechtlicher Regelungen die Mitwirkung von Beamten bei der Aufgabenbesorgung im Bundesdienst vorsieht, darf das Beamtentum keinesfalls zur Gänze abgeschafft oder auch nur in eine völlig unbedeutende Rolle gedrängt werden.

and public employees under labour law in the Austrian federal public service. However, the distinction between both legal regimes has become blurred during the last decades. The Austrian Länder have their own civil services and enjoy wide discretion in regulating the working conditions of their civil servants. This has led to an interesting (but also inconsistent) laboratory of civil service reforms. Whereas some Länder have abolished a specific public law of civil servants within their jurisdictions, others have kept it. However, this overlap of different legal regimes and different types of public employment on the federal and Länder level have provoked the question about the future of the civil service status as such. Moreover, the existing civil service law is seen as fragmented, non-transparent, highly regulated and complex and – even for experts – not easy to understand[370]. So far the experts are split in two groups. Whereas the first group of experts believes that a specific status and specific working conditions are still needed in order to have an impartial, loyal and professional civil service[371], the other group points to the argument that all requirements as to an apolitical, ethical, committed and professional civil service can also be attained if the Austrian public employees are employed under labour law. Furthermore, EU law does not put any obstacles here since all EU legal instruments are either applicable to the private sector or to the public and private sector – but almost never solely to the public sector[372].

Anderes gilt für die Vertragsbediensteten. Diese sind in der Bundesverfassung zwar erwähnt, aber nicht vor Abschaffung geschützt. Daraus folgt, eine einheitliche Rechtsform für alle Bundesbediensteten könnte –auf Basis der geltenden Verfassungsrechtslage –nur eine öffentlich-rechtliche sein".Bundeskanzleramt (Hrsg.), Wege zu einem neuen einheitlichen Dienstrecht für den Bund, Wien 2008, p. 9 .

370 "Das Dienstrecht ist zudem sehr zersplittert, sehr unübersichtlich und in vielen Punkten auch für fachkundige Juristen nicht immer nachvollziehbar und vielfach schlicht überreguliert ". Bundeskanzleramt (Hrsg.), Wege zu einem neuen einheitlichen Dienstrecht, op. cit.

371 Sie schützen sowohl vor willkürlich benachteiligenden als auch vor willkürlich begünstigenden Personalmaßnahmen. Dadurch wird ein Gefühl persönlicher Unabhängigkeit erzeugt, das dem Allgemeininteresse, der Gesetzmäßigkeit, Objektivität und Unparteilichkeit der Amtsführung dient und mittelbar zur Qualität der Vollziehung beiträgt. Dies spielt vor allem in jenen Vollzugsbereichen eine Rolle, wo eine erhöhte Verantwortlichkeit für die Rechtsverhältnisse von Bürgern besteht, wie etwa bei Ermächtigungen zu Grundrechtseingriffen oder besonderer Korruptionsgefahr. Bundeskanzleramt (Hrsg.), Wege zu einem neuen einheitlichen Dienstrecht, op. cit., p. 10.

372 Anders ist die Situation aber bereits im Lichte des Europarechts. Denken Sie nur an die Vorgaben zu Betriebsübergang, Arbeitszeit, Arbeitsschutz, Gleichbehandlung oder Antidiskriminierungsrecht. Bei all diesen Fragen umfasst der Geltungsbereich der einschlägigen EU-Richtlinien den privaten und öffentlichen Bereich meist gleichermaßen. Nur vereinzelt finden sich punktuelle Ausnahmen, wo wirklich ganz

In fact, the ultimate test for any public service system seems to be whether it contributes to a stable, non-corrupt, ethical and effective public service. Therefore, the question is whether a more traditional bureaucratic system or a reformed post-bureaucratic system will produce a more or less ethical public service. This question is difficult to answer for various reasons: Generally, discussions about ethics and unethical behaviour are becoming more complex. Linking "Privatisation of Civil Services" to unethical behaviour" is not easy as many variables for unethical behaviour need to be examined. So far we are not aware of any existing empirical correlation between bureaucratic and post-bureaucratic systems and the level of corruption. However, there is a considerable amount of research on the impact of new public management reforms on civil servants' ethics[373]. According to these studies, the relation between NPM reforms and civil service ethics is ambivalent. It could be argued that in general NPM reforms aim towards post-bureaucratic organisational structures. Although they have similar features, the level of post-bureaucracy cannot be considered to match an NPM type of system. In order to find out whether the level of post-bureaucracy has any ethical implications, we correlated it with the Transparency International's Corruption Perception Index (see Figure 13).

---

spezifi sche staatliche Aufgaben wahrzunehmen sind. Es gibt auch genügend Instrumente, mit denen der Sorge begegnen werden könnte, dass dann Mitarbeiterinnen und Mitarbeiter den Vor-gesetzten oder gar der politischen Willkür ausgesetzt wären. Wir haben im Arbeitsrecht ein weit reichendes Antidiskriminierungsrecht, wir haben Gleichbehandlungsvorschriften und vor allem Instrumente der kollektiven Rechtskontrolle. Zur Vermeidung von Willkür gegenüber den Mitarbeiterinnen und Mitarbeitern bedarf es also nicht unbedingt öffentlich-rechtlicher Vorschriften. (...) Hingegen muss man dem Druck Rechnung tragen, dem öffentlich Bedienstete ausgesetzt sein können und manchmal sicherlich ausgesetzt sind, insbesondere auch von politischer Seite. Hier bedarf es eines wirksamen Schutzes vor Versetzungen, vor Kündigungen oder Entlassungen. Ebenfalls unverzichtbar ist eine Absicherung bei besonderen Gefahren. Hier ist insbesondere an den Bereich der Exekutive zu denken, da sich Exekutivorgane nicht wie normale Arbeitnehmer entfernen können, wenn es eng wird, sondern gegebenenfalls sogar – wie heißt das so schön – aktiv die Gefahr aufsuchen müssen. Hier bedarf es natürlich entsprechender Vorkehrungen, Wege zu einem einheitlichem Dienstrecht, op. cit., p. 14 and 16.

373 See for example: Jeroen Maesschalck, The Impact of New Public Management Reform on Public Servants Ethics: Towards a Theory, in: Public Administration, Vol. 82, 2004, pp. 465-489; Emile Kolthoff, Ehics and New Public Management, 2007; H.G. Frederickson, Public Ethics and the New Managerialism, in: Public Integrity, 1999, No. 1, pp. 265-278.

Figure 13: Relation between the traditional bureaucracy - post-bureaucracy continuum and the corruption perception index

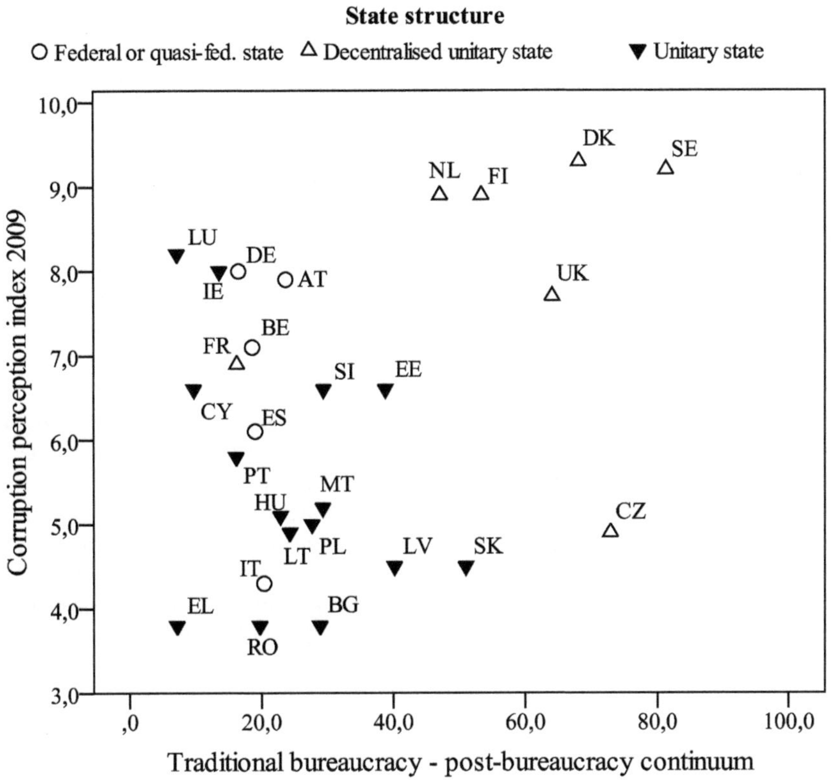

Based on the above figure it seems that the degree of post-bureaucracy itself does not seem to have a direct influence on the degree of corruption. If we divide the X-axis into two equal groups, the average score for the traditional bureaucracies is 6.3 and for the post-bureaucratic countries it is 6.4. Traditional bureaucracies such as Luxembourg can have a very high CPI score, but so can post-bureaucracies like Sweden. Although it is evident that many Scandinavian post-bureaucratic countries have a rather low level of corruption, the same is also true for many bureaucratic countries like Germany, Ireland and Austria. Therefore, the administrative reform as such does not have ethical implications, i.e. it does not increase or decrease the integrity of the officials. One could interpret as an argument that bureaucratic features as such are not necessary to ensure ethical government. In fact, this could be a strong argument against many classical bureaucratic principles. Institutional aspects alone are not sufficient for establishing a link between ethics, corruption and civil service system.

In fact, in the last decades, the public standard of morality has become much stricter in all European countries, independent of what civil service system they have. "Previously accepted conduct...is now deemed unethical and previously unethical conduct is now deemed criminal"[374]. At the same time the public maintains in almost all EU countries that the classical public service ethos is changing and levels of unethical behaviour are on the rise. However, at the same time the growing interest in public ethics reflects a growing interest in clear values, standards and norms. Apparently there is a trade-off between the growing complexity of our societies and the need for better, clearer and stricter rules. Moral and ethical standards are changing more rapidly than ever. Concepts of conflicts of interest and corruption have also changed over the years to include more types of official and private conduct. What was legal a generation ago is considered corrupt today[375]. Because of the increasing number of ethical rules and standards "there are many more laws to be broken nowadays."[376] Modern approaches to ethics do result in more rules and more standards and – at the same time – more insecurity about the right standards. At the same time regulation in the field of ethics takes a stronger prophylactic approach. Prohibitions are regulated for an increasing variety of circumstances. At the same time requirements for disclosure of interests have shifted from (original) concentration on financial issues into other non-pecuniary commitments. Public opinion has also shifted towards an objective conception of conflict and a subjective conception of interest

The present trend shows a general tendency in all public service systems towards higher expectations of the public regarding the quality of public services. The "days of unquestioned trust and admiration on the part of (...) the general public are over."[377] These expectations do not only concern the field of ethics. Rather, they reflect a general tendency towards higher expectations in fields such as good governance, public performance, legitimacy and accountability,

374 Frank Anechiarico/James Jacobs, The Pursuit of Absolute Integrity – How Corruption Control Makes Government Ineffective, University of Chicago Press, 1996, p. 16.

375 Alan Rosenthal, The Effects of Legislative Ethics Law: An Institutional Perspective, in: Dennis Saint-Martin/Fred Thompson (eds.), Public Ethics and Governance, 2006, p. 163.

376 Ibid, p. 163.

377 Mark. S. Frankel, Professional Codes: Why, How, and with What Impact?, in: Journal of Business Ethics, Vol.8, No. 2-3, 1989, p. 109.

transparency and openness, diversity, non-discrimination and policies on unwelcome behaviour and harassment.

Moreover the discussions on ethics and conflicts of interests should also be understood within the context of new discussions about the corporate responsibility of internationally operating companies, the salaries of top managers, the medical benefit of genetic engineering, euthanasia, the ethics of green shareholding, the social and cultural impact of the new media, our responsibility for climate change, etc. "Achieving an ethos of honesty and transparency.

Today, not a day goes by without extensive media coverage of corruption, fraud and unethical behaviour of civil servants and Holders of Public Office. Consequently discussions about ethical behaviour, conflicts of interests and integrity issues require answers to some very simple but fundamental questions: what is good and proper behaviour in times of changing and reforming government, decentralisation trends, the emergence of public-private partnerships, ongoing internationalisation trends, new threats (terrorism), new challenges (best practices), new opportunities (more and better information technologies) and new values in our societies? These developments show that any discussion about ethics and corruption cannot be separated from an analysis of ethical behaviour in general in our societies.

Our present understanding of ethics seems to be more and more paradoxical: on the one hand there have never been so many (regulatory) activities, reforms and studies in this field, including in all different civil service systems, bureaucratic or post-bureaucratic systems. On the other hand, public service reforms seem to produce ever new insecurities as to their effects on ethics. Ethics experts also face many difficulties in answering whether ethical challenges are increasing, decreasing – or both? Another development is also striking: whereas the media and the wider public call for the introduction of more rules and standards in the field, many experts indicate the potential negative effects of more rules, pointing, for example, to the fact that public discussions on ethics pay too little attention to the impact of ethics policies on administrative reactions, procedures, processes monitoring requirements, costs and civil rights. The first experts to address these problematic issues in detail were Anechiarico and J.B. Jacobs in the year 1996! Thus, literature on the challenges and paradoxes of conflicts of interest policies is still fairly recent.

In fact, it seems that ethics policies are becoming more important precisely because the public services are changing so much. The underlying reasons for this worldwide development can be summarised as follows:

- Firstly, governments are increasingly expected to ensure that civil servants do not allow their private interests to compromise official decision-making;
- Secondly, society is becoming increasingly demanding as to behaviour of civil servants and Holders of Public Office. Consequently potential conflicts of interest may weaken public trust;
- Thirdly, new forms of relationship have developed between the public and private sector and give rise to increasingly close forms of collaboration between the two sectors;
- Fourthly, new forms of mobility between the public and private sector may provoke more potential conflicts of interests as regards post-employment issues;
- Political scandals and increasing media attention put more pressure on the political actors to do even more in the field of public ethics.

On the other hand, there is little empirical evidence about the development of ethical behaviour and whether countries with traditional bureaucracies have more or less ethical problems. The Transparency International's Corruption Perceptions Index indicates that the Scandinavian countries (who belong to the group of post-bureaucratic countries) are those countries with the lowest level of corruption. The first EU country that comes relatively close to a traditional bureaucratic model (Luxemburg) ranks amongst the top ten of the list. However, this does not mean a lot since levels of corruption have many causes and underlying reasons.

In the above-mentioned survey "*Are Civil servants different because they are civil servants?*" the Member States were asked to give their comments to the following statement which concerned the link between privatisation, politicisation and mobility. "*Total privatisation of the civil service would lead to a decline in organisational loyalty, more ethical problems and more politicisation. In addition, it would increase mobility between the public and private sector and lead to less continuity and stability in the public service*". In fact, about half the Member States (France, Cyprus, Lithuania, Malta, Slovenia, Belgium, Germany, Poland, Spain, Finland) were of the opinion that a total privatisation would produce more problems. For example, according to the answer from Slovakia (which is representative for many others), "*There is a chance that total privatisation of the civil service would lead to a decline in organisational loyalty, more ethical problems and more politicisation, but it is not necessary, that such a situation will supervene/happen*". The Irish reply stated that "*The introduction of a significant number of employees on short term contacts could have an impact on organisational loyalty as such employees may not have such a strong connection with or commitment to the organisation as an employee with more secure tenure".* Surprisingly, a relatively high number of respondents (Denmark, Slovakia, Greece, Estonia, the Netherlands, Portugal, Latvia, Italy) considered the positive effects of privatising the public service, either wholly or in part. The Italian answer to the question argued that privatisation as such does not have negative effects: "*Much depends on the behaviour of the single agents"*.

Table 47: Would total privatisation of the civil service lead to a decline in organisational loyalty, more ethical problems and more politicisation?

Agree or partly agree	Disagree (more positive effects of privatisation)
France	Denmark
Cyprus	Slovakia
Lithuania	Greece
Malta	Estonia
Slovenia	The Netherlands
Belgium	Portugal
Germany	Latvia
Poland	Italy
Spain	Ireland (only partly)
Finland	
Czech Republic	
Luxembourg (but no link to ethical problems)	
Ireland (only partly)	

Note: Not all Member States have replied to this question

The consensus amongst the EU countries is relatively thin: all Member States accept that every country needs effective and efficient public officials with high ethical standards. However, there is much less consensus as to the question of whether these requirements can be achieved with only one category of public employees who are employed under an 'ordinary" labour contract or whether a specific civil service status is needed. Another question relates to the question of how working conditions should be designed and how working conditions relate to work behaviour. For example, is it still necessary to offer lifetime tenure because it is hoped that this correlates positively with impartiality, independency and performance?

So far the Member States have adopted three solutions to these challenges.

> Model 1: Those Member States who believe that public tasks are specific and require a specific ethical behaviour. Therefore, a specific group of civil servants with a specific public law status and specific working conditions is still needed for most or all public employees.
>
> Model 2: Those Member States who believe that public tasks are specific and require a specific ethical behaviour. Therefore a specific group of civil servants with a specific public law status is still needed for a small group of core public employees (mostly on the central level, for judges etc.). For all other public employees, working conditions are aligned and some features of private sector practices adopted.
>
> Model 3: However, a specific status is no longer needed since all job and ethical requirements can also be regulated under labour law contracts. These countries are in a process of abolishing the statutory civil service and aligning the working conditions of the different groups of public employees or even between public- and private sector employees.

In most Member States current reform trends move between the second and the third model. What is striking is the fact that no country is privatising the public service. Therefore, it is difficult to find evidence relating to the ethical implications of a privatised civil service. Looking for benchmarks in this field is no easy task and will lead us to the other side of the Atlantic.

In the United States "Texas nullified its merit system in 1985, making all state employees employees-at will; a 1996 Georgia law mandated that all new civil servants be hired on at-will basis; and in 2001 Florida eliminated job tenure....South Carolina and Arkansas recently abolished their merit systems (....). Such strategies are often mutually reinforcing in a manner that promotes the ongoing deterioration of career public service; the effect is that the status and role of the public employee today is not too different than that found in business..."[378].

The American State of Georgia passed a radical reform in 1996 that, in effect, removed all new employees from the traditional career service and made them "at-will" employees. In fact, this was less of a reform than a straightforward elimination of the traditional civil service, explicitly intended to make it easier for state agencies to fire employees who do not satisfy performance standards or

---

378 Bowman/West, Removing Employee Protection: A "See No Evil" Approach to Civil Service Reform, in: Huberts/Maesschalck/Jurkiewicz, op. cit., p. 185.

who do not respond to executive policies. Another objective of the reform was to decentralise almost every basic personnel function from the central offices to the individual agencies including compensation, hiring and affirmative action.

Another underlying reason for the reform was that traditional administration was seen as overregulated, too centralised, too slow and unresponsive. In contrast, a business model was seen as bringing increased efficiency, flexibility and alternative service delivery mechanisms[379]. "What we've got is a rigid inflexible system. It's antiquated. And it needs to be changed. . . . We don't believe that public employees should have any protection that the private employees don't have. Why should government be any different?[380] Similar but less drastic reforms were undertaken in Florida, Arizona, Washington D.C. and Texas.

In Georgia, after the introduction of the new reform act, new civil servants had no seniority rights and no rights to appeal against disciplinary actions such as a reduction of salaries, dismissal or bad personnel evaluation. Annual salary increases were abolished. Furthermore, agencies were free to write their own job descriptions and pay what they wished. "So if an agency wants to pay more to attract a higher-quality candidate to some-low level clerical position, it can simply create a new title and pay scale".[381]

According to a survey by Walters, positive outcomes of the reform in Georgia were clearly the reduction in the length of time for hiring, firing, promotion and re-assignment of tasks. In addition, the satisfaction level of personnel managers increased and more responsibilities were given to agency personnel, recruitment was made more flexible, hiring was more timely, and pay and promotions became more flexible[382]. Negative outcomes were that "the state has seen a proliferation of job titles – a one third increase..."[383] and the lack of uniformity and even divisions within departments for similar work[384]. Furthermore, the abolition of careers and seniority has to some extent stifled career advancement[385]

379 Jonathan West, Georgia on the Mind of Radical Civil Service Reformers, in: Review of Public Personnel Administration, Vol. 22, No. 2 Summer 2002, pp. 79-93.

380 Charles W. Gossett, Civil Service Reform in Georgia, in: Review of Public Personnel Administration, Vol. 22, No. 2, Summer 2002, p. 101.

381 Walters, J., Life After Civil Service Reform: The Texas, Georgia, and Florida Experiences, IBM Endowment for The Business of Government, Human Capital Series, October 2002, p. 24.

382 Ibid., p. 27.

383 Ibid., p. 25.

384 Ibid., p. 28.

385 Ibid., p. 25.

and employees were not very supportive of the reforms[386]. Regarding the number of lay-offs, they have doubled, but remain "pretty low"[387].

Other surveys, mainly by Kellough and Nigro, relating to the attitudes of classified and unclassified employees "at will"[388], and a survey by Sanders[389] revealed a mix of views (although many were rather negative) toward the Georgia reforms, suggesting that they have not been particularly effective. According to Kellough and Nigro, "our results raise doubt that the reforms were successful in developing more effective personnel processes or more motivated public employees. Large majorities of classified and unclassified employees found that most of the measures implemented were not working as reform proponents had expected. We believe that this outcome raises a fundamental question of the relationship between theory and practice in public service reform. Simple theories of motivation or of organisational change may not be adequate. More careful thought must be given to what it takes to build a productive and dedicated public workforce"[390].

In another study, Coggburn revealed serious doubts as to whether a simple deregulation policy would lead to improved performance. "The important thing to remember is that deregulation, just like any other type of personnel reform, will produce effects, some anticipated and desirable, others unanticipated and undesirable".[391] In addition, a study by Klopp revealed problematic results. "Also, a substantial number of employees viewed promotions and pay increases as being bestowed upon favoured employees under performance standards that are often vague and arbitrary. Meanwhile (...) employees were upset that the previous administration's promise to raise pay didn't materialise (...) While changes in

---

386 Ibid., p. 29.

387 Ibid., p. 26.

388 See especially Edward Kellough and Lloyd G. Nigro, Dramatic Reform of the Public Service: At Will Employment and the Effort to Create a New Public Workforce, Manuscript, January 28, 2005.

389 Robert M. Sanders, GeorgiaGain or Georgia Loss? The Great Experiment in State Civil Service Reform, in: Public Personnel Management, Vol. 33, Summer 2004, pp. 151-162.

390 Edward Kellough and Lloyd G. Nigro, Dramatic Reform of the Public Service: At Will Employment and the Effort to Create a New Public Workforce, unpublished paper, University of Georgia/Georgia State University, 2005, pp. 19-20.

391 Jerrell D. Coggburn, Deregulating the Public Personnel Function, in: Steven W. Hayes/Richard C. Kearney (eds.), Public Personnel Administration, Fourth Edition, 2003, p. 87.

the system may have been significant, thus far it does not appear that improvements in productivity or public service have been significant"[392].

In Georgia most employees agreed that there had been little if any real change in the human resources practices in their agencies following enactment of the civil service reform law[393] and "over 75% disagreed with the idea that Act 816 had resulted in a state workforce that is now more productive and responsive to the public..."[394]. On the other hand, fears that the shift "of large numbers of employees to the unclassified service would lead to the abuse or manipulation of workers for political reasons" could not be confirmed[395]. Most employees were of the opinion that they are not "exposed to partisan political coercion on the job"[396].

The studies of Kellough and Nigro, in particular, reveal some very interesting and unexpected outcomes of the Georgia reforms. The first is that "for the most part, they are not convinced that the act has done much to improve human resources practices or performance on the agency level"[397]. The second is that negative outcomes dominate the positive outcomes of the reform. And the third is that political coercion has not increased significantly and the number of dismissals is still rather low.

One could derive two interesting hypotheses from these conclusions. Firstly, that alignment of working conditions may have an adverse effect on – rather than improve – working conditions, performance and motivation. Secondly, alignment does not necessarily result in more insecurity for employees and will not increase political pressure on them. "Predictions that removing the protections (...) from employees would have a significant negative impact on their loyalty when compared to employees who did have such protection are not supported by the findings ... On most of the specific issues investigated here – profession of concern for the agency, likelihood of changing jobs in the near future, interest in

---

392 Klopp, B., Civil Service Reform, in: Collective Bargaining Reporter, http://www.afscme.org/wrkplace/cbr102_1.htm, p. 4.

393 Ibid.

394 Ibid.

395 Edward Kellough and Lloyd G. Nigro, Administrative Theory and Civil Service Reform; A Review of the Georgia Experience, University of Georgia, Manuscript, May 1, 2003, p. 17.

396 Ibid., p. 12.

397 Ibid., Administrative Theory, p. 14.

having employee organisations represent them, and responsiveness to managers' direction – there are no significant differences"[398].

398 Gossett, Charles W., The Changing Face of Georgia's Merit System: Results from an Attitude Survey in the Georgia Department of Juvenile Justice, in: Public Personnel Department, Vol. 32, No 2, 2003, p. 277.

VIII. CONCLUSIONS

1. Towards a better theoretical understanding of change processes

In the discussions and the analysis of the various civil service systems, much insight and many fascinating developments have been found. However, the results of this comparative analysis also represent a remarkable challenge regarding a theoretical understanding of the discussed change processes in the field of civil service reforms. In fact, many reform outcomes confirm the assumptions of path-dependency, political culture, rational choice, neo-institutionalism, Europeanisation and convergence theories at the same time. Moreover, because of the growing fragmentation of the national public services, the increasing diversity of the public sector workforce and the differences in structure and size of the national civil services, this study also challenges uniform public motivation theories. On the other hand, our findings do not challenge the existence of public service motivation as such. However, we agree with Perry and Hondeghem that it is necessary to investigate the influence of the country/region/civil service structure as an institution of public service motivation. In addition, it is also important to carry out more research on public service motivation in different parts of the public sector. Do civil servants (still) have a different public service motivation than other public employees? Are civil servants in the ministries different to those in the agencies? Do civil servants in "bureaucratic" countries have different motivations and values than civil servants in post-bureaucratic countries? And – are civil servants more ethical because they are civil servants?

This study has given evidence that different historical traditions and cultures as well as HR systems have a considerable impact on public management modernisation paths and on the outcomes of HR reforms. In a way, the findings in this study give a fascinating picture about the differences and similarities of the public service systems in Europe at the same time. It also illustrates the difficulties in identifying country models and geographical similarities in times of decentralisation, differentiation and flexibilisation. At the same time it also gives an overview about Europeanisation, convergence and common reform and fashion trends in some areas.

In fact, whereas in some policies similar reform trends and reform outcomes can be observed, in other fields differences are prevailing or even increasing. Almost all Member States follow the same grand reform paths: decentralisation of HR responsibilities and responsibilisation of managers, flexibilisation of recruitment and career development policies, a stronger focus on individual and organisational performance management and a general trend towards debureaucratisation. The relevance of context and diversity in European public administrations has important implications for the concept of mutual learning and good practice. Because of this it is almost impossible to offer a European definition of the term *civil services* and good practices in civil service reform. Only in rare cases can foreign reforms be purchased as standard off-the-shelf products without taking into account their roles and repercussions in the respective administrations. Success is only possible if new reform instruments are shaped to the needs of the specific administration, taking the particularities of the administrative culture into account. At the same time, benchmarking may only be possible in those areas which are marked by a) common reform trends, b) common reform fashions, c) the adoption of common reform instruments in a d) similar administrative culture/structure. For example, whereas decentralisation of HR policies can mean very different things in different countries, national efforts in the field of reducing administrative burdens or in implementing EU legislation in the field of anti-discrimination can be comparable and become subject of comparative analysis in a selected group of countries. This again may result in very interesting benchmarking or even best practice studies.

Despite all current developments away from the bureaucratic model, it is difficult to say whether our findings confirm the end of the bureaucratic paradigm or the beginning of a new post-bureaucratic paradigm. For certain, the classical bureaucracies are about to change. However, some bureaucratic features are not vanishing. It is not yet clear what the post-bureaucratic paradigm is, apart from remedies to the weaknesses of the classical bureaucratic model. Still, developments like decentralisation, responsibilisation, flexibilisation, deregulation and more openness are too wide and too fluid concepts. These developments are also full of paradoxes and ambivalences. Consequently, they represent alternatives to the classical models. But does this also mean improvements?

What is clearly noticeable is that the post-bureaucratic reform of the national civil services is gaining importance in all Member States. As a result, the current international reform process is leading to a boost in innovation that could also be of great interest in the respective national practice. The international comparison provides a multitude of options for learning from the experiences and problems of others, without ignoring the particularities of the national administrative structures. Hence, the nature and effects of public service reforms must be seen much more in the context of the different public administrative traditions, geographical and cultural differences as well as the importance of different organisational structures. At the same time it must be seen in the context of worldwide reform trends, reform fashions, political interests and the importance of the European integration process.

2. The need for better country clusters

As the results of our study suggest, it is also important to find better and more fine-tuned classifications for the national civil service systems. As our findings show, it becomes increasingly difficult to classify the Member States into country traditions, geographical or civil service clusters. In fact, similarities exist only with regard to some institutional and structural issues. One example may illustrate this all: all Mediterranean countries have a career structure in their civil services; whilst none of the Scandinavian countries has a career system. This could be interpreted as the existence of two different models. However, this is problematic for various reasons. In fact, other institutional features may be very diverse within the different country clusters and administrative traditions. For example, continental countries differ sharply as regards the issue of civil servants' job security.

Figure 14: Similarities amongst administrative traditions and country clusters

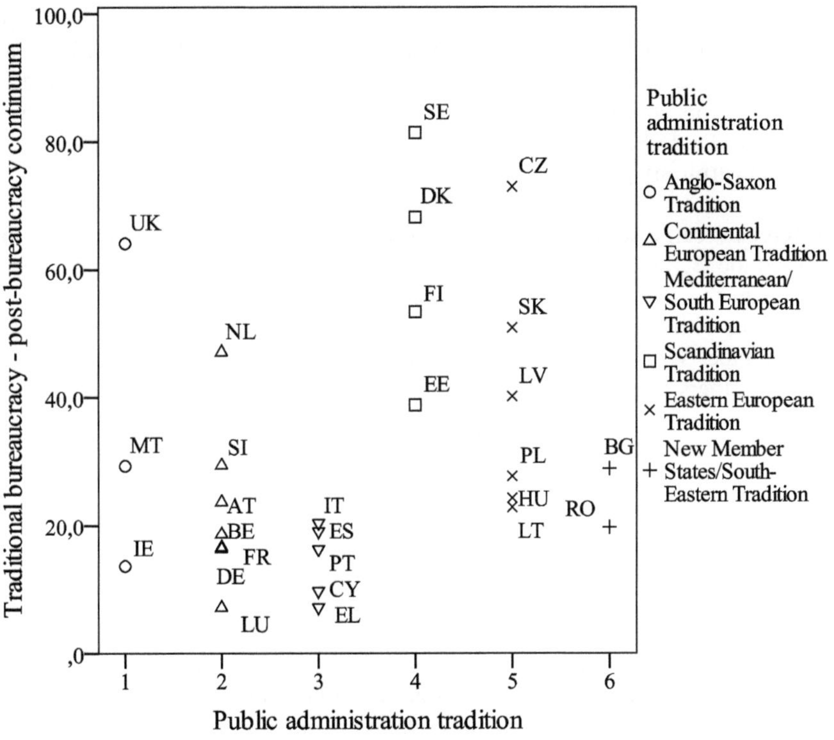

From our clusters, only the third group, Mediterranean countries, indeed represents a number of homogeneous civil service systems. However, the trend seems to be rather in the direction of more differentiation. In the meantime, especially after the most recent reforms in Portugal, this group of countries (Greece, Cyprus, Portugal, Spain and Italy) is becoming increasingly diverse. Although most of these countries still share the fact that they have much more bureaucratic features than the Scandinavian group, they are also relatively diverse. The bureaucratic and "privatised" Italian civil service is very different from the still relatively traditional and bureaucratic Greek civil service. On the other hand, the reformed Portuguese civil service cannot be compared with the Spanish civil service which still resembles the traditional French model (although the Spanish reform process has introduced – similar to Germany – many different and diverse reform initiatives on central and regional level). Contrary to this and despite some significant differences between Estonia on the one hand and Denmark, Finland and Sweden on the other hand, the latter three Scandinavian countries can also be seen to form a relative homogenous administrative tradition. The Netherlands combine features of the Scandinavian states with classical bureaucratic states. Our data suggests that it would be problematic to include it into the same category as Belgium, Germany, Luxemburg and France, which still have more traditional bureaucratic systems. The Anglo-Saxon countries and the Eastern European countries represent the most diverse groupings of countries. Thus, the Anglo-Saxon cluster and Central European cluster are relatively diverse and arbitrary groupings.

Differences can also be seen in relation to the former communist countries that entered the EU in 2005. Most of them adopted a traditional bureaucratic career system in the early nineties. However, many Eastern European states are still struggling with many different reform concepts and do not know which reform path to take. Whereas some take very different reform concepts (Lithuania vs. Latvia), others have opted for more similar strategies (Slovakia, Hungary). At the time of writing the conclusions for this study the Czech Republic did not have a civil service law (a draft bill was still being debated). Today, most of the Eastern European states have hybrid systems with fragile career systems (if at all), less job security for civil servants than in other Member States, no specific pension systems for civil servants, flexible recruitment systems and too large mobility flows (given the fact that work in the public services is not very attractive).

Overall, this study confirms the existence of a great variety of systems. Whereas most countries move away from the traditional bureaucratic career systems, our study cannot confirm that all Member States are moving towards the same direction. There is no clear development towards the emergence of a European post-bureaucratic model. Instead, most Member States seem to be keeping some traditional elements whilst throwing away others. The decision on what to keep and what to abandon is closely connected with national traditions, habits, beliefs and the national political interests. Overall, the result is a paradox: whilst all Member States want to move away from the bureaucratic model, they have not found yet a final reform destination.

Thus, this study gives a fascinating insight into the differences and similarities of the HR systems in Europe. However, it illustrates much more a new stage of civil service reform and experimentation. The reform focus varies greatly amongst the Member States. Whereas some introduce new civil service laws (Portugal and Germany), others focus on HR reforms and mobility policies (France), coordination policies (Sweden) or the fight against corruption (many Eastern European states). Bureaucratic career systems and post-bureaucratic systems produce their own reform agendas. The same can be said for country clusters: Continental, Eastern European, Scandinavian, Anglo-Saxon, South-Eastern and Mediterranean countries produce their own successes and failures as a result of public service reforms.

Still it is very difficult to say whether post-bureaucratic countries produce more or less efficiency, effectiveness, citizen orientation, fairness, good administration, performance, less patronage and corruption than the bureaucratic countries. So far it seems that many civil service models have their own strengths and weaknesses. However, as this study shows, many Eastern European countries face challenges that do not exist in old Member States (and even less in the Scandinavian countries). In general, the older Member States seem to be more successful in fields such as anti-discrimination, equality and diversity policies. Many continental career-system countries also have more competitive salary systems. However, overall the Scandinavian countries are seen as more successful with regard to a number of individual HR policies. Eastern European states and the two new Member States face more challenges than the older Member States.

3. The future of the national civil services

As could be seen in this study, contemporary civil services are increasingly complex. In the future, public administration will most likely become more complicated and probably more contradictory all the time[399]. While expectations of government are increasing, the resources available to meet these expectations are diminishing. Civil servants of the future will have to be at ease with more complexity and flexibility. They will have to be comfortable with change, often rapid change. At the same time they will take more autonomous decisions, be more responsible, accountable, performance-oriented, and subject to new competency and skill requirements. Despite the popularity to criticise the over-emphasis on laws and rules in contemporary civil services, the primacy of law is likely to remain in the future. However, it will be complemented by other tools for resolving conflicts, new integrity-based approaches, new regulatory techniques, new informal instruments, an enhanced access to IT information, and a delicate balance between more citizen rights and a general stronger concern for governmental risks.

The civil service workforce will be better qualified and more diverse than ever before. At the same time, civil servants will face more value conflicts and dilemmas although they are also better aware of the existence of ethical rules, conflicts of interest issues and conflict resolution techniques.

Despite all alignment trends, civil servants will never be able to compete with private sector companies in terms of flexibility. In fact, some specific bureaucratic features will remain in place in order to sustain core democratic values like equality, fairness and legal security. According to Peters and Pierre, "the challenge in the longer term....is to design organisations that combine the efficiency and service capacity of decentralised organizations with the uniform and legalistic nature of hierarchical organisations"[400].

Overall, despite all popular images, work in the civil services will remain interesting, challenging, important and "a key to a better society and world"[401]. Overall, the Member States will – due to different national political agendas – continue to differ sharply as regards reform pressure and reform priorities. For example, the response from Sweden to this study showed that most reform issues are currently of little significance because they were already implemented a long time ago. However, reform policies such as diversity, anti-discrimination, reducing administrative burdens and performance-related pay are likely to continue to have a high priority on the reform agenda of many countries. At the

399 David H. Rosenbloom/Robert S. Kravchuk/Richard M. Clerkin, Public Administration, Understanding Management, Politics, and Law in the Public Sector, 7th edition, Mc Grawhill, Singapore 2009, p. 541.

400 Peters/Pierre, Handbook of Public Administration, 2nd edition, op. cit., p. 6.

401 Rosenbloom/Kravchuk/Clerkin, Public Administration, op. cit., p. 548.

same time, budgetary constraints will lead to a deterioration of working conditions in some countries and not enhance the attractiveness of work in the national civil services. Moreover, growing financial constraints and budget pressures will force the national governments to further cut resources in more areas and policies, and this may have negative results on the effectiveness of public policies. Many Member States will continue to employ a specific category of public law civil servants. However, the number of civil servants will be reduced as will the sectors that employ civil servants.

Although this research did not deal explicitly with the role of politics in the reform process, it is likely that politics will continue to have a strong impact on reform fashions and reform agendas. The overall definition of what public administration should be in the future is likely to continue to be politically determined. As we have seen in this study, the case of reducing administrative burdens as a political reform priority represents one example for the importance of the political class in defining the reform agenda.

Today, the national civil services no longer have a single, coherent paradigm or conceptual framework. "Disaggregation promotes decomposition of the civil service. Two concepts central to traditional management are now disappearing. One is that any particular government, whether federal, state, or local, should act as a single, unified employer. The other is the concomitant idea of a unified civil service"[402]. Consequently, "we may soon find ourselves with a hollow administrative structure processing huge transfers", but with service provision increasingly conducted under the auspices of non-governmental actors[403]. Whereas once perhaps 80 to 90% of national public employees were subject to the same statutes and working conditions, today the number is declining[404]. "Information technology also promotes decomposition. The workplace of the future may be no 'place' at all"[405].

Overall, these changes may also have positive effects after all; "the problems of the old 'one-size-fits-all' approach are well documented and real. However, they will also fundamentally alter the concept of civil service and further fragment government"[406]. For example, if reliance on decentralisation and outsourcing grows, "as seems likely, the demands for personal responsibility are likely to

402 Ibid., p. 545.
403 Peters/Pierre, Handbook of Public administration, 2nd edition, op. cit.
404 Rosenbloom/Kravchuk/Clerkin, Public Administration, op. cit., p. 546.
405 Ibid.
406 Ibid.

increase and reach private individuals engaged in government work"[407]. Therefore, good leadership will become more important than ever before. At the same time, people will also become more critical towards bad leadership and poor performance of their leaders.

Without a doubt, the future will see the emergence of a growing paradox. On the one hand, various factors (e.g., growing financial and demographic pressures as well as value changes) will continue to put pressure on the civil services to continue with radical reforms. On the other hand, the pace of change and growing uncertainties about the reform results will generate more discussions on the need to preserve traditional values, to keep the identity of civil servants and to maintain some specific features that are different to the private sector.

In all Member States, accusations that the civil services are not innovative, not ready to reform and suffering from reform inertia are clearly wrong. Contrary to this, reforms have led to many changes. The ongoing reforms in the national public services promote the change, deconstruction and the decentralisation of the public services on all fronts. As a consequence, the traditional concept of the public service as a single, unified employer is slowly disappearing. At the same time, HR management is also becoming more flexible and decentralised. Moreover, the public employees and their values are also changing.

Today, the changing role of the state requires a changing conception of the public services and the civil servants. Despite the many changes that are taking place in many countries, the public perception is still that civil servants work in an environment, which is clearly separated from the private sector. In some countries civil servants are seen as a protected group, set apart from the outside world. In reality, customer- and citizen- orientation have increased, and working conditions have been aligned to those in the private sector. Nowadays the differences between public and private employees in terms of their status, working time, pay, pensions, holidays, recruitment and competency requirements are lesser than they were previously.

Reforms are implemented everywhere and at great speeds. Overall, this study has shown that the current reform process in the national civil services can be identified as an opening-up process of the national civil services. Instead of being separated from the society and citizens, the trend is towards the blurring of public and private boundaries as well as between civil servants and public employees. Also physically, the walls between the civil service and the labour mar-

---

407 Ibid., p. 548.

ket are coming down. Almost all Member States have started to facilitate recruitment procedures, reform or even abolish careers, reduce internal hierarchies, support more mobility, delegate more responsibilities to line managers and align the working conditions between civil servants and other public employees. More and more public tasks are carried out by non-state bodies and more tasks which have traditionally been carried out by civil servants are carried out by other public employees or private service providers.

In the future the national civil services will look more aligned as was ever the case before. To state that the times of the traditional bureaucracy are over is tempting. In fact, it is highly unlikely that the traditional bureaucracy is coming back. However, it cannot be excluded that specific principles and aspects may return to the agenda. For example, the current trend towards decentralisation and fragmentation has resulted in new discussions about the need for a new public service ethos and the need for common values. Much depends on the outcomes of reforms. As this study shows, many HR reforms in the national civil services do not show clear results. Whereas some reform trends produce improvements, others simply bring about alternation or even deteriorations of working conditions and reform results. Thus, the reform outcomes do not indicate that the post-bureaucratic times are much better - in many cases they are simply different.

Also in the coming years, most Member States will maintain the public law status of civil servants. At the same time they are introducing reforms which put into question the very sense of it. Civil servants are still numerous; however, their numbers are diminishing. They still enjoy greater job security. However, the difference between public employees and civil servants' job security is fading. Member States are abolishing careers and seniority. However, they still want to value experience, competence and stability. Member States are eager to promote the traditional civil service ethos. However, many modern reform trends are generating a new set of values which are producing value dilemmas.

The future will be a constant strive towards finding the right balance amongst competing values and principles: between standardisation and citizen-orientation, flexibility and the need for stability, autonomy, individualism and fairness, centralisation and decentralisation, secrecy and openness, hierarchy and responsibilisation, the call for new rules and deregulation, individual performance and equality etc.

If the traditional bureaucracy is slowly disappearing what will happen to the bureaucrats, the civil servants? Will they disappear like the classical concept of the bureaucracy? In this study we could not find that civil servants carry out their tasks differently than other public employees. However, we also could not find any evidence that they perform their tasks differently (or worse) because they are civil servants. Nevertheless, this study reveals one important paradox: all Member States continue to employ civil servants; however, they see fewer reasons as to why civil servants with specific working conditions are needed. In fact, all they need are professional and competent public employees.

La Bureaucratie est morte. Vive la Bureaucratie.

The Civil Service is dead. Long live the Civil Service.

IX. LITERATURE

Joel D. Aberbach/Bert A. Rockman, In the Web of Politics – Three Decades of the U.S. Federal Executive, Brookings Institution, Washington D. C., 2000

Advies van de Raad voor het Overheidspersonnelsbeleid inzake de Ambtelijke Status, Adviesnummer 17, The Hague, 16 December 1998 (official document without author)

Christopher W. Allinson, Bureaucratic Personality and Organisation Structure, University of Leeds, 1984

Pablo Alonso/Gregory Lewis, Public Service Motivation and Job Performance: Evidence from the Federal Sector, in: American Review of public Administration, Vol. 31, No. 4, 2001, pp. 363-380

Frank Anechiarico/James B. Jacobs, The Pursuit of Absolute Integrity – How Corruption Control Makes Government Ineffective, University of Chicago Press, 1996

J. Norman Baldwin, Are We Really Lazy?, in: Review of Public Personnel Administration 4, Spring 1984, pp. 80-89

Ulrich Beck, Risikogesellschaft - Auf dem Weg in eine andere Moderne, 1986

Hans A.G.M. Bekke/Frits M. van der Meer (eds.), Civil Service Systems in Europe, Edward Elgar Publishing, 2000

Arthur Benz, Status und Perspektiven der Politikwissenschaftlichen Verwaltungsforschung, in: Die Verwaltung, Nr. 3/2003, pp. 361-388.

L. Bordogna, Industrial Relations in the Public Sector, European Foundation for the Improvement of Living and Working Conditions, Dublin, 2007

Danielle Bossaert/Christoph Demmke/Koen Nomden/Robert Polet/Astrid Auer, Civil Services in the Europe of 15, Trends and New Developments, EIPA, 2001

Danielle Bossaert/Christoph Demmke/Marie-Laure Onnée-Abbruciati, L'evolution des fonctions publiques en Europe – une approche comparée des dévelopments récents, in: Marie-Laure Onnée-Abbruciati, Le fonctionnaire est-til un salarié comme les autres? Pensions de retraite dans les fonctions publiques en Europe, Bruylant, Bruxelles 2003

Geert Bouckaert/John Halligan, Managing Performance, Routledge, 2008

James S. Bowman, The Success of Failure: The Paradox of Performance Pay, in: Review of Public Personnel Administration, Vol. 30, No. 1, March 2010, pp. 70-89

Barry Bozeman, Bureaucracy and Red Tape, New Jersey, 2000

Barry Bozeman/Hal Rainey, Organizational Rules and the "Bureaucractic Personality", in: American Journal of Political Science, Vol. 42, No 1, January 1998, pp. 163-189.

Gene A. Brewer/Sally Colman Selden/Rex L. Facer II, Individual Conceptions of Public Service Motivation, in: Public Administration Review, Vol. 60, No. 3, May/June 2000, pp. 254-264

Bundeskanzleramt Österreich, Das Personal des Bundes, Wien 2009

Bundeskanzleramt Österreich (Hrsg.), Wege zu einem neuen einheitlichen Dienstrecht für den Bund, Wien 2008

Roberto Caranta, Point de vue sur les réformes récentes en matières de fonction publique en Italie, in Council of State (Conseil d'Etat), Public report of the Council of State, Studies and Documents, Reflections on the Civil Service, Paris, 2003, p. 405

Dalton Conley, Elsewhere U.S.A. – How We Got from the Company Man, Family Dinners, and the Affluent Society to the Home Office, BlackBerry Moms, and Economic Anxiety, Pantheon, New York, 2008

Conseil d'Etat, Public Report of the Council of State, Studies and Documents, Reflections on the Civil Service, Paris, 2003

Terry Cooper, The Responsible Administrator, Jossey Bass, 5th Edition, 2006

Danish Ministry of Finance, State Sector Personnel in Denmark, Copenhagen, 2002

Danish Ministry of Finance, State Sector Personnel, 2005, Copenhagen 2006. http://www.perst.dk/Publications/2006/State%20Sector%20Personnel%20in%20 Denmark%202005.aspx

Roger H. Davidson (ed.), Workways of Governance – Monitoring Our Government's Health, Brookings Institution Press, Washington D.C., 2000
Charles Debbasch, La fonction publique en Europe, Paris, 1981

L. DeHart-Davis/S.K. Pandey, Red Tape and Public Employees: Does Perceived Rule Dysfunction Alienate Managers, in: Journal of Public Administration Research and Theory, Vol. 15, No. 1, 2005, pp. 133-148

Christoph Demmke/Uta Linke, Who's a National and Who's a European? Exercising Public Power and the Legitimacy of Art. 39 4 EC in the 21st Century, in: EIPASCOPE 2003/2, pp. 2-10.

Christoph Demmke, Civil Services in the Accession States – New Trends and the Impact of the Integration Process, EIPA, Maastricht, 2004

Christoph Demmke, European Civil Services between Tradition and Reform, EIPA, Maastricht, 2004

Christoph Demmke, Are Civil Servants Different Because they are Civil Servants? EIPA, Maastricht, 2006.

Christoph Demmke/Gerhard Hammerschmid/Renate Meyer, Decentralisation and Accountability as Focus of Public Modernisation Reforms, Office of Official Publications of the EU, Luxemburg, 2006

Christoph Demmke/Thomas Henökl/Timo Moilanen, What are Public Services Good at? Success of Public Services in the field of Human Resource Management, Slovenian EU-Presidency, EIPA, 2008 (not published)

Christoph Demmke/Mark Bovens/Thomas Henökl/Timo Moilanen, Regulating Conflicts of Interest for Holders of Public Office in the European Union – A Comparative Study of the Rules and Standards of Professional Ethics for the Holders of Public Office in the EU-27 and EU Institutions, Office of Official Publications of the EU, Luxemburg 2008

Christoph Demmke, Leistungsbezahlung in den Oeffentlichen Diensten der EU-Staaten, in: Der moderne Staat, No. 1/2009, pp. 53-73

Janet V. Denhardt/Robert B. Denhardt, The New Public Service, Sharpe, 2007

Hans-Ulrich Derlien/B. Guy Peters (eds.), The State at Work, Comparative Public Service Systems, Edward Elgar Publishing, 2008

John D. Donahue/Joseph S. Nye (eds.), For the People, Can We Fix Public Service? Brookings Institution Press, Washington D.C. 2003

Francois Dubet, Ungerechtigkeiten, Hamburger Edition, Hamburg, 2008

Yves Emery/David Giauque, Dilemmes de la GRH publique, LEP, Lausanne 2007

Yves Emery/Carole Wyser, Identities of Public Sector Employees as a Source of Inspiration for Differentiating HRM Practices: the Swiss case, paper presented at the EGPA Conference, 2.-5 September 2009

European Commission, White Paper on European Governance, Report of the Working Group on "Better Regulation", May 2001

European Foundation for the Improvement of Living and Working Conditions, Effect of Performance-related Bonuses on Gender Pay Gap, Dublin 2008

Ewan Ferlie/Laurence E. Lynn/Christopher Politt, The Oxford Handbook of Public Management, Oxford University Press, 2005.

Anthony Foley, The Size, Cost and Efficiency of the Public Service, in: Administration, Vol. 57, No.1, pp. 69-101

Fonction Publique Francaise, Rapport annuel 2007-2008, http://www.fonction-publique.gouv.fr/article1488.html (last time checked on 9 January 2010)

Melissa Forbes/Laurence E. Lynn Jr., How Does Public Management Affect Government Performance? Findings from International Research, Bush School Working Paper, No. 420, October 2004

Virginie Forest, Performance-related Pay and Work Motivation: Theoretical and Empirical Perspectives for the French Civil Service, in: International Review of Administrative Sciences, Vol. 74, 2009, No. 2, pp. 325-329

France, The Public Employment Observatory, Annual report 2003, Speech by Mr Jean-Paul Delevoye at the Meeting of the Steering Committee of the Public Employment Observatory, 9 December 2003, Paris 2003, pp. 28-29

Mark S. Frankel, Professional Codes: Why, How, and with What Impact?, in: Journal of Business Ethics, Vol. 8, No. 2-3, 1989, pp. 109-115

H. G. Frederickson, Public Ethics and the New Managerialism, in: Public Integrity, 1999, No. 1, pp. 265-278

Francis Fukuyama, State Building Governance and World Order in the 21st Century, Ithaca, New York, Cornell University Press, 2004

Edgar Norman Gladden, Civil Services of the United Kingdom 1853-1970, Frank Cass, London 1967

Edgar Norman Gladden, A History of Public Administration, Frank Cass, London, Vol. II, 1972

Daniel Goleman, Working with Emotional Intelligence, Bantam, New York, 2000

Charles E. Goodsell, Red Tape and a Theory of Bureaucratic Rules (Review of the Book by Bozeman), in: Public Administration Review, Vol. 60, No. 4, July/August 2000, pp. 373

Charles E. Goodsell, The Case for Bureaucracy, A Public Administration Polemic, Third Edition, Chatham, New Jersey, 1994

Charles W. Gossett, Civil Service Reform in Georgia, in: Review of Public Personnel Administration, Vol. 22, No. 2, Summer 2002, pp. 94-113

Charles W. Gossett, The Changing Face of Georgia's Merit System: Results from an Attitude Survey in the Georgia Department of Juvenile Justice, in: Public Personnel Management, Vol. 32, No 2, 2003

Anneke Goudswaard, Flexible Labour-sustainable Labour?, The Situation in the Netherlands After Twenty Years of Increasing Flexibility, Dissertation, Catholic University of Nijmegen, 7 October 2003

Gerhard Hammerschmid/Renate E. Meyer/Isabell Egger-Peitler, Das Konzept der Public Service Motivation – Status Quo der internationalen Diskussion und erste empirische Evidenzen für den deutschsprachigen Raum, in: Der moderne Staat, No. 1/2009, pp. 73-92

Charles Handy, Understanding Organizations, Fourth Edition, London 1999

Harvard Business Review, Motivating People, Special Issue 2003

Steven W. Hayes/Richard C. Kearney (eds.), Public Personnel Administration, Fourth Edition, Prentice Hall, New Jersey, 2003

Johnny Hellgren/Markus Sverke/Kerstin Isaksson, A Two–dimensional Approach to Job Insecurity: Consequences for Employees Attitudes and Well-being, in: European Journal of Work and Organizational Psychology, 1999, Vol. 8, pp. 179-195

Joachim Jens Hesse/Christopher Hood/B. Guy Peters, Paradoxes in Public Sector Reform – An International Comparison, Duncker/Humblot GmbH, Berlin, 2003

Geert H. Hofstede, Culture's Consequences – Comparing Values, Behaviors, Institutions and Organizations Across Nations, Sage Publications, 2001

Christopher Hood, The Art of the State, Clarendon Press, Oxford 1998

Christopher Hood/David Heald, Transparency: The Key to Better Government, Oxford University Press, 2006

David Houston, Public Service Motivation: A Mutivariate Test, in: Journal of Public Administration Research and Theory, Vol. 10, No. 4, October 2000, pp. 713-727

Leo W.J.C. Huberts/Jeroen Maesschalck/Carole L. Jurkiewicz, Ethics and Integrity of Governance, Edward Elgar Publishing, Massachusetts, 2008

Patricia Ingraham/ Barbara, S. Romzek, New Paradigms for Government, Jossey Bass Publishers, San Francisco, 1994

Hans Jung, Personalwirtschaft, München/Wien, 3rd Edition, 1999

Devorah Kalekin-Fishman/Pirkko Pitkänen (eds.), An Emerging Institution? Multiple Citizenship in Europe – Views of Officials, Peter Lang, Bern, 2008

J.Edward Kellough/Lloyd Nigro, Pay for Performance in Georgia State Government: Employee Perspectives on Georgia Gain after Five Years, University of Georgia, Manuscript, July 16, 2001

Edward Kellough/Lloyd G. Nigro, Administrative Theory and Civil Service Reform; A Review of the Georgia Experience, University of Georgia, Manuscript, May 1, 2003

Edward Kellough/Lloyd G. Nigro, Dramatic Reform of the Public Service: At Will Employment and the Effort to Create a New Public Workforce, unpublished paper, University of Georgia/Georgia State University, 2005

Edward Kellough/Lloyd G. Nigro (eds.), Civil Service Reform in the States – Personnel Policy and Politics at the Subnational Level, Suny Series in Public Administration, State University of New York Press, 2006

Walter J.M. Kickert (ed.), The Study of Public Management in Europe and the US., Routledge, London and New York, 2008

Walter J.M. Kickert/Richard J. Stillman, The Modern State and its Study, Edward Elgar Publishing, Cheltenham 1999

J. J. Kirlin, Big Question for a Significant Public Administration, in: Public Administration Review, No. 2, March/April 2001, pp.140-143

Bert Klandermans/Tinka van Vuuren, Job Insecurity – Introduction, in: European Journal of Work and Organizational Psychology, Vol. 8, 1999, pp. 145-153

B. Klopp, Civil Service Reform, in: Collective Bargaining Reporter, http://www.afscme.org/wrkplace/cbr102_1.htm (last time checked on 7 January 2010)

Emile Kolthoff, Ethics and New Public Management, Boom Juridische uitgevers, 2007

Reinhart Kosselleck, Begriffsgeschichten, Suhrkamp, Frankfurt/M., 2006

Robert Kriegel/David Brandt, Sacred Cows Make the Best Burgers – Developing Change-ready People and Organizations. Harper Business, 1996

Georg Lakoff/Elisabeth Wehling, Auf leisen Sohlen ins Gehirn, Politische Sprache und ihre heimliche Macht, Carl-Auer, Heidelberg 2008

Torbjörn Larsson, Governing Sweden, Statskontoret, Stockholm, 1995

Edward Lawler III, Treat People Right! How Organizations and Individuals Can Propel Each Other into a Virtuous Spiral of Success.. Jossey-Bass 2003

Paul C. Light, Government’s Greatest Achievements of the Past Half Century, in: Reform Watch, Brookings Institute, Vol. 2, November 2000

Charles E. Lindblom, The Science of Muddling through, in: Public Administration Review, 1959, pp. 79-88

Zsuzsanna Lonti, OECD, Government at a Glance, Presentation to EUPAN, 17 June 2009

Zsuzsanna Lonti/M. Woods, "Towards Government at a Glance, OECD, Paris, 2008

Jürgen Lorse, Personalmanagement im öffentlichen Dienst, Luchterhand, Neuwied und Kriftel, 2001

Niklas Luhmann/Renate Mayntz, Personal im öffentlichen Dienst, Baden Baden, Nomos-Verlagsgesellschaft, 1973

L. E. Jr. Lynn, The Myth of the Bureaucratic Paradigm: What Traditional Public Administration Really Stood For, in: Public Administration Review, March/April 2001, pp. 144-160

Elke Löffler, The Modernisation of the Public Sector in an International Comparative Perspective – Implementation Strategies in Germany, Great Britain and the United States, Speyerer Forschungsberichte 174, Forschungsinstitut für öffentliche Verwaltung, Speyer, 1997.

Jeroen Maesschalck, The Impact of New Public Management Reform on Public Servants Ethics –Towards a Theory, in: Public Administration, Vol. 82, 2004, pp. 465-489

Siegfried Magiera/Heinrich Siedentopf (eds.), Das Recht des öffentlichen Dienstes in den Mitgliedstaaten der Europäischen Gemeinschaft, Duncker & Humblot, Berlin,1994.

Siegfried Magiera/Karl-Peter Sommermann/Jacques Ziller (Hrsg.), Verwaltungswissenschaft und Verwaltungspraxis in nationaler und transnationaler Perspektive, Dunker und Humblot, Berlin, 2008

Herbert Mandelartz, Sisyphos Lebt, Berliner Wissenschafts Verlag, Berlin, 2009

Robert Maranto, A Brief Against Tenure in the U.S. Civil Service, Praising Civil Service but not Bureaucracy, Review of Public Personnel Administration, Sage, Vol. 22, No. 3, Fall 2002, pp. 175-192

Ellen Mastenbroek, De postmoderne overheid: wens of werkelijkheid?, in: Bestuursweten-schapen, No. 2, 2003

Yves Mény, Politique comparée, les démocraties: Allemagne, Etats-Unis, France, Grande-Bretagne, Italie, 5th Edition, Paris, 1993

Jan-Hinrik Meyer-Sahling, Sustainability of Civil Service Reforms in Central and Eastern Europe – Five Years After EU Accession, Sigma Paper No. 44, Paris 2009

Ministerie van Binnenlandse Zaken en Koningsrijksrelaties (ed.), The Dutch Civil Service, Kluwer, Netherlands, 2004

Ministère de la Fonction Publique de l'Etat, La fonction publique de l'Etat, Paris 1999

Ministerio de Administraciones Públicas, Civil Service in Spain, Madrid 2002

Henry Mintzberg , The Structuring of Organizations, Prentice Hall, 1979

Ferdinand Müller-Rommel/Jean Blondel/Darina Malova, Governing New European Democracies, London, Palgrave Macmillan, 2007

National Centre for Social Research/Centre for Research into Elections and Social Trends, Guiding Principles –Public Attitudes towards Conduct in Public Life, January 2003

C.R. Niessen, Preliminary report to the Dutch Government, Bestaat er aanleiding de rechtspositionele verschillen tussen ambtenaren en civielrechtlijke werknemers te handhaven? [Is it necessary to maintain a distinction between civil servants and private sector employees regarding legal status?], 1982

Stafford Northcote/C E Trevelyan, The Organisation of the Permanent Civil Service, Parliamentary Papers, Volume XXVII, 1854

Barry J O'Toole/Jordan, Grant, (eds.) Next Steps, Improving Management in Government, Dartmouth, Aldershot, 1995, pp. 99-118

OECD, La mesure de l'emploi public dans les pays de l'OCDE. Sources, Methodes et Résultats, Paris, 1997

OECD Observer, Policy Brief, from Red Tape to Smart Tape: Administrative Simplification in OECD Countries, June 2003

OECD, Management in Government: Feasibility Report on the Development of Comparative Data, Paris, 31 October 2005

OECD Reviews of Human Resource Management in Government, Executive Summary, Paris, 2007

OECD, Challenges of Human Resources Management for Multi-level Government, Paris, December 2008

OECD, Employment in Government in the Perspective of the Production costs of Goods and services in the Public Domain, Paris, January 2008

OECD, The State of the Public Service, Paris, 2008

OECD, Government at a Glance 2009, Paris, 2009

OECD, Measuring Government Activity, Paris, 2009

Johan P. Olson, Maybe It Is Time to Rediscover Bureaucracy, in: Journal of Public Administration Research and Theory, Vol. 16, No. 1, 2006, pp. 1-24

Dwight Osborne/T.Gaebler, Reinventing Government, Cambridge M.A., 1992

Laurence J. O'Toole Jr./Kenneth J. Meier, Plus ca change. Public Management, Personnel Stability, and Organizational Change, in: Journal of Public Administration Research and Theory, Vol. 13, No. 1, p.43-64

Matthias Pechstein/Rudolf Summer (Hrsg.), Beiträge zum Beamtenrecht, Mohr Siebeck, 2007

James L. Perry, Measuring Public Service Motivation: An Assessment of Construct Reliability and Validity, in: Journal of Public Administration Reearch and Theory, Vol. 6, No. 6, 1996, pp. 5-22

James Perry/Annie Hondeghem (eds.), Motivation in Public Management – The Call of Public Service, Oxford University Press, 2008

B. Guy Peters, The Politics of Bureaucracy, 5th edition, Routledge, 2001

B. Guy Peters/Jon Pierre (eds.), Handbook of Public Administration, 1st edition, Sage, 1995

B. Guy Peters/Jon Pierre (eds.), Handbook of Public Administration, 2nd editon, SAGE, 2003

B. Guy Peters/Donald J. Savoie, Governance in the Twenty-first Century – Revitalizing the Public Service, McGill-Queen's University Press, Montreal, Buffalo, London, 2000

Christopher Pollitt, Convergence. The Useful Myth?, in: Administration Vol. 79, No. 4, Winter 2001, pp. 933-947

Christopher Pollitt, Clarifying Convergence –Striking Similarities and Durable Differences in Public Management Reform, in: Public Management Review, Vol. 4, Issue 1, 2002, pp. 471-492

Christopher Politt, Bureaucracies Remember, Post-bureaucratic Organizations Forget?, in: Public Administration, Volume 87, Number 2, June 2009, pp. 198-218

Christopher Pollitt/Geert Bouckaert, Public Management Reform, A Comparative Analysis, Oxford University Press, 1st edition, 2000

Christopher Politt/Geert Bouckaert, Public Management Reform: A Comparative Analysis, Oxford University Press, 2nd edition, 2004

Report of the United Nations Expert Group Meeting, Improving Public Sector Effectiveness, Dublin, Ireland 16-19 June 2003

Hal Rainey, Understanding and Managing Public Organizations, San Francisco, 2003

Rapport annuel sur l'Etat de la Fonction Publique, Vol. 1, 2007/2008, Paris http://www.fonction-publique.gouv.fr/article1258.htmlp. (last time checked on 7 January 2010)

Rapport annuel sur l'Etat de la Fonction Publique, Vol. 1, 2008/2009, http://www.fonction-publique.gouv.fr/article1488.html (last time checked on 7 January 2010)

Christoph Reichard, Assessing Performance-oriented HRM Activities in Selected OECD Countries, A Review of Ten Years of Modernisation, The HRM Perspective, PUMA/HRM (2002) 9, 24 September 2002

Christoph Reichard/Eckhart Schröter, Der Öffentliche Dienst im Wandel der Zeit: Tradierte Probleme, aktuelle Herausforderungen und Reformperspektiven, in: Der moderne Staat, No. 1, 2009, pp. 17-36

David H. Rosenbloom/Robert S. Kravchuk, Public Administration, Fifth Edition, New York, 2002

David H. Rosenbloom/Robert S. Kravchuk/Richard M. Clerkin, Public Administration – Understanding Management, Politics, and Law in the Public Sector, 7th edition, Mc Grawhill, Singapore 2009

Dennis Saint-Martin/Fred Thompson (eds.), Public Ethics and Governance, Volume 14, Standards and Practices in Comparative Perspective, Amsterdam/Boston/Heidelberg/New York/Oxford/Paris, 2006

Robert M. Sanders, GeorgiaGain or GeorgiaLoss? The Great Experiment in State Civil Service Reform, in: Public Personnel Management, Vol. 33, Summer 2004

Kuno Schedler/Isabella Proeller (eds.), Cultural Aspects of Public Management Reform, Vol. 16, JAI Press, 2007

Jürgen Schwarze, European Administrative Law, First Revised Edition, London, 2006

Joanne Scott/David M. Trubek, Mind the Gap – Law and New Approaches to Governance in the European Union, in: European Law Journal, Vol. 8, No. 1, 2002, pp. 1-18

Gerhard Schulze, Die Beste aller Welten, Carl Hanser Verlag, Wien 2003

Hagen Schulze, Staat und Nation in der europäischen Geschichte, Munich, 2nd Edition, 2004

Sally Coleman Selden/Gene A. Brewer, Work Motivation in the Senior Executive service: testing the High Performance Cycle Theory, in Journal of Public Administration Research and Theory, 2000, Vol. 10. No 3, pp. 531-550

Jay M. Shafritz./Albert C. Hyde, Classics of Public Administration, The Dorsey Press, Chicago, Illinois, 2nd Edition 1987

Jay M.Shafritz/Albert C. Hyde (eds.), Classics of Public Administration, Moore, First Edition, 1978

Jay M.Shafritz./ Albert C.Hyde, Classics of Public Administration, The Dorsey Press, Chicago, Illinois, Second Edition 1987

Heinrich Siedentopf (ed.), Bewertungssysteme für den öffentlichen Dienst, Nomos, Baden-Baden 1978

Herbert Simon/Victor A. Thompson/Donald W. Smithburg, Public Administration, New York 1961

Herbert Simon, Public Administration, Alfred Knopf, New York, 1973

Ria Janvier/ Katleen Janssens, De mythe van het statuut voorbij? De nieuwe overheidswerknemer is opgestaan! Brugge 2003

Social Research Institute, Survey of Public Attitudes Towards Conduct in Public Life, London 2006

Statskontoret, Principles of Good Administration, Stockholm, 2005

Richard, J. Stillman, Public Administration, Fourth Edition, Houghton Company, Boston 1988

Larry D. Terry, Leadership of Public Bureaucracies: The Administrator as Conservator, Sage, Thousand Oaks, 1995

Victor A. Thompson, Modern Organisation, Alfred A. Knopf, 1961

United Kingdom, Cabinet Office, Personnel Statistics, Media Brief, 1 April 2004

United Kingdom, Cabinet Office, A Draft Civil Service Bill, A Consultation Document

United Kingdom, House of Commons, Public Administration Select Committee, On Target? Government by Measurement, Fifth Report, 2002-2003, London, Vol. 1, 22 July 2003

US Office of Personnel Management, Performance Related Pay, Washington D.C, April 2002

Steven van de Walle, Perceptions of Administrative Performance: The Key to Trust in Government?, Dissertation at the Catholic University of Leuven, 2004

Steven van de Walle, Measuring Bureaucratic Quality in Governance Indicators, Paper presented at the 8th Public Management Research Conference in Los Angeles, 29 September to 1 October 2005

Steven van de Walle/Mierkatrien Sterck/Wouter van Dooren/Geert Bouckaert, What You See Is Not Necessarily What You Get, Instituut voor de Overheid, Leuven, July 2004

Wouter van Dooren, Performance Measurement in the Flemish Public Sector: A Supply and Demand Approach, PhD at the University of Leuven, 2006

Guurtje van Sloten, Work Organisation, Technology and Working Conditions, European Foundation for the Improvement of Living and Working Conditions, Dublin 2002

Tony Verheijen /Alexander Kotchegura_(eds.), Civil Service Systems in Central and Eastern Europe, Edward Elgar, 2000

Jill Wakefield, The Right to Good Administration, Kluwer, Alphen aan den Rijn, 2007

Dwight Waldo, The Administrative State, Ronald Press, New York, 1948

Dwight Waldo (ed.), Ideas and Issues in Public Administration, Greenwood Press, Westport, 1953

J. Walters, Life After Civil Service Reform: The Texas, Georgia, and Florida Experiences, IBM Endowment for The Business of Government, Human Capital Series, October 2002

Michael Walzer, Sphären der Gerechtigkeit, Ein Plädoyer für Pluralität und Gleichheit (English version: Spheres of Justice. A Defense of Pluralism and Equality, 1983), Köln 1996

Max Weber, Politik als Beruf, Reclam, Stuttgart 1999

Max Weber, Wirtschaft und Gesellschaft, Grundriß der verstehenden Soziologie, 1922

Martin Wehrle, Der Feind in meinem Büro, Berlin 2005

Jonathan West, Georgia on the Mind of Radical Civil Service Reformers, in: Review of Public Personnel Administration, Vol. 22, No. 2, Summer 2002, pp. 79-93

Hans de Witte, Job Insecurity and Psychological Well-being – Review of the Literature and Exploration of Some Unresolved Issues, in: European Journal of Work and Organizational Psychology, Vol. 8, 1999, pp. 155-177

Manfred Zach, Gauner, Pinsel, Chicaneure – Eine kleine Geschichte der Bürokratie, Klöpfer und Meyer, Tübingen, 2003

Jacques Ziller, Administrations comparées, Paris, Montchrestien, 1993

Jacques Ziller, European Models of Government – Towards a Patchwork with Missing Pieces, in: Parliamentary Affairs, No. 54, 2001, pp. 102-119

http://web.worldbank.org/WBSITE/EXTERNAL/TOPICS/EXTPUBLICSECTORANDGOVERNANCE/EXTADMINISTRATIVEANDCIVILSERVICEREFORM/0,,contentMDK:20133489~menuPK:286372~pagePK:148956~piPK:216618~theSitePK:286367,00.html (last time checked on 1 February 2010)

http://web.worldbank.org/WBSITE/EXTERNAL/TOPICS/EXTPUBLICSECTORANDGOVERNANCE/EXTADMINISTRATIVEANDCIVILSERVICEREFORM/0,,contentMDK:20133489~menuPK:286372~pagePK:148956~piPK:216618~theSitePK:286367,00.html (last time checked on 1 February 2010)

Annex 1: First questionnaire

Civil Services in the Europe of 27 – Reform and Innovation in Public Service Systems: Towards new public service models in Europe?

The European Institute of Public Administration (EIPA) is launching the "European Observatory of Public Administration", an online platform making it possible for the Member States to easily and regularly analyse new reforms and developments within their national public services compared to those of the other EU Member States.

To begin with, EIPA has developed a questionnaire available to all Member States of the EU as well as to the European Commission. All respondents are invited to answer to the questions until 30 January 2009.

EIPA will analyse the incoming data and inform the Member States on its webpage about the results of this study, offer new public service comparisons and discuss new developments in the field.

For the future it is planned that EIPA will continuously analyse comparative data in specific policy areas. The results will be placed on the webpage and be at the disposal of the Member States (and the wider public).

Member state

Please make your selection * [Please select ▾]

Validation Code

Please fill the validation code you have been given * [ ]

1. Definition and structure of civil services

Is the civil service in your country organised according to governmental levels?	Yes	No
Central level	☐	☐
Local level	☐	☐
Regional level	☐	☐

Is the civil service in your country organised according to governmental sectors?	Yes	No
Security (Police, Defence)	☐	☐

Justice	□	□
Health (Hospitals)	□	□
Education	□	□
Other (please specify)	□	□

Are legal competences in the civil service divided according to these governmental levels?	Yes	No
Central level	□	□
Local level	□	□
Regional level	□	□

Are legal competences in the civil service divided according to these governmental sectors?	Yes	No
Security (Police, Defence)	□	□
Justice	□	□
Health (Hospitals)	□	□
Education	□	□
Other (please specify)	□	□

2. Legal Status of Civil Services

Do civil servants in your country have a public law status?	Yes	No, we do not have a system based on public law
Please make your selection	□	□

Are the existing civil service rules (constitutional provisions, civil service law, regulations, statutes) applicable to all public employees ?	Yes	No
Please make your selection	□	□

If not, what is the approx. percentage of civil servants with public law status in your public administration?	<20%	20-40%	41-60%	61-80%	>80%
Please make your selection	□	□	□	□	□

What are the main differences between civil servants (with a public law status) and other public employees (under labour law status)?	Yes	No

Different legal status (nomination, oath, constitution requirement)	☐	☐
Different recruitment requirements	☐	☐
Different organisational and career system	☐	☐
Higher job security	☐	☐
Different pension rights	☐	☐
Different Salary System (regulated by law)	☐	☐
Distinct Disciplinary rules	☐	☐
Distinct Ethical rules	☐	☐
Different Social Dialogue	☐	☐
Right to strike (restricted for some civil service categories)	☐	☐

Is there a trend towards increasing or decreasing the number of civil servants?	increasing	decreasing	neither
Please make your selection	☐	☐	☐

Does a specific senior civil service exist in your country?	Yes	No
Please make your selection	☐	☐

3. Legal, political and organisational competences in the field of public administration and HRM

During the past years is the reform trend towards	Yes	No
further centralising legal and political competences at central government level	☐	☐
decentralising competences to regional/local authorities	☐	☐
decentralising competences to other sectors	☐	☐
delegating and outsource competences to NGOs and semi-public bodies	☐	☐
delegating and outsource competences to Public Private Partnerships (PPP)	☐	☐
privatising competences	☐	☐

During the past years have managerial tasks and responsibilities in the field of HRM been increasingly delegated?	to individual departments/organisations/agencies	delegated to individual managers

Please make your selection	□	□

4. Leadership issues

Have top managers and middle managers been given more/less responsibilities within the last years?	Yes, a lot more	Some more	Same	Less	A lot less
Please make your selection	□	□	□	□	□

If so, in which field are top-and middle managers and line managers given more/less responsibilities in Human Resource Management?	More	Same	Less
Design of codes of conduct and ethical norms	□	□	□
Decision-making on training needs for employees	□	□	□
Determining performance related pay	□	□	□
Decision-making powers in recruitment matters	□	□	□
Decision on a disciplinary procedure in case of misconduct	□	□	□
Decision-making and recommendation for promotions	□	□	□
Determining career development needs	□	□	□
Design and adoption of poor performance plans	□	□	□
Performance plans for line department	□	□	□
Changing working time arrangements for employees	□	□	□
Introducing diversity policies in the organisation	□	□	□
Relocating staff due to structural changes	□	□	□
Dismissal of employees	□	□	□

5. Conditions for access to the civil service

Do you have a civil service which is structured in careers and/or corps?	Yes	No
Please make your selection	□	□

If so, are reforms under way to modify the present structure?	Yes	No
Introduce new career/corps structures?	□	□
Reduce the number of careers/corps?	□	□
Abolish careers/corps?	□	□

Is entrance/recruitment in the civil service generally taking place at the lowest level/rank/position in the relevant career/corps/hierarchical level?	Yes, always	Yes, but exceptions are possible	No, access/recruitment can take place at any time at all levels
Please make your selection	☐	☐	☐

Is professional experience in the private sector taken into account in the recruitment process and in the classification in the (salary) hierarchy?	Yes, no restrictions	Yes, but restrictions	No, generally not	No
Please make your selection	☐	☐	☐	☐

Is professional experience in the private sector recognised in the calculation of pension rights?	Yes, no restrictions	Yes, but restrictions	No, generally not	No
Please make your selection	☐	☐	☐	☐

Is it possible to recruit senior managers from the PRIVATE sector for a limited period of time (limited and/or flexible contracts)?	Yes	Yes, rarely taking place	No, senior managers must be recruited from the public sector	No, constitutional requirements to offer unlimited contracts in the public sector
Please make your selection	☐	☐	☐	☐

Is it possible to recruit senior managers from the PUBLIC sector for a limited period of time (limited and/or flexible contracts)?	Yes	Yes, rarely taking place	No, senior managers must be recruited from the public sector	No, constitutional requirements to offer unlimited contracts in the public sector
Please make your selection	◻	◻	◻	◻

6. Recruitment requirements

Are there specific formalised recruitment requirements in the civil service?	Yes, specific concours	Yes, specific preparat paratory procedurs	Yes, state exam	Yes, training	Yes, others	No, recruitment procedures are similar to those used in the private sector	Others
Please make your selection	◻	◻	◻	◻	◻	◻	◻

7. Promotion System

Is it necessary to pass a specific internal concours/exam before a promotion can take place?	Yes	In some cases	No
Please make your selection	◻	◻	◻

Generally speaking, do promotions take place to the next higher rank/level?	Yes	No
Please make your selection	◻	◻

Is it also possible to promote candidates to other positions at mid-career or top-level?	Yes	No
Please make your selection	◻	◻

8. Remuneration System

Is the basic salary regulated by law?	Yes	No
Please make your selection	□	□

Is the basic salary centrally and/or decentralised managed?	Centralised and applicable to the whole civil service	Centralised but applicable only to the federal/central level	Centralised elements but decentralised discretion by departments/agencies	Decentralised and subject to individual negotiations in departments/agencies
Please make your selection	□	□	□	□

Do you have a wage system which is based on seniority, age and experience?	Absolutely	Rather yes	To some extent	Rather not	Not at all
Please make your selection	□	□	□	□	□

Do you have a wage system which is based on performance and target agreements?	Absolutely	Rather yes	To some extent	Rather not	Not at all
Please make your selection	□	□	□	□	□

Do you have a hybrid wage systems which combines seniority elements with performance related pay?	Absolutely	Rather yes	To some extent	Rather not	Not at all
Please make your selection	□	□	□	□	□

9. Mobility

Is functional (inter-ministerial and intra-ministerial) mobility obligatory/voluntary?	Obligatory (e.g., every four years change of function)	Voluntary but important element/condition in career development policies (promotion)	Voluntary and widely accepted	Voluntary but not yet frequently applied in practice
Please make your selection	□	□	□	□

10. Job Security

Do civil servants enjoy life-tenure/employment for life?	<20%	20-40%	41-60 %	61-80%	>80%
Yes, dismissal is only possible for disciplinary reasons	◻	◻	◻	◻	◻
Yes, but dismissal is possible in cases of poor performance (subject to negative performance assessments)	◻	◻	◻	◻	◻
No, but civil servants have a high job security and unlimited contracts	◻	◻	◻	◻	◻
No, civil servants have the same contractual situation as employees in the private sector	◻	◻	◻	◻	◻

11. Change Management and Future Challenges

How influential/important are the following modernisation topics in your country?	Very important	Important	Neutral	Not very important	Not important at all
Reform of civil service law (legal status)	◻	◻	◻	◻	◻
Reform of principals of good administration/good governance	◻	◻	◻	◻	◻
Anticipating demographic change	◻	◻	◻	◻	◻
Diversity policies	◻	◻	◻	◻	◻
Equality	◻	◻	◻	◻	◻
Leadership	◻	◻	◻	◻	◻
Citizen orientation	◻	◻	◻	◻	◻
Quality management	◻	◻	◻	◻	◻
Reducing administrative burdens	◻	◻	◻	◻	◻
Decentralisation of HR competencies	◻	◻	◻	◻	◻
Ethics and fight against corruption	◻	◻	◻	◻	◻

Salary reform	□	□	□	□	□
Career system reform	□	□	□	□	□
Performance management	□	□	□	□	□
Addressing poor performance	□	□	□	□	□
Competency management	□	□	□	□	□
Reform of working conditions	□	□	□	□	□
Alignment with the working condidtions of other public sector employees	□	□	□	□	□
Reducing public personnel / savings policies	□	□	□	□	□
Open government and transparency	□	□	□	□	□
Enhancing mobility: PUBLIC - PRIVATE	□	□	□	□	□
Enhancing mobility: PUBLIC - PUBLIC	□	□	□	□	□
Enhancing mobility: INTERNATIONAL	□	□	□	□	□
Training	□	□	□	□	□
Measures in order to raise attractiveness of public service employment	□	□	□	□	□
Reform of HR departments	□	□	□	□	□
Deregulation of HR rules	□	□	□	□	□
Reform of working time	□	□	□	□	□

Annex 2: Second questionnaire

Civil Services in the Europe of Twenty Seven: Towards New Public Service Models in Europe?

Dear Colleagues,

As promised during the last HRWG meeting in Prague on 28 April 2009, please find enclosed some additional questions regarding our study on "Civil Services in the Europe of Twenty Seven". We are very hopeful that the new questions will help clarify earlier questions in our survey which were less clear and difficult to respond to (questions 1, 2 and 10). In a separate mail, we will also contact some of you as we need further clarification about some unanswered/unclear issues left in your first response to the survey. We kindly ask you to submit your response to us by email until 30 May 2009.

As mentioned earlier, the aim in this survey is to improve our knowledge of the different civil service systems and our understanding of how civil service system is defined in different national contexts. Another objective is to provide for the first time comparative and analytical data on the national recruitment, pay, mobility policies, promotion and HRM policies. Thus, this intensive and innovative piece of research should be seen as complementary to the earlier studies which were conducted by the French EU Presidency .

As always, we will inform you as soon as possible and provide you with the up-to-date findings. Please do not hesitate to contact us if you need any help.

Best regards,
- Christoph, c.demmke@EIPA-nl.com
- Timo, timo.moilanen@helsinki.fi
- Thomas, thomas.henokl@gmail.com

1. Contact information

1.1 Member State:

1.2 Respondent's email address:

2.1 Do the following administrative sectors belong to the central civil service or do they have their own civil service systems?

	Central Civil Service	Specific Civil Service	Other (not part of CS)
a) Central Government (ministries)	☐	☐	☐
b) Governmental agencies	☐	☐	☐
c) Judiciary	☐	☐	☐
d) Diplomatic service	☐	☐	☐
e) Police	☐	☐	☐
f) Military	☐	☐	☐
g) Education	☐	☐	☐
h) University	☐	☐	☐
i) Hospitals	☐	☐	☐

Comments:

2.2 Generally speaking, do you have a highly centralised civil service system, or is it decentralised to various levels (e.g., regions, Länder, counties) that have their own civil service systems?

highly centralised system ☐ ☐ ☐ ☐ ☐ highly decentralised system
(same rules apply to most civil servants) (different rules for different groups of civil servants)

2.3 Please check the option that is applicable

Yes No Cannot say or does not apply

☐ ☐ ☐ legal status of civil servants defined by law on the central level and applicable to the whole civil service

☐ ☐ ☐ (if existing) career structure is regulated by the law and it is applicable to the whole civil service

☐ ☐ ☐ basic salary is regulated by law and applicable to all civil servants

☐ ☐ ☐ recruitment procedure (concours, state exam, assessment center) for different job positions are regulated centrally

☐ ☐ ☐ career development policies (promotions) are regulated centrally

☐ ☐ ☐ pension system for civil servants is decided on the central level and is applicable to the whole civil service

☐ ☐ ☐ central rules about how and when to carry out performance appraisals

☐ ☐ ☐ rules on equality, antidiscrimination and diversity policies are regulated by law and they are applicable to the whole civil service

2.4. Do the regions or Länder have their own legislative power to regulate their civil service systems (e.g., recruitment, salary systems, pensions)?

wide legislative powers ☐ ☐ ☐ ☐ ☐ no power

Comments:

3.1 Are there different categories of public employees in the public service?
(e.g., civil servants, other public employees)

☐ yes, please explain
☐ no

3.2 If you have several categories of public employees, what is their approximate percentage in your public service? Please write the name of the category and its possible percentage. (e.g., civil servants 80%, other public employees 20%)

Categories:
1. (%)
2. (%)
3. (%)
…

Comments:

4.1 What is the legal status of <u>civil servants</u> in your country?

☐ public law status ☐ civil law status (labour law)

Comments:

4.2 What is the legal status of other <u>public employees</u> in your country?

☐ public law status ☐ civil law status (labour law)

Comments:

5.1 Generally, do civil servants with public law status have

life-time tenure ☐ ☐ ☐ ☐ ☐ limited, fixed-term contract
(high job security) (low job security)

Comments:

5.2 Can civil servants employment be terminated due to:

Please choose as many options as you prefer.

☐ disciplinary reasons
☐ poor performance
☐ economic difficulties
☐ restructuring
☐ re-organisation
☐ downsizing
☐ other, what

Comments:

5.3 If you have different categories of public employees, do they differ with respect to job security?

☐ yes, please explain how they differ
☐ no, they do not differ

☐ no, we do not have different categories of public employees

5.4 If you have different categories of civil servants, how do they differ with respect to job security?

☐ yes, please explain how they differ
☐ no, they do not differ

☐ no, we do not have different categories of civil servants

5.5 Does civil servants' job security differ from the private sector job security?

☐ yes, it differs. Please explain:
☐ no, it does not

5.6 Is the trend regarding civil servants' job security towards

Increasing ☐ ☐ ☐ Decreasing

Comments:

6.1 How is civil service defined in your country? To answer this question, you could refer to relevant legislation and other rules that define civil service. We shall greatly appreciate if you could provide us extracts of these documents.

Comments:

Peter Lang · Internationaler Verlag der Wissenschaften

Yunus Dauda

Managing Technology Innovation

The Human Resource Management Perspective

Frankfurt am Main, Berlin, Bern, Bruxelles, New York, Oxford, Wien, 2009.
XVII, 155 pp., 3 tab., 12 graph.
Labour, Education & Society. Edited by György Széll. Vol. 12
ISBN 978-3-631-57012-8 · pb. € 39,00*

Technology in the world today has contributed to promote organisational competitiveness and national development. But most developing countries have not substantially benefited from science and technology, hence their underdevelopment and poverty. They could not harness and manage their scientific and technological innovations and use their human and material resources to meet basic needs of their people, reduce socio-economic inequalities, create employment opportunities and improve national security. The achievement of these is considered in this book to be dependent on provisions of conducive environments for effective human resource management for scientific and technological innovations. Human resource management concepts and practices were used to evolve frameworks and processes for the generation, acquisition, adoption, and transfer of technology, depending on the objectives of different countries and organisations.

Contents: Technology and Human Resource Innovation · Managing Technology Innovation · Human Resource and Technology Work System Management · Human Resource and Technology Change Management · Strategic Human Resource Innovation Management · Strategic Technology Innovation Management · Technological Innovation and Employee Relations · Technological Innovation and Human Resource Management · Research and Development (R & D) for Technology Innovation · Technology Innovation and Human Resource Performance Management · Team Building for Research and Development (R & D) Technology Innovation · Management of Research and Development (R & D) for Technology Innovation · Technology Innovation and National Development

www.ingramcontent.com/pod-product-compliance
Ingram Content Group UK Ltd.
Pitfield, Milton Keynes, MK11 3LW, UK
UKHW021831100926
8556IPUK00004B/277

9 783631 604663